Feng Shui History

221 BC to 2012 AD

Other Books on Feng Shui by Stephen Skinner

Feng Shui Before & After - Haldane Mason, Tuttle
Feng Shui for Everyday Living aka *Feng Shui for Modern Living* - Cico
Feng Shui History – Golden Hoard
Feng Shui Style - Periplus
Feng Shui the Traditional Oriental Way - Haldane Mason
Feng Shui: the Living Earth Manual - Tuttle
Flying Star Feng Shui - Tuttle
Guide to the Feng Shui Compass – Golden Hoard
K.I.S.S. Guide to Feng Shui (Keep it Simple Series) – Penguin, DK
Key San He Feng Shui Formulas – Golden Hoard
Living Earth Manual of Feng Shui – RKP, Penguin, Arkana
Mountain Dragon – Golden Hoard
Original Eight Mansion Formula – Golden Hoard
Practical Makeovers Using Feng Shui – Haldane Mason, Tuttle
Water Dragon – Golden Hoard

Selected Books on the Western Esoteric Tradition by Stephen Skinner

Agrippa's Fourth Book of Occult Philosophy – Askin, Ibis
Aleister Crowley's Astrology – Spearman, Ibis
Complete Magician's Tables – Golden Hoard, Llewellyn
Dr John Dee's Spiritual Diaries: the fully revised edition of 'A True & Faithful Relation of what passed...between Dr John Dee...& some Spirits' - Golden Hoard
Geomancy in Theory & Practice – Golden Hoard, Llewellyn
Goetia of Dr Rudd: Liber Malorum Spirituum (with David Rankine) – Golden Hoard
Grimoire of Saint Cyprian: Clavis Inferni (with David Rankine) – Golden Hoard
Key to the Latin of Dr John Dee's Spiritual Diaries - Golden Hoard, Llewellyn
Keys to the Gateway of Magic (with David Rankine) – Golden Hoard
Magical Diaries of Aleister Crowley – Spearman, RedWheel Weiser
Michael Psellus 'On the Operation of Daemons' - Golden Hoard
Millennium Prophecies: Apocalypse 2000 - Carlton
Nostradamus (with Francis King) – Carlton
Oracle of Geomancy – Warner Destiny, Prism
Practical Angel Magic of Dee's Enochian Tables (with David Rankine) – Golden Hoard
Sacred Geometry – Gaia, Hamlyn
Search for Abraxas (with Nevill Drury) – Spearman, Salamander
Sepher Raziel: Liber Salomonis (with Don Karr) – Golden Hoard
Techniques of High Magic (with Francis King) – Daniels, Inner Traditions, Askin
Terrestrial Astrology: Divination by Geomancy – Routledge
Veritable Key of Solomon (with David Rankine) – Golden Hoard, Llewellyn

Stephen Skinner also launched and published the world's largest selling glossy feng shui magazine *Feng Shui for Modern Living* in both English and Chinese language editions.

Feng Shui History

the story of Classical Feng Shui
in China and the West
from 221 BC to 2012 AD

Stephen Skinner

GOLDEN HOARD PRESS

2012

Published by Golden Hoard Press Pte Ltd
PO Box 1073 Robinson Road
Singapore, 902123.

www.GoldenHoard.com

First Edition

ISBN 978-0-9568285-4-5

Printed in Malaysia

Dedicated to my extraordinary wife Navaneeta Das
who learnt Flying Star feng shui
more rapidly than anyone I have ever taught

史帝芬

Contents

List of Half-Tone Plates

List of Figures

Acknowledgements

I would like to point out that this book contains historical material drawn from my earlier book *Guide to the Feng Shui Compass: a Compendium of Classical Feng Shui.* It has been reorganised so that it is now in a more reader-friendly chronological order, without the continuing requirement of needing to explain the technical aspects of the construction of the lo p'an. In addition, a lot of new material has been added about the progress of feng shui in the 20th-21st centuries, both in China and in the rest of the world.

I specially want to thank Tony Holdsworth for help with the details of the growth of feng shui in the UK. Both he and Derek Walters contributed significantly to that very growth. Without the input from Denny Fairchild I would not have been able to do justice to the history of the development of feng shui in the US over the last 30 years. His help was supplemented by Elliott Tanzer and Kartar Diamond who let me have the benefit of their memories of how feng shui developed in the US. My thanks to Jami Lin for the photograph of James Moser. Raymond Lo's input on the background of feng shui in Hong Kong was invaluable. The inimitable Tyler Rowe contributed much of the material about feng shui in Australia. Being an Australian myself I should feel ashamed that I did not have that material at my finger tips, but instead I am delighted at the job he made of it. To Janene Laird for facilitating my own recent trip back there to teach San He feng shui. To Victor Garza for additional information on Korea.

To friends and feng shui Masters including (in alphabetical order) Chen Chein Lee, the late Victor Dy, Vincent Koh, Peter Leung, Francis Leyau, Raymond Lo, Dr Michael Oon, Dr Jin Peh, Tan Khoon Yong, Dr Yang Kim Voon, Joey Yap, Yap Boh Chu and Yap Cheng Hai, and especially to the late Master Wu of Hong Kong, as well as to many others too numerous to mention, I extend my heartfelt thanks for their assistance and ongoing friendship.

I would like to admit to a dilemma in putting together this book, and that is the use of the term 'Master.' In dynastic times, feng shui Masters were acknowledged by common consent, based on their lineage or their particular skills. Nowadays the term Master has been somewhat devalued by the proliferation of self-appointed masters whose range of experience and knowledge of feng shui is very varied. A trawl through Google will literally turn up thousands of modern day feng shui practitioners claiming this title, and "feng shui Master" produced 269,000 hits at my last count.

This is even further complicated by the fact that many of the practitioners mentioned in this book did not use the title 'Master' when I first knew them decades ago. Others who have a competency equal to many of their colleagues have not bothered to adopt this title. The increasing frequency of award of 'Grand Master' titles has also blurred the distinctions, although many of those awards are undoubtedly deserved.

I have vacillated between the two extremes of placing 'Master' or 'Grand Master' as a prefix to anyone who has contributed anything to the world of Feng Shui albeit in big or small ways, or limiting the title just to the great masters of the past like Yang Yun Sung.

I have limited the title of Master to the great masters of the past and a few contemporary masters who have contributed much to the spread of feng shui knowledge. The real masters know who they are, and they will not be offended by this decision.

I would like to acknowledge the unstinting assistance over the years of Wei Loon Soo and Er Choon Haw for help with translations of Chinese feng shui texts. Er Choon Haw helped with the research and is responsible for some of the painstaking illustrations of lo p'ans used in this book. Also Kate Sullivan for her painstaking sub-editing of this book.

On a corporate level I wish to thank the staff of the British Library; British Museum; Library of the National University of Singapore; Museum of Science, Oxford; National Library Board of Singapore; Pitt-Rivers Museum, Oxford; Royal Geographical Society, London; Science Museum, London; SOAS, London University; Wellcome Institute; American Anthropological Museum of Philadelphia and lastly but definitely not least the Whipple Museum of the History of Science, University of Cambridge for their willing assistance in my quest for information and images of early lo p'ans.

I would also like to thank the heads of various companies and of two government departments, in the UK, Europe and Asia who have employed me to do their feng shui analysis, but who do not wish their usage of feng shui to be known to the world at large. Some of the less publicity-shy US corporations are mentioned in the chapter on feng shui in the US.

Introduction

It may sound preposterous that architectural and geographic changes can bring about an increase in fertility and luck, but I believe than any system that did not deliver concrete results over such a long period, to an essentially pragmatic race such as the Chinese, would not have survived for centuries. For feng shui to have had such a long history, and been so jealously guarded by Imperial edict, it must have been able to deliver repeatable and concrete results. My own experience of feng shui and its effects over the last 36 years leads me to believe that the practice, correctly applied, definitely works.

Many of my readers already know my history, but a quick summary here may not go amiss. I introduced feng shui to the West with the publication of the first 20th century English book on feng shui in 1976. With the publication from 1998-2001 of the magazine *Feng Shui for Modern Living* both in English and also later in Chinese (through a Chinese language co-edition published in Taiwan), I have helped to spread interest in feng shui worldwide and outside of the Chinese-speaking world. As interest has progressed further, there are now many more Westerners who not only know what traditional feng shui is, but also want to know how to use it practically.

My intention has always been to propagate accurate knowledge about feng shui, so that feng shui is seen as a practical rather than a mystical knowledge. Feng shui is not a religion, but a discipline as precise in its practice as surveying or geography, and more precise in its application, calibration and formulae than many 'soft' Western sciences (such as psychology or sociology). My intention is to have feng shui understood as a scientific practice, one with repeatable results which can be reliably applied to all habitations to improve the lives of those living there, rather than as a mass of semi-mystical doctrines.

The *lo p'an* is the main instrument of feng shui. It is to feng shui what the telescope is to astronomy. Anyone who tells you they can do feng shui without a lo p'an is working at about the same level as mediaeval astronomers were in the sixteenth century, compared with the techniques of modern day astronomers. The lo p'an uses the Earth's magnetic field and precise astronomical data to determine alignments and direction. It is provided with a number of tightly-packed rings which relate to the many theorems of time and change that make up this fascinating subject. It is amazing that since the writing of my first book on feng shui in 1976 where the lo p'an was briefly described, that none of the more than one thousand books published on feng shui in English since then have more than touched lightly upon the lo p'an or even noticed its existence.

This is rather like devoting so much energy to astronomy, without bothering to describe how to use, or even mentioning the existence of the telescope.

I therefore published *A Guide to the Feng Shui Compass* to make up for that omission. For the first time in English it explains what the lo p'an really is, describes all of its rings, and some of the methods for using this amazing instrument. The lo p'an is also the forefather of the Western maritime and hiking compass, as the Chinese discovered how to use the compass some 1500 years before any European usage. In its present form the lo p'an is a much more complicated instrument than any Western compass.

The study of feng shui has never been easy. In the 19th century the approach to feng shui by Western missionaries and colonial administrators was largely anecdotal and anthropological. Even in the 20th century, questioning non-expert practitioners is a common approach to researching feng shui. As Joseph Needham once remarked "the 'anthropological' method of de Groot would be exactly paralleled by the efforts of a Chinese scholar to find out what Englishmen knew of nuclear physics, by interrogating fishwives and traditional Morris dancers." I was very lucky in 1976 to have instead found an old Kowloon 'street master,' Master Wu, who was happy to share with me his practical knowledge and experience, in exchange for a little of my help with his negotiations with unsympathetic Western architects.

But I also took the Western approach to any complex subject and read the classics of feng shui in SOAS and other collections. The written source materials of feng shui are in traditional Chinese, hard to find, and couched in technical language. Even now the Chinese classics of feng shui are only slowly appearing in English, a process I am attempting to speed up.

Until the 1980s it was not even possible to attend classes in English given by Chinese practitioners, and the history of the subject is seldom mentioned in these classes beyond a minimal summary of the supposed lineage of the teacher concerned. I have to admit that I have never attended such a class, but learned what I know of feng shui from working with Chinese practitioners such as the late Master Wu in Hong Kong in 1976. Any gaps were then filled in by painstakingly reading the Chinese classics feng shui clasics. Because of the paucity of material in English on the history of feng shui, I make no apology for repeating passages from my previous book on the lo p'an.[1]

Some may feel that I have devoted a disproportionate amount of space to the history of the last four decades, particularly to the people involved. It could also be said a balanced history of feng shui should have devoted more space to the ancient masters. I have to admit that is true, but in my defence, I should point out that I have lived through this history and been personally involved. I was hoping that someone else would write a full account of this period, but as nobody has stepped forward, I felt that I should at least record whatever details I can recall.

[1] Stephen Skinner, *Guide to the Feng Shui Compass,* Golden Hoard, Singapore, 2008.

Plates

The history of feng shui is intimately bound up in the development of its prime instrument, the lo p'an, and so it is essential to be able to see in detail the rings of the lo p'an mentioned in the text, and to be able to distinguish between the different sorts of lo p'an as they changed over the centuries. For a full analysis of the lo p'an see my *Guide to the Feng Shui Compass: a Compendium of Classical Feng Shui*, GHP, Singapore, 2006.

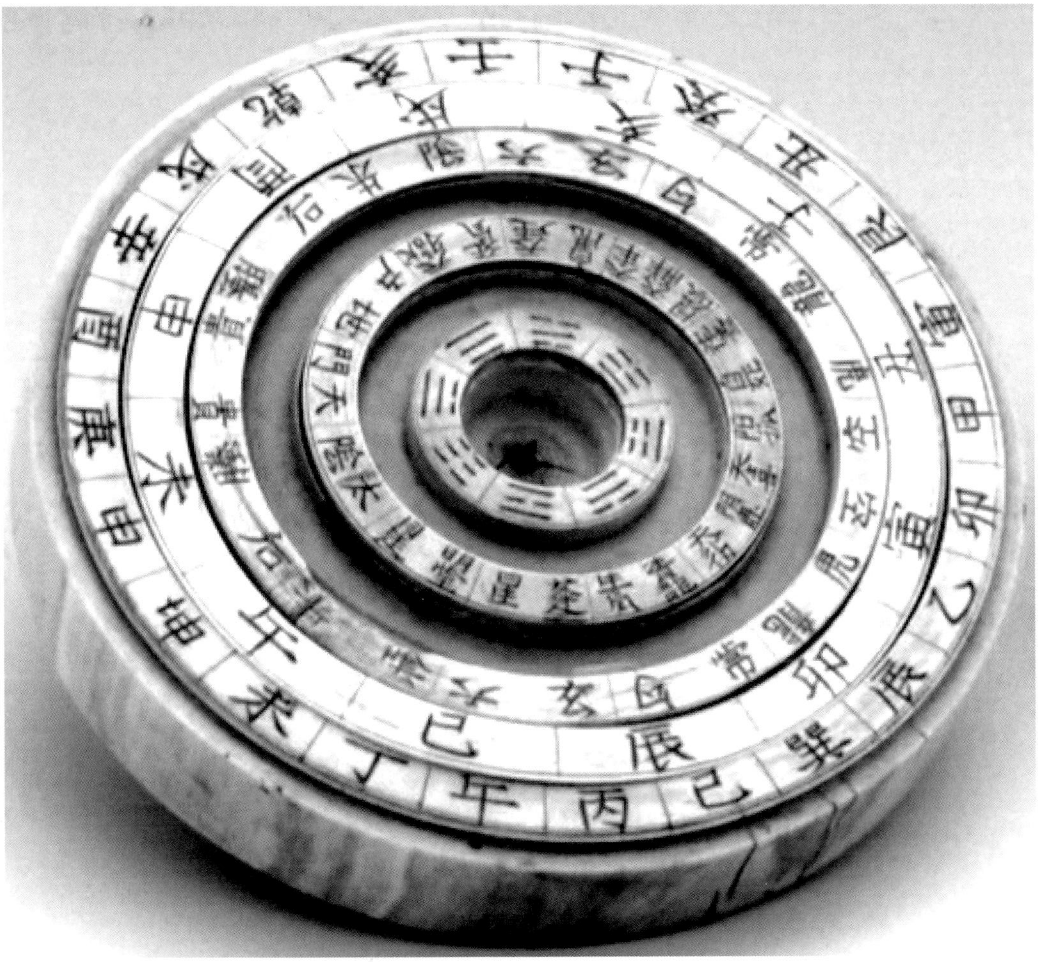

Plate 1: A 13th century Sung dynasty lo p'an made of mammoth tusk ivory, with two fixed rings and five separately rotating rings (two are missing). Approximately 1250 CE.[1]

[1] Courtesy of the Museum of the History of Science, Oxford [item 47707].

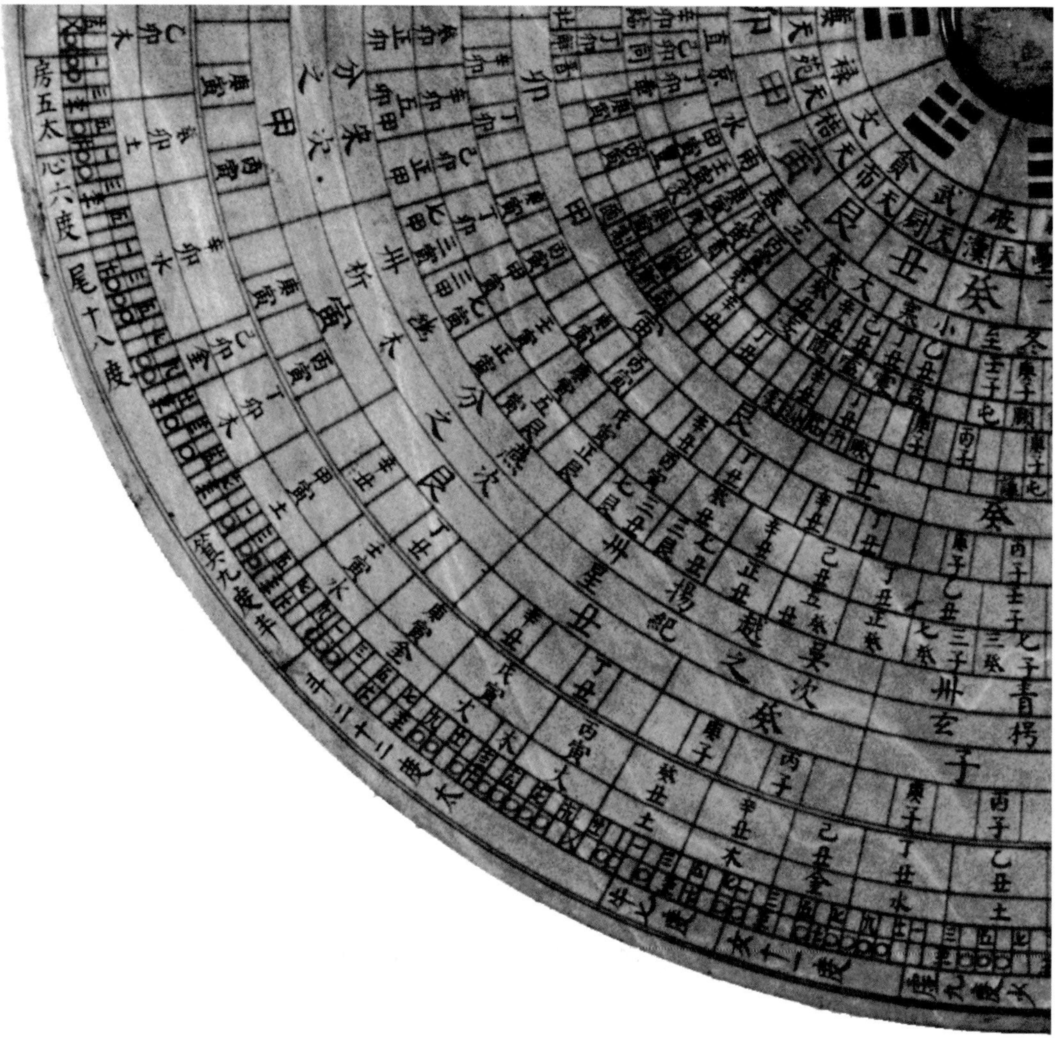

Plate 2: A 22 ring Ch'ing dynasty San He lo p'an made by Chou Yi Tsan c. 1800.[1] The rings 5, 7, 9, 13, 14 and 15 do not occur on modern lo p'ans. Note the double line which separates the Heaven Plate from the Astronomical rings. There is no 64 hexagrams ring.

[1] By Zhou Yi Zan. Courtesy of the Whipple Museum of Science, Cambridge University. [1203]

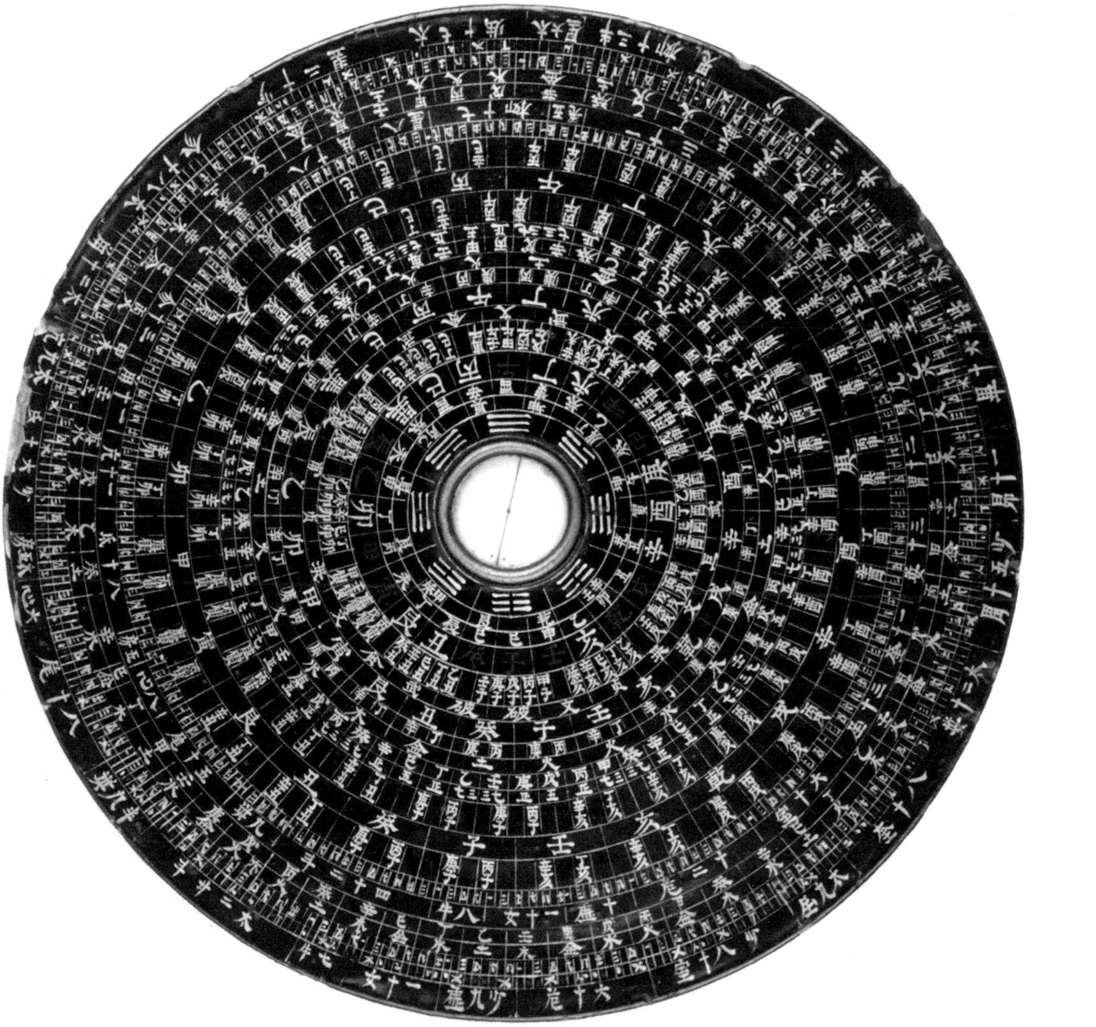

Plate 3: A 21 ring San He Ch'ing dynasty black lacquer lo p'an circa 1890 made by Lin Chun Chou.[1] The rings are:

1. 8 trigrams in Former Heaven Sequence.
2. Yellow Springs.
3. Robbery *sha.*
4. 24 Mountains **Earth Plate**
5. The 72 Dragons.
6. Nine Stars.
7. 24 Mountains Outer Heaven **(Man) Plate**.
8. 120 *fen chin.*
9. The 5 Elements of the *fen chin.*
10. The 60 Dragons.
11. 60 Threes and Sevens riding the ch'i.
12. Man Plate 90 *fen chin.*
13. 24 Mountains **Heaven Plate**.
14. Heaven Plate 90 *fen chin.*
15. **Astronomic Plate** day-degrees.
16. 28 *Hsiu* (using Ch'ing dynasty epoch).
17. 60 Uneven Dragons or *ying so.*
18. 61 Elements of the Uneven Dragons.
19. The 365.25 day-degrees of the *Hsiu*.
20. The auspiciousness of the day-degrees.
21. The 28 *Hsiu* with their extents.

---

[1] Lin Jun Zhou. Courtesy of the Whipple Museum, University of Cambridge [0075]. Note that the Heaven Pool was misaligned when it was repaired and re-set incorrectly into the lo p'an. It should be vertical with the double dots aligned with the middle of the K'un trigram. The needle itself is also missing.

Plate 4: A Classical San He Ch'ing dynasty lo p'an from the Fang Hsiu Shui workshop, circa 1890 CE, from the author's collection. See Figure 50 for details of its rings.

Plate 5: Detail from a Ch'ing dynasty 19 ring lo p'an from the Wu Lu Heng workshop, circa 1890.[1] Ring 12 shows the 'Threes and Sevens Riding the ch'i,' a ring that does not appear on modern lo p'ans. Yin/yang markings are shown in a separate ring.

[1] Courtesy of the Science Museum, London [A642257/10462855]

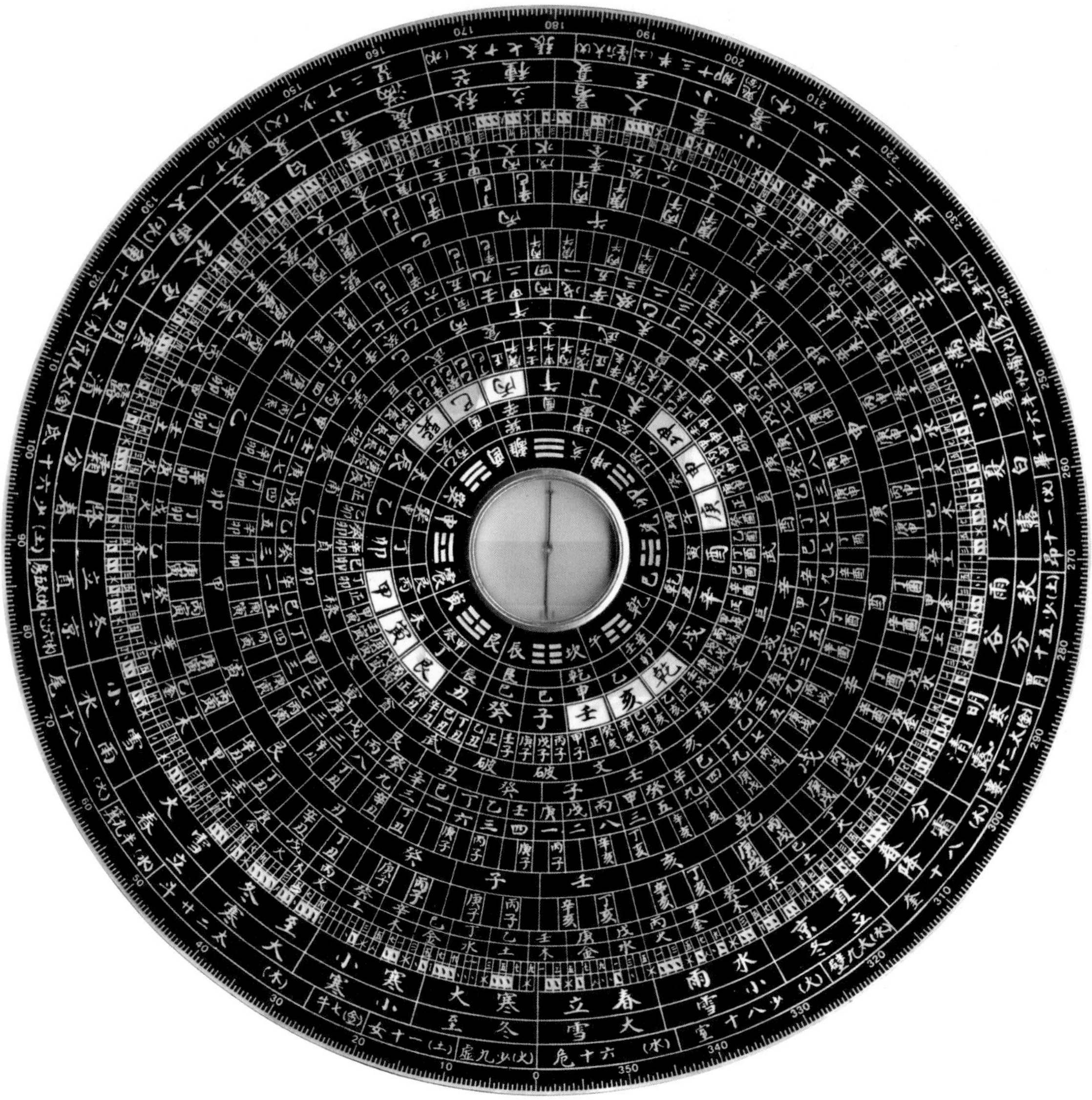

Plate 6: Full 'standard' San He lo p'an.[1] Circa 1980.

[1] Manufactured by Cheng Yi T'ang 正易堂.

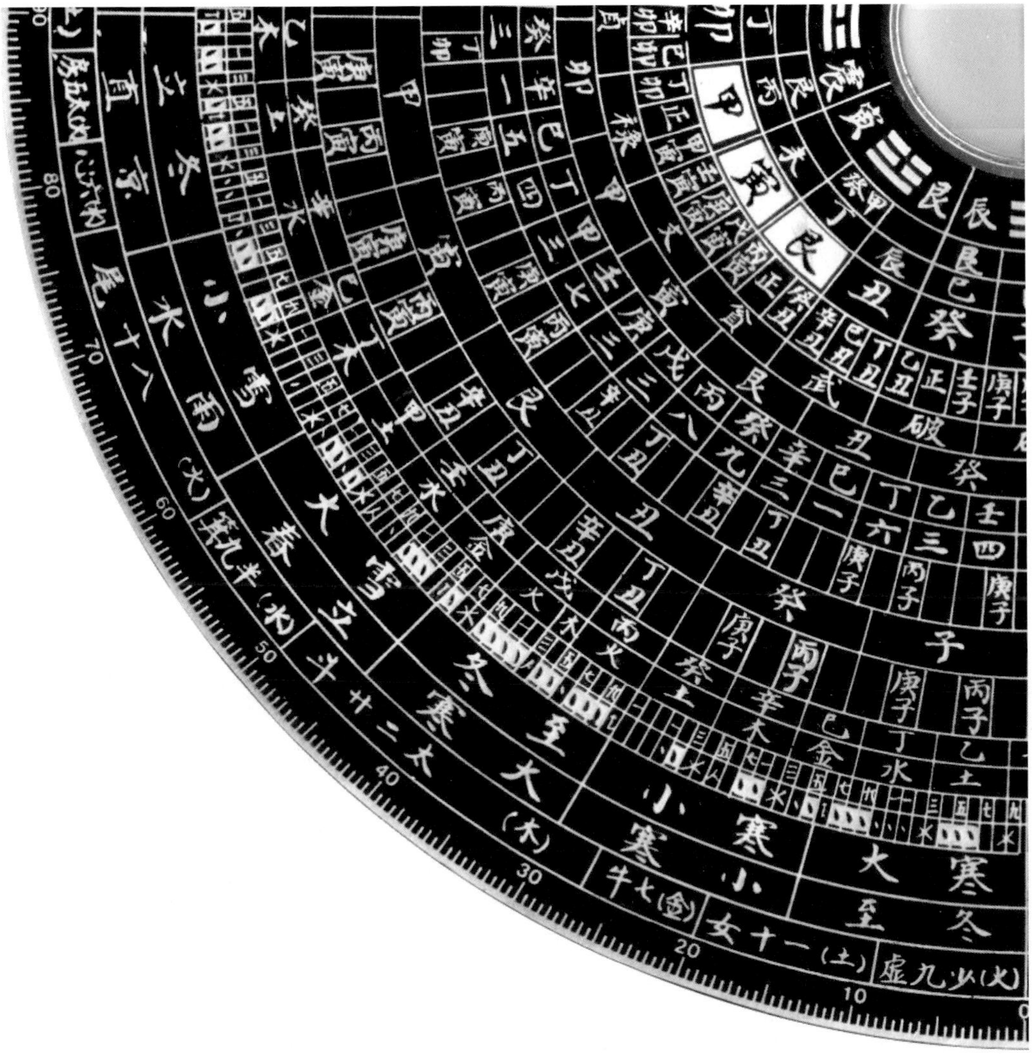

Plate 7: Detailed quarter view of the 'standard' San He lo p'an.[1] Circa 1980.

[1] Manufactured by Cheng Yi T'ang 正易堂.

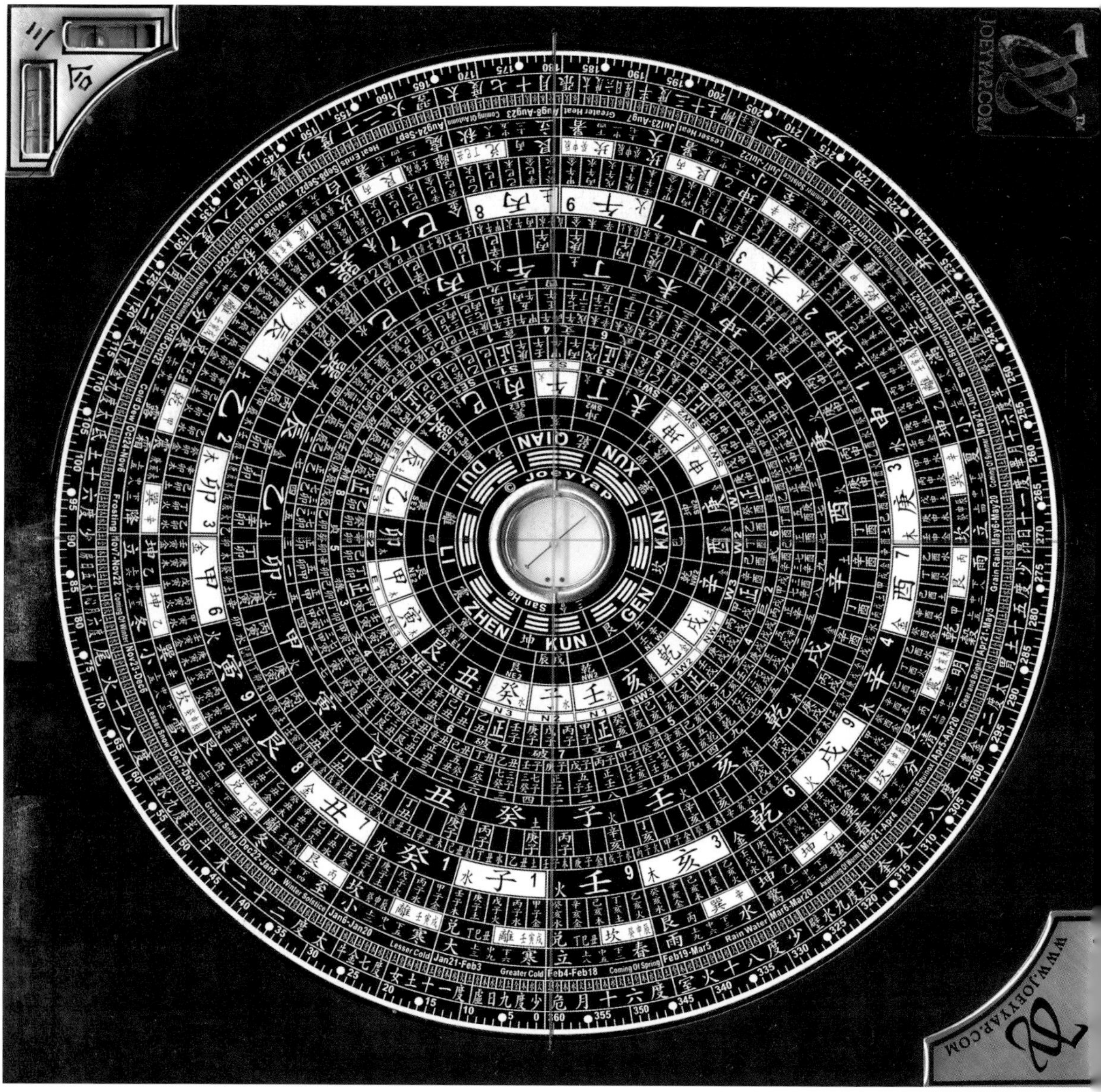

Plate 8: Master Joey Yap's modern semi-English 22 ring San He lo p'an circa 2005.[1]

[1] Courtesy of Master Joey Yap. Available from www.JoeyYap.com.

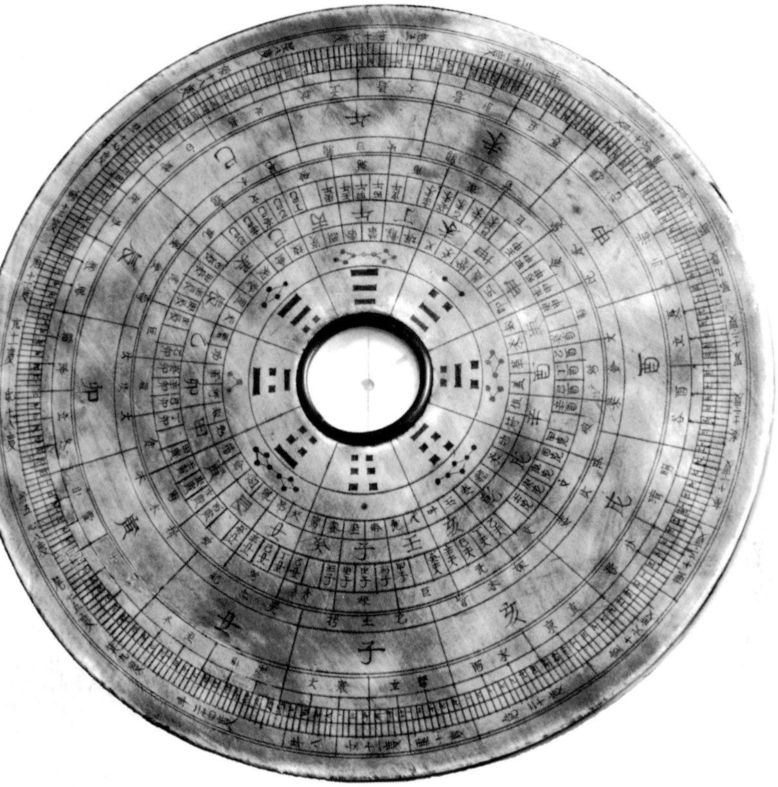

Plate 9: An early 13 ring Chiang P'an probably dated from 1804-1824 CE.[1] It reflects the design from Chiang Ta Hong's time, which has not changed much. The rings are:

1. Former Heaven Sequence 8 trigrams.
2. Lo Shu numbers.
3. 24 *yuan yün* Changing Heaven Stars.
4. 24 Mountains **Earth Plate** (with San Yuan yin/yang markings).
5. 72 Dragons.
6. 24 Nine Stars.[2]
7. 12 Jupiter Stations with the Element.
8. 12 Earthly Branches.
9. 24 Mini-Seasons (starting at Tzu and going anti-clockwise).
10. Blank sectors representing the 72 *hou* (5 day time periods).
11. [**Astronomical Plate**] Star day-degree numbers for each *Hsiu*.
12. 365.25 blank sectors.[3]
13. 28 *Hsiu* with their extent in day-degrees.[4]

[1] This lo p'an might be dated to 1804-1824 as the Lung Lou Heaven Star (ring 3) is at Ch'ien. The *Hsiu* ring is incomplete. Courtesy of the Division of Anthropology, American Museum of Natural History [70_2567].

[2] Note there is a double line Plate division between rings 6 and 7 and again between rings 8 and 9.

[3] This unfinished ring which was meant to carry the auspicious/inauspicious markings of the *Hsiu*.

[4] Also unfinished as only six *Hsiu* have been marked, the last one was marked with a boundary mistake, which probably caused this particular lo p'an to be completely discarded by its maker. Because of this it is unlikely that it was ever used as a working lo p'an.

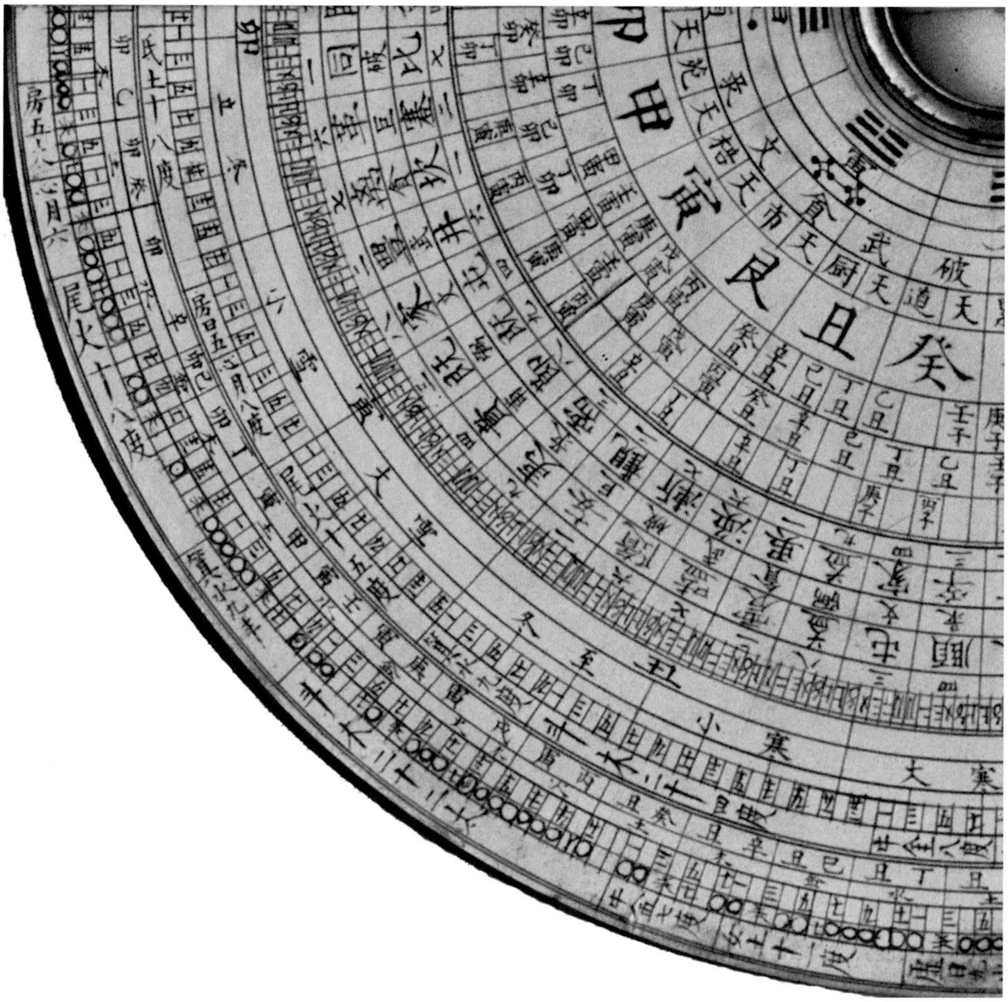

Plate 10: Detail from a Ch'ing dynasty San Yuan lo p'an c. 1880. This lo p'an clearly shows the segregation between Plates marked by double lines.[1] The rings are:

1 **San He Plate** 8 trigrams Former Heaven Sequence
2 *Yao sha*
3 Lo Shu numbers
4 San He Nine Stars in 24 sectors
5 24 Fixed Heaven Stars (two sectors for each star)
6 **Earth Plate** 24 Mountains (with San He yin/yang)
7 72 Mountain-Piercing Dragons
8 60 Earth-Penetrating Dragons
9 120 *fen chin*
10 **San Yuan Plate** Period Number for Nine Stars
11 Inner Plate 64 hexagram names
12 San Yuan Nine Stars in 64 sectors
13 Outer Plate 64 hexagram names
14 Lo Shu Element number
15 Hexagram *yao* numbers with auspicious in red
16 **Astronomical Plate** 12 Earthly Branches
17 24 Mini-Seasons (with 72 blank *hou*)
18 Day-degrees of each *Hsiu*
19 *Hsiu* with number of day-degrees extent and Element
20 60 *ying so* Uneven Dragons
21 61 *ying so* Uneven Dragons Elements
22 365.25 *Hsiu* day-degrees of each *Hsiu*
23 365.25 *Hsiu* day-degrees auspiciousness markings
24 *Hsiu* with number of day-degrees extent and Element[2]

[1] Courtesy of the Science Museum, London [10253278].
[2] Ring 24 starts from the K'ai Hsi epoch, but ring 19 reflects the epoch of the lo p'an circa 1880 CE.

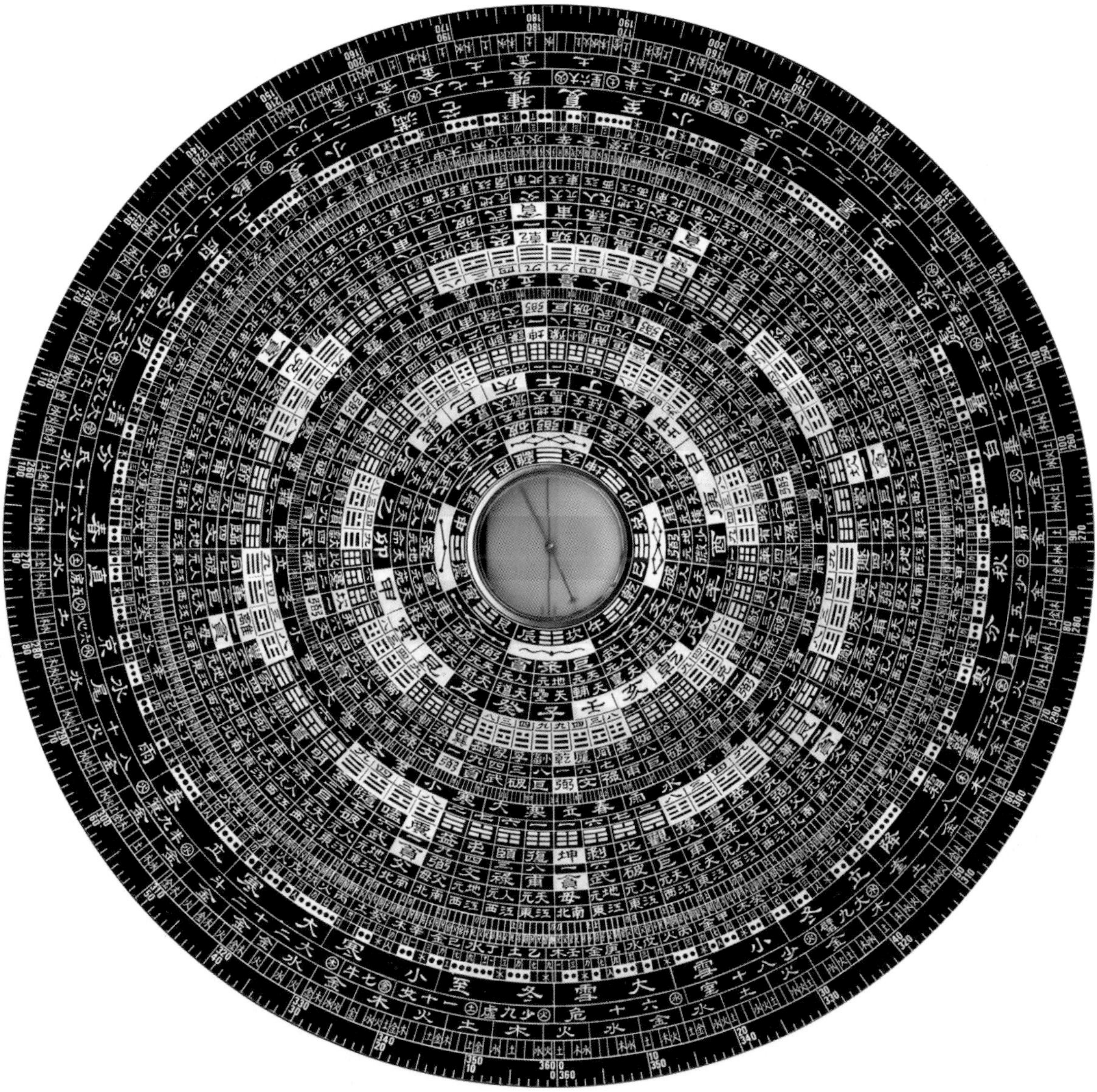

Plate 11: Full 'standard' San Yuan lo p'an.[1] Circa 1990.

[1] Manufactured by Wen Hsiang T'u Shu Kung Ssu 文翔圖書公司.

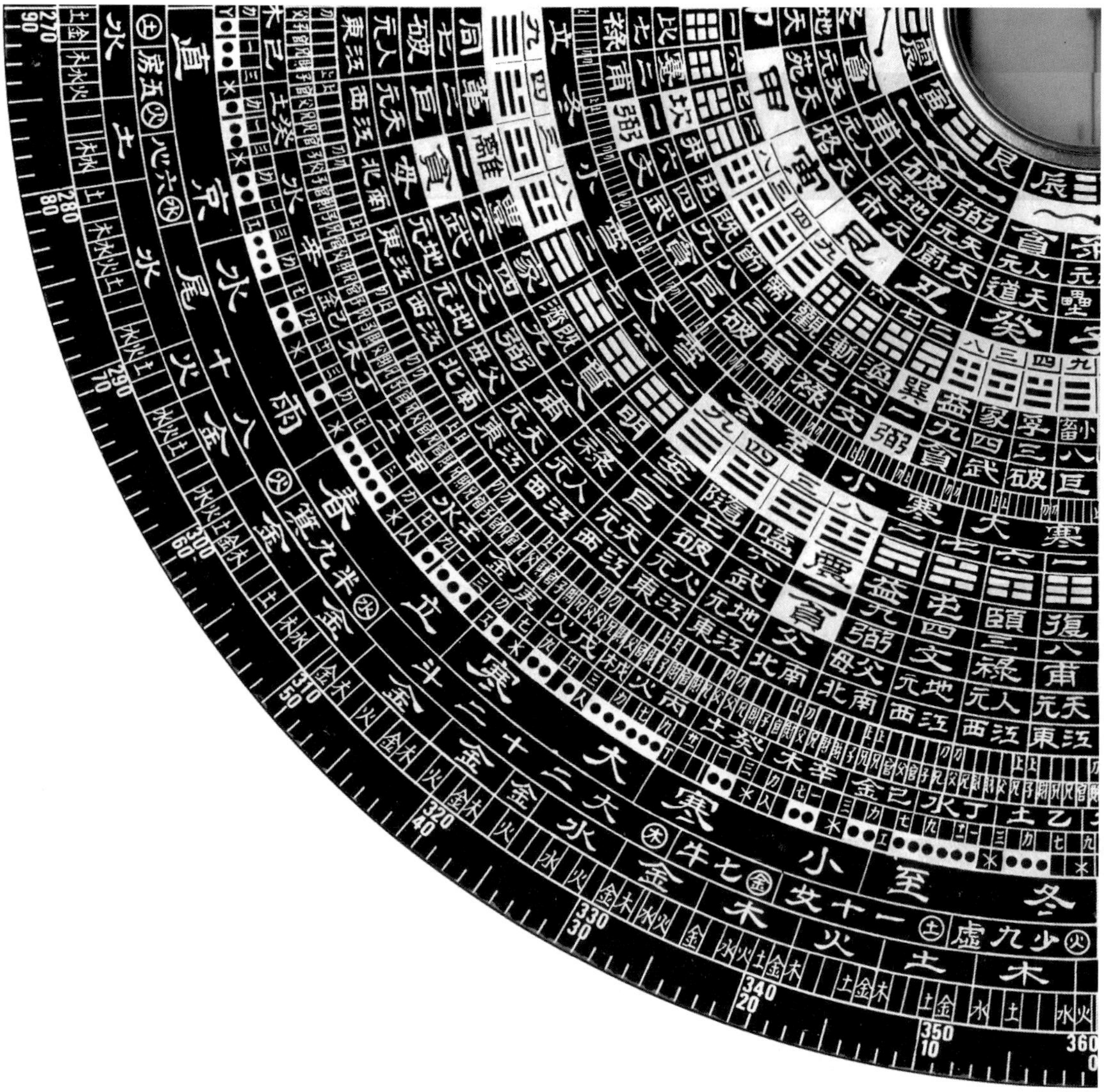

Plate 12: Detailed quarter view of the 'standard' San Yuan lo p'an.[1] Circa 1990.

[1] Manufactured by Wen Hsiang T'u Shu Kung Ssu 文翔圖書公司.

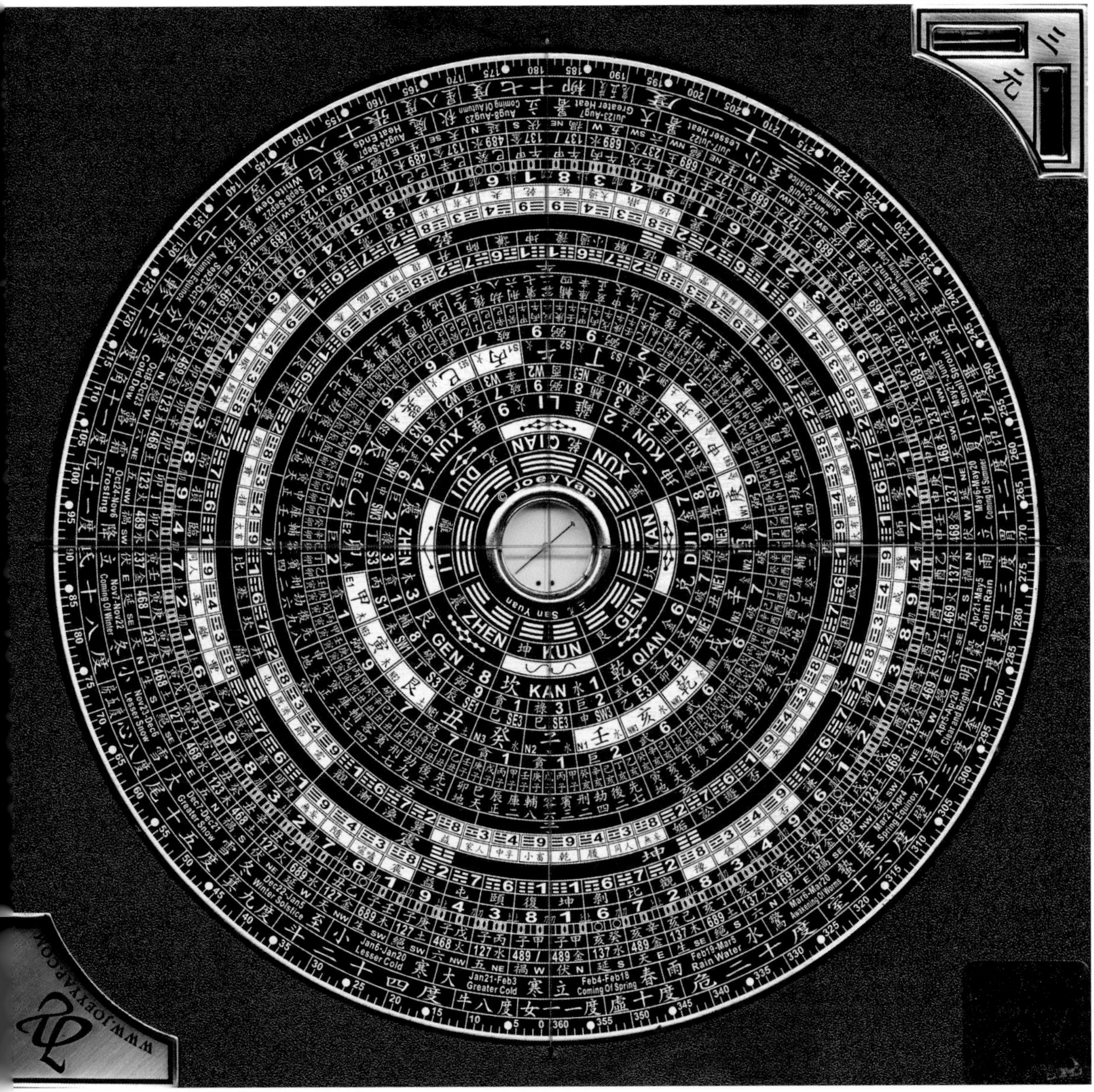

Plate 13: Master Joey Yap's modern semi-English 24 ring San Yuan lo p'an, circa 2005.[1]

[1] Courtesy of Master Joey Yap. Available from www.JoeyYap.com.

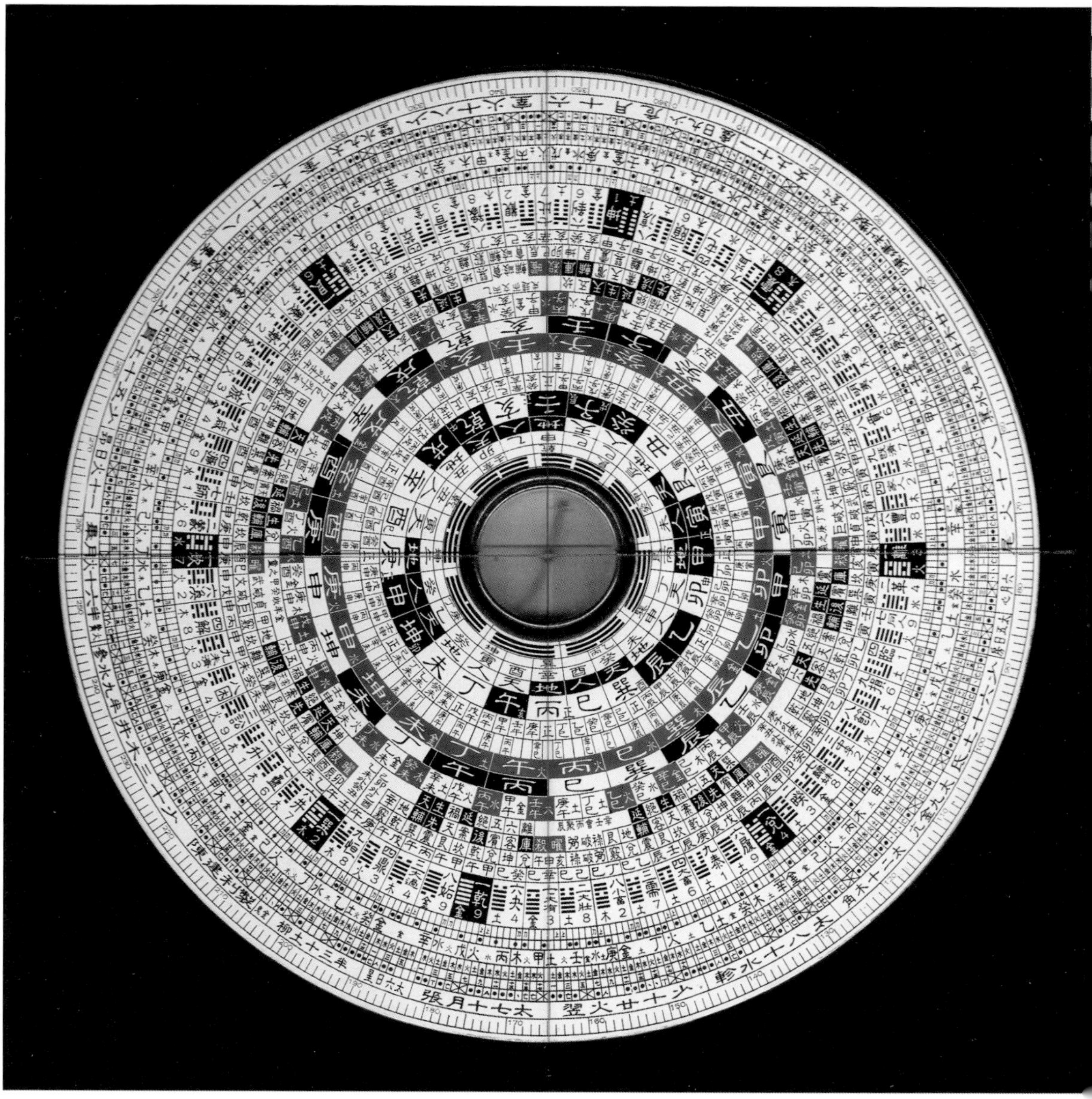

Plate 14: Full Tsung He or mixed lo p'an circa 2000.[1]

[1] Chin Yuan Shu Chü 進源書局.

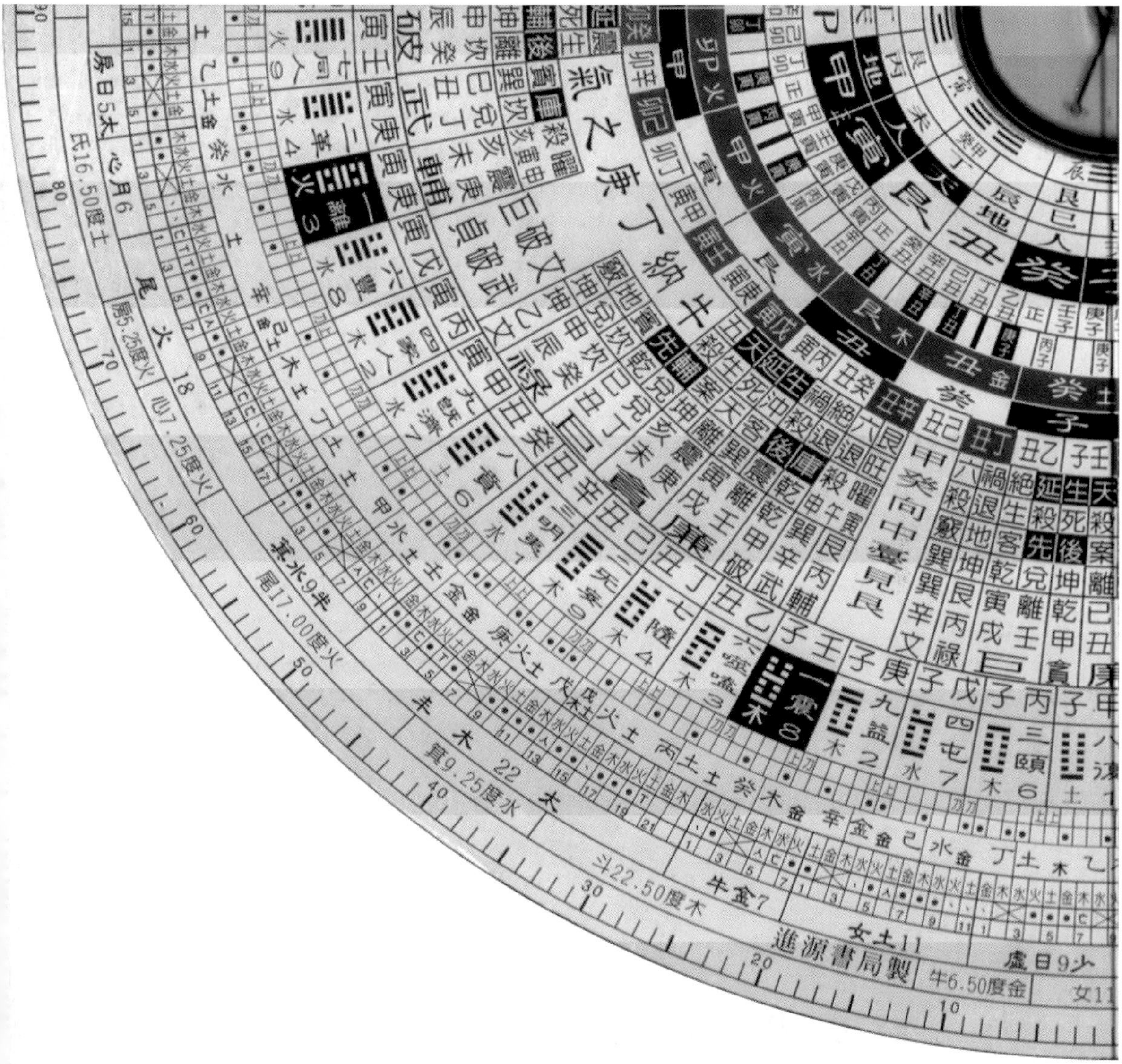

Plate 15: Detailed quarter view of the same Tsung He or mixed lo p'an circa 2000.[1]

[1] Chin Yuan Shu Chü 進源書局.

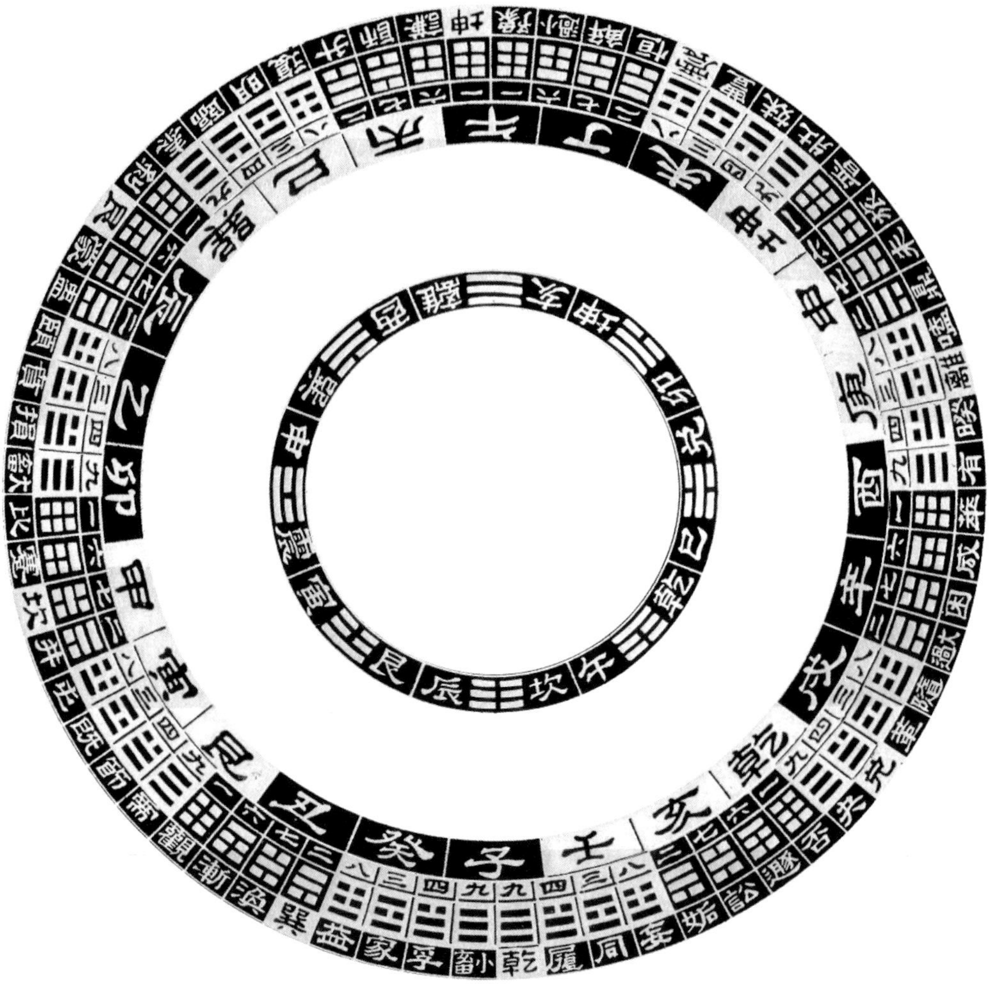

Plate 16: The Inner 64 hexagram ring of a Tsung He or San Yuan lo p'an, with just the Lower trigrams. Chinese names of the hexagrams in the outermost ring, and the Lo Shu number on the inner ring. The 8 trigrams and 24 Mountains are shown for reference.

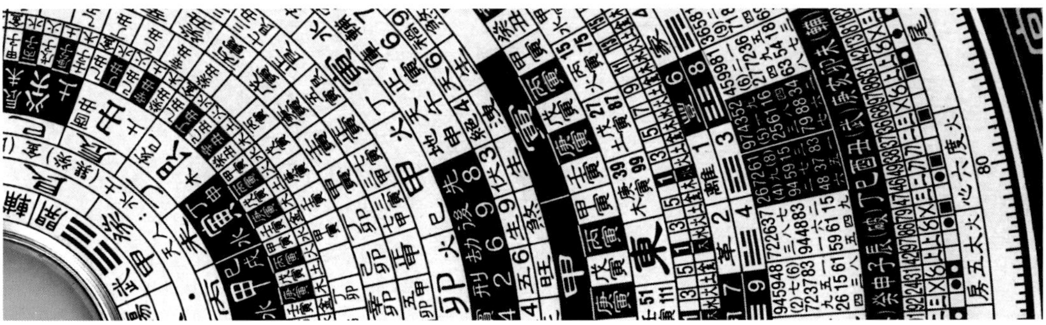

Plate 17: A slice taken from a modern mixed lo p'an with a full Flying Star chart ring incorporated in the 22nd ring showing Periods 5, 6, 7, 8 and 9 for the *Chia* (E1) Mountain.

The Early History and Mythology of Feng Shui

Symbols which are important to Chinese culture and also to feng shui, such as the Green Dragon[1] or the White Tiger date back to at least 4000 BCE. The famous M45 Yangshao tomb with a tiger and a dragon marked out with clam shells has often been cited as proof that feng shui is 6000 years old. But of course these astronomical symbols are Chinese cultural symbols and not wholly the province of feng shui. They definitely do *not* prove that feng shui dates back that far, as many have claimed, despite the fact that the dragon is shown on the East and the tiger shown on the West of a grave orientated to the South.

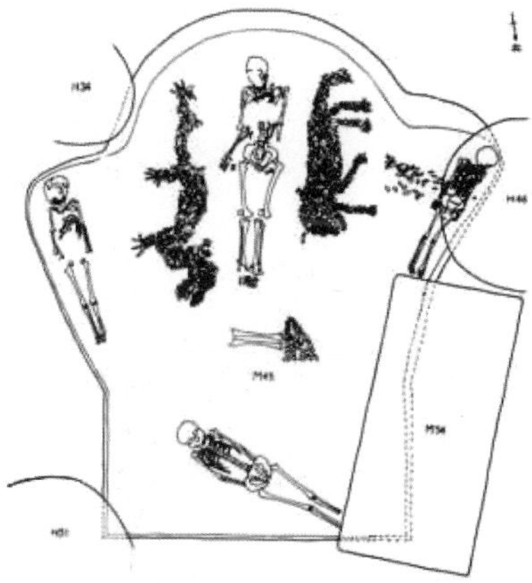

Figure 1: Dragon and tiger outlined in clam shells in a Yangshao grave.

Legendary Emperors

It is often thought that the hexagrams of the *I Ching/Yi Jing* are an important part of the lo p'an, but these did not enter into its construction until a relatively late date. The earliest form of the *Shih* (a predecessor of the *lo p'an)* did not even have the trigrams, and only later did it use just 4 of the trigrams, which it passed along to the early *lo p'an*. Instead, it is true to say that the hexagrams are an important part of Chinese science and philosophy, but not initially a part of feng shui at all. Traditionally Fu Hsi[2] (2852-2737 BCE) was the discoverer or inventor of the eight trigrams. The trigrams are not very important till the rise of the San Yuan School in the late Ming dynasty, being only a minor part (or completely absent from) pre-Ming dynasty lo p'ans. The full 64 hexagrams were only finally added to the lo p'an in about 1817.

---

[1] The colour of the Ch'ing Lung 青龍 *Qing Long* is sometimes rendered as 'green' sometimes as 'blue.' The ancient meaning of the Chinese 青 was blue but the modern use is green. 'Azure dragon' is a translator's compromise.

[2] 伏羲 Fu Xi.

Hsüan Nü, the Mysterious Girl

The history (or more accurately the mythology) of feng shui begins with Hsüan Nü[1] the Dark or Mysterious Girl, or as she is sometimes called, the Lady of the Nine Heavens, who remains a patron goddess of feng shui to this day. At the dawn of Chinese pre-history a story is told of the Yellow Emperor, Huang Ti[2] (2697–2597 BCE) which is supposed to outline the origins of the main instrument of feng shui, the compass or lo p'an. Huang Ti fought a battle against Ch'ih Yu.[3] The latter being a master of magic, tried many tricks during this battle, one of which was to blanket the Emperor's troops with a thick and swirling fog This caused them to completely lose their way, and break rank. Of course clouds and similar phenomena rely upon wind and water (both being the constituents of feng shui) to form, and so we have an initial hint of feng shui being used in this story. The Emperor was on the verge of defeat when Heaven sent him Hsüan Nü, the Mysterious Girl. She gave him a charm in the form of a compass which enabled the Emperor to navigate out of the fog and win the battle.

This myth is subtly enshrined in the titles of later feng shui classics, such as 'A South-pointer to Dispel the Fog about the Lo Ching.'[4] Hsüan Nü also turns up in the Classic called 'The Nine Heavens Mysterious Girl's Universe and Ocean Corner Classic.'[5] Notice the stress upon the corner directions. As we will see later the 'corner directions' NW, NE, SW, SE are marked on the ancient *Shih* board (a forerunner of the feng shui compass) by the 4 important Gates of Heaven, Ghosts, Earth, and Man, and much later by the only 4 trigrams to be incorporated into the 24 Mountains ring. The lo p'an became the supreme tool of feng shui, and more than one feng shui practitioner has had cause to thank the Mysterious Girl for her help and assistance.

It is said of the Mysterious Girl that during the day she determined the directions by the movement of the sun, but at night by the 28 Mansions of the Moon.[6] This clearly shows that there were two different bases for feng shui (lunar and solar): the 28 constellations or Mansions of the Moon, and the directions as determined by the sun. The School of feng shui called Hsüan

---

[1] 玄女 Xuan Nü. Hsüan 玄 Xuan in this name is the same character as that is found in Hsüan K'ung 玄空 Xuan Kong, one of the main Schools of feng shui practice.

[2] 黃帝 Huang Di, the Yellow Emperor. Not to be confused with the first Emperor of the Ch'in (Qin) dynasty, 皇帝.

[3] 蚩尤 Chi You.

[4] *Lo Ching Chih Nan P'o Wu Chi* 羅經指南潑霧集 *Luo Jing Zhi Nan Po Wu Ji* by Yeh Chiu Sheng 葉九升 (incorrectly attributed to Wu T'ien Hung). *Lo ching* is an older name for the *lo p'an*.

[5] *Chiu T'ien Hsüan Nü Ch'ing Nang Hai Chio Ching* 九天玄女青囊海角經 *Jiu Tian Xuan Nü Qing Nang Hai Jiao Jing.*

[6] The 28 *Hsiu* 宿 *Xiu* are sometimes translated as 'constellations,' but are more accurately the 28 unequal divisions of the sky which make up the Mansions of the Moon.

K'ung[1] reflects this myth by using the same word, '*Hsüan*' or Mysterious in its title, but of course this School doesn't date from that period. The exact quote is:

> In the daytime Hsüan Nü [the Mysterious Girl] determined the directions [of the lo p'an] by the rising and setting of the sun.[2] In the night she determined the directions by the divisions of the [28] *Hsiu*.[3]

Or in other words, she behaved just as sailors or astronomers have done for centuries.

Later the Emperor Shun (2255–2205 BCE) attempted to regulate the rivers, and his legendary knowledge of flood control reflects the control of ch'i associated with water. Emperor Yü (2205-2197 BCE) succeeds in this task and discovers the Lo Shu.[4] In the Hsia 夏 (Xia) dynasty (2150-1557 BCE) the solar calendar, which is still used for feng shui calculations, was supposedly first established. In fact this dynasty has given its name to the Hsia Calendar.[5]

Shang Dynasty (1557-1027 BCE)

In the Shang 商 dynasty the 60-fold cycle made up of the permutations of the 10 Heavenly Stems and the 12 Earthly Branches was allegedly established. This cycle of Sexagenary (60-fold) Combinations is fundamental to the construction of a number of rings on the lo p'an, and to the measurement of time cycles of both 60 days and 60 years, used to this day in all areas of Chinese culture. It is also basic to the use of Four Pillar *pa tzu* (*bazi*) astrology. It was used to mark the years until 1929, when it was replaced in the People's Republic of China. Other Chinese communities continue to use it, so for example, 2011 is accounted the year of the Water Dragon.

Chou (Zhou) Dynasty (1027 - 221 BCE)

In the Chou 周 (Zhou) dynasty, there is evidence from oracle bones that solar and lunar eclipses were recorded. Constellations were recorded in the *Book of Odes* (9th century BCE) and a system of divination called *chan pu*[6] was used to determine the auspiciousness of sites. *Chan pu* also dealt with the nature of water on a site, and the effect of underground streams, amongst other things.

In the *Chou Shu*[7] ('Annals of the Chou Dynasty') the founding of the city of

---

[1] 玄空 Xuan Kong.
[2] This is a reference to the use of the *gnomon* to establish directions from shadow position readings.
[3] *I Shu T'ien*, Chapter 651, *Hui K'ao* I, page 16a, as translated by Needham (1962), Volume 4, Part 1, page 303, but with some minor translational amendments by the present author.
[4] Emperors 舜 Shun and 禹 Yu.
[5] 夏歷 Xia Li.
[6] 占卜 *zhan bu*.
[7] 周書 *Zhou Shu*.

Luoyang is recorded. Soon after he came to power in 1027 BCE, the second King of the Chou dynasty, Chou Ch'eng Wang[1] came to examine the site. The record is very detailed, and records him arriving in the morning of the 21st day of the 2nd lunar month of the year of the founding of Luoyang.[2] Before that Master T'ai Pao Chao Kung[3] surveyed the site for its suitability. He used *chan pu* divination to determine the correct positioning for the fortifications, and probably an early form of *ti li* for the overall positioning of the city. He chose a position at the confluence of streams for the location of Luoyang.[4]

After making appropriate sacrifices, construction work on the new city began. Although it is clear to what extent *chan pu* involved locational divination, this probably ranks as the first detailed documented use of feng shui-like principles. When the Ch'ing editors came to portraying this ancient event in the late 19th century, their romanticised illustration very clearly shows a feng shui consultation complete with a lo p'an (see Figure 51), but this is probably more of a Ch'ing vignette than an accurate portrayal of Chou dynasty feng shui.

What did Confucius know about Feng Shui?

During the historic period called the Spring and Autumn Period[5] (770-476 BCE) in the middle of the Chou dynasty, Confucius edited the *I Ching*, whose hexagrams later formed the major rings of the San Yuan lo p'an. Slightly before then Lao Tzu[6] composed the *Tao Teh Ching*[7] the fundamental text of Taoism.

Feng shui derives its theoretical background from Taoist cosmology. Connected to this are a number of key contributing elements that make up feng shui: water; the heavens; the five Elements and magnetism. And it is during this dynasty that connections began to be made between them.

Water

In 510 BCE, King Hoh Lü[8] buried his daughter, who had committed suicide. When building the tomb the workmen cut huge water tanks connected to the tomb indicating that, even in this period, water was intimately connected with the feng shui of graves.

---

[1] 周成王 Zhou Cheng Wang.

[2] 洛邑 Luo Yi.

[3] 太保召公 Tai Bao Zhao Gong.

[4] It was apparently not till 250 years later in 772 BCE that the Chou dynasty actually moved their capital to Luoyang.

[5] 春秋 Chun Qiu.

[6] 老子 Lao Zi.

[7] 道德經 *Dao De Jing*.

[8] 闔閭 He Lü, reigned 514-496 BCE.

> The grave of Hoh Lü's daughter was situated outside the Ch'ang gate (of the capital), on the north side of the road. Its lower square [water] tank was forty-eight *pu* wide and had a water depth of twenty-five feet. The other tank measured sixty *pu*, with a depth of ten feet five inches. The grave tunnel opened upon the road which led to the temple and which ran further in a southern direction through the Ku-su gate. The whole ground had a circumference of six miles.[1]

This does not mean that feng shui existed at this point in time, but the association between graves, water, and possibly ch'i was known.

The Heavens

Archaeologists have found grave artefacts marked with the Northern Ladle[2] constellation dating from 433 BCE and before. This constellation, which is a very important constellation for Taoists, also has its applications in feng shui and Taoist magic, and is at the root of the Flying Star School of feng shui. This use of the Northern Ladle does not however prove that fully fledged feng shui dates back to that time. However, one fragment on which the Northern Ladle was marked was part of a *Shih* plate, which was a forerunner of the lo p'an.

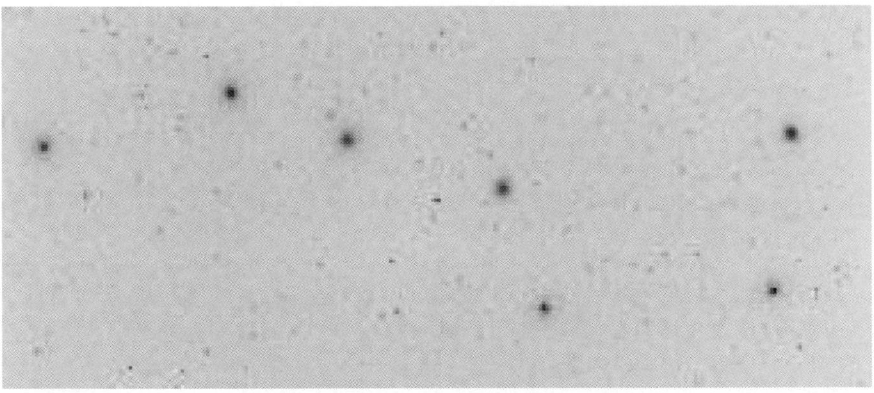

Figure 2: The Seven Stars of the Northern Ladle photographed as they actually appear in the night sky. You can use a ruler to check the completely straight alignment of stars 1, 5 and 7 and also of stars 4, 5, and 6, counting from the right. You can see how these star alignments could be used as very precisely aligned pointers. Stars 2 and 1 also point to the North Pole star.

---

[1] From the *Yueh Tsueh Shu*. A *pu* 步 *bu* is defined as a pace or step, so these water tanks were substantial. *Li* is often translated 'miles,' as in this passage, but it is now thought to be 1/3 of a mile. So the site may have been two miles in circumference and therefore have a diameter of about 1100 yards (1024 metres).

[2] *Pei Tou* 北斗 *Bei Dou*. This is a very important constellation (or more accurately, asterism) for Chinese astronomy, astrology, feng shui and Taoist magic. It has a unique position near the North Pole Star around which it rotates over the course of the year, in such a way that you can tell the time, or the season, simply by observing the position of its 'handle.' It is part of the constellation of Ursa Major, or the Great Bear. In the US it is usually referred to as the Big Dipper, which is a name I have refrained from using here because of its English connotation of fairground and fun-park rides.

The Five Elements

The philosopher Tsou Yen (c. 350-270 BCE) was the first to distinctly mention the Five Elements, Fire, Water, Earth, Metal and Wood, although undoubtedly they were known well before his time.

The patterns of interaction between the Elements, successively destroying or creating each other are the basis for many feng shui formulae.

Magnetism and Magnetic North

Another element which feng shui seeks to measure is magnetism. The compass is perhaps the most amazing of all ancient Chinese instruments. Joseph Needham stated that the discovery of the compass:

> was the greatest Chinese contribution to physics [and was of] incalculable importance…as the first and oldest representative of all those dial and pointer readings which play so great a part in modern scientific observation.[1]

The discovery of the connection between ferrites (oxides or salts of iron) and the magnetic field of the Earth is lost in the mists of times. Ferrites were first discovered thousands of year ago. One of the areas where large deposits were found was the district of Magnesia[2] in Turkey, giving the mineral's English name of magnetite (Fe_3O_4). Magnetite was later nicknamed lodestone.[3] In China the stone was called the *tz'u shih*[4] or 'loving stone' a reference no doubt to its power of attraction. Another Chinese name for it is even more interesting, *hsüan shi*[5] the 'mysterious stone.' *Hsüan* 玄 is the same Chinese character as in *Hsüan K'ung* 玄空 *Xuan Kong*, later the name of a famous School of feng shui practice.

It became apparent that this stone would attract iron, and iron stroked by it would align itself with the Earth's magnetic field if allowed to swing freely. Stroking this mineral against a freely rotating iron needle, would cause this needle to readily and precisely align itself North-South. This magnetised iron needle is at the heart of the compass. The key step in the creation of a compass was to mark directional indicators around this magnetised free-swinging needle. The Chinese were aware of this phenomenon probably well before the 4th century BCE, and therefore 1500 years before the compass was known or used in Europe or the rest of the word.

---

[1] Needham (1962), Volume 4, Part 1, page 229.

[2] Magnesia was the site of the ancient and celebrated temple of Artemis Leucophryene, goddess of love and attraction. The nearby city, Ephesus, was also important for its temple of Artemis.

[3] There is no dispute that the attractive power of the lodestone was known in both China and the West since at least 500 BCE. Thales, 6th century BCE is quoted by Aristotle on the attractive powers of the magnet.

[4] 慈石 *ci shi.* Now more usually 磁石.

[5] 玄石 *xuan shi.*

Ancient Astronomical Beginnings

The earliest ring on the lo p'an is almost certainly the ring of the 28 *Hsiu* or Mansions of the Moon,[1] which is found on the outer edge of most lo p'ans, amongst the Astronomical rings.

There are many scattered traces of these *Hsiu* on oracle bones and in early Chinese tombs inscribed on astronomical and divinatory material. The earliest material includes crude star maps of the 28 *Hsiu* together with images of the 4 Celestial Animals, both of which later form part of feng shui practice. The ancient tomb box lid shown in Figure 3 is perhaps the most well known. It dates from 433 BCE and shows both the 28 *Hsiu* and two out of the 4 Celestial Animals.

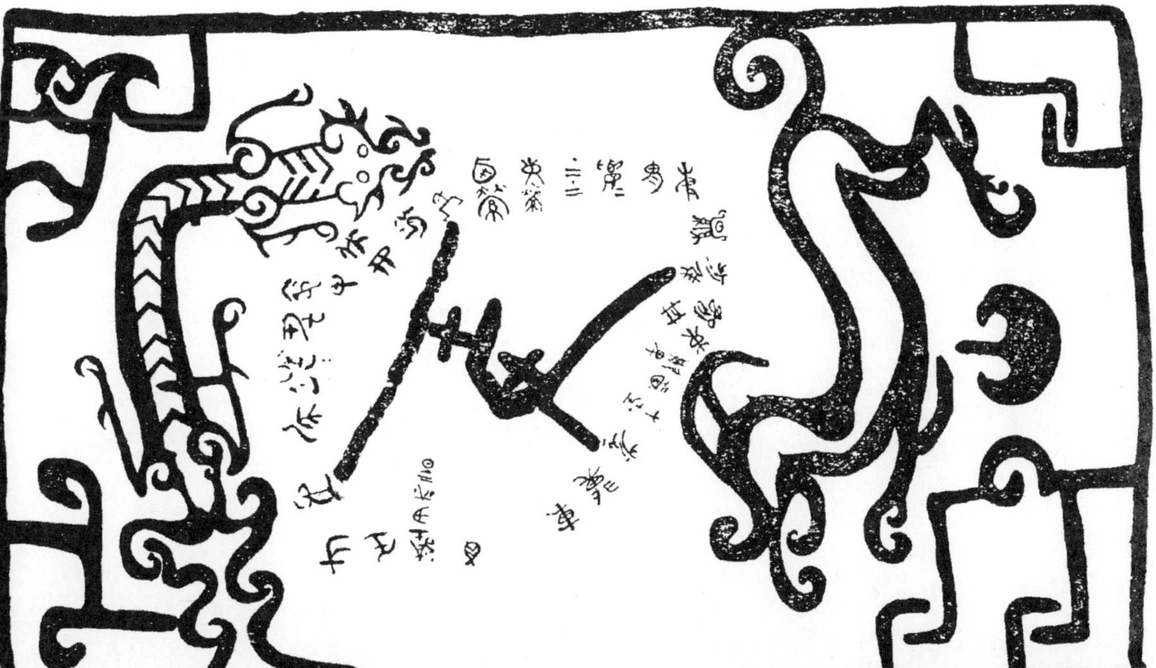

Figure 3: Lid of a lacquer chest found in the tomb of the Marquis Yi of the Tsêng (Zeng) State dating from 433 BCE.[2]

The main figures on the chest lid are the Green Dragon (head upwards on the left) and White Tiger (head downwards on the right). North is top left and South is bottom right. The small characters are the 28 *Hsiu* or Mansions of the Moon which rotate in a *clockwise* direction, a tradition which will be later reversed on the lo p'an. The character in the centre is the Northern Ladle or

[1] 宿 *Xiu*.

[2] Discovered in 1978 in Hubei Province, now in the Hubei Museum.

Pei tou (*bei dou*) 北斗 with its major lines just touching the 4 *Hsiu* near the 4 Cardinal Points.[1] This lid clearly demonstrates that the Celestial Animals and the 28 *Hsiu* were a major part of Chinese cosmology almost 2500 years ago, but this does not prove that feng shui existed at that date.

Early Masters

One possible point of origin for some of the techniques of feng shui is the military strategist Chang Liang[2] (c.230-185 BCE). He is supposed to have learned feng shui from the Taoist priest 'Red Pine Master' or Ch'ih Sung Tzu[3] who is sometimes held to be the inventor of the 'Eight Stars, Eight Gates' method of feng shui.

The next important figure is the delightfully named Kuei Ku Tzu[4] (flourished 220 BCE) a name which literally means 'Ghost Valley Master.' This could refer to either his special powers or to his geographical origin. Whichever it is, his mother is reputed to have conceived him after spending the night weeping over the grave of his dead father. In her sleep she dreamed that her husband was once more alive, and came to her and impregnated her with a son, whose name could very well imply 'son of the ghost.' A more likely story is that he was originally called Wang Hsü,[5] but because he came from Kuei Ku mountain, was renamed Kuei Ku Tzu, the 'Kuei Ku Mountain Master.' Either way Kuei Ku Tzu became a master of the arts of divination, astrology, military strategy and magic.

The Chinese use of the compass (not necessarily the lo p'an) for feng shui and other dry land purposes can be traced back with certainty to the 4th century BCE. The following quote is from a book by Kuei Ku Tzu which clearly states:

> when the people of [the State of] Chen go out to collect jade, they carry a 'South-pointer' with them so as not to lose their way.

So as the 'South-pointer' or *ssu nan*,[6] is conveniently portable, it is therefore not some kind of observatory equipment or South-pointing carriage, and it is therefore most likely to have been a compass. Another quote from the 3rd century BCE in Han Fei Tzu's *Yu Tu P'ien* helps to reinforce the importance of south-seeking compasses for land navigation:[7]

---

[1] From Cheng (1998), page 179.

[2] 張良 Zhang Liang.

[3] 赤松子 Chi Song Zi. Sometimes rendered as the Red Peach Master. Also known as, the 'Yellow Stone Master' or Huang-Shih Kung 黃石公 Huang Shi Gong. These may have been different people.

[4] 鬼谷子 Gui Gu Zi. Kuei 鬼 literally means 'ghost.'

[5] 王詡 Wang Xu.

[6] 司南 *si nan*. See Needham (1962).Volume 4, Part 1, page 269.

[7] 韓非子 《有度篇》 Han Fei Zi's *You Du Pian*.

> This makes the prince forget his position and confuse West and East, until he really does not know where he stands. So the ancient kings set up a 'South-pointer,' in order to distinguish between the directions of dawn [East] and sunset [West].

As the reference is to *ancient* kings, we may reasonably expect that this device originated at least a century before this quote, in the 4th century BCE. This device sounds if it was a larger and more institutional construction than a pocket compass, but it was still a 'South-pointer.' Some academics have suggested that this refers to the *gnomon,* but I think that is unlikely.

The Gnomon and Astronomic North

Although the *gnomon* was extensively used for defining astronomical directions (by plotting the shadows it casts at different times of the day or year)[1] it could not by any stretch of the imagination be described as a 'South-pointer.' Just as the compass is used to find Magnetic North, so the gnomon is used to find Astronomic North.

The gnomon is basically a shadow stick, and its function is not to find magnetic north, but to find true or Astronomic north. The gnomon was regularly used in ancient China (and still is today) as the simplest way of tracking the movement of the Sun, and marking its sunrise and sunset positions. It is not easy to look directly at the Sun, as everybody knows, but you can easily examine its shadow. Hence, marking shadow points on the ground cast by an eight foot[2] high gnomon, has been a technique used by the ancient Chinese since before even the Han dynasty.

As well as tracking the daily and seasonal movement of the sun in the sky, you can also use a gnomon for determining True North. To do so, you need to plot a range of shadow points made at, say, half hour intervals during the course of a day. Then connect up the points to form a shadow point plot line (see dotted line in Figure 4). Then draw a circle with its centre at the base of the gnomon (C) which will intersect the shadow point plot line at two points (A and B).

Then bisect the angle made at the centre by these two points of intersection (as shown in Figure 4), and you will produce a line that points directly to Astronomic North (CD). This was the daytime method that was used by the astronomers of ancient China to find Astronomic North. It can still be used today.

---

[1] See Figure 5.

[2] Eight Han feet is about 192 cm or about 6 feet 3.6 inches. The height of gnomon varied, up to 7 feet 10.5 inches.

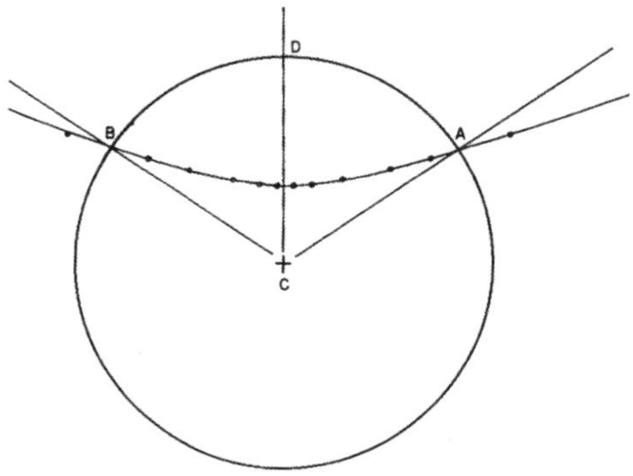

Figure 4: The geometry used to find Astronomic North from the gnomon points.

A simpler method described in the 'Gnomon of the Chou dynasty' confirms that the method pre-dates 221 BCE.[1]

> At dawn set up a gnomon and observe its shadow. At sunset observe its shadow once more. The ends of the shadow align to indicate due east-west. [The line drawn from] their midpoint to the gnomon indicates due north-south.

Figure 5: The Ancient Chinese Gnomon. Note the short shadow to the left of the base of the gnomon (because the time is close to noon) and the sun almost directly above.[2]

---

[1] *Chou Pi Suan Ching* 周髀算經 *Zhou Bi Suan Jing*, Section 2:8a. See Major (1993) page 277; and Cullen (1996), pages 101-117.

[2] *Shu Ching T'u Shuo* 書經圖說 *Shu Jing Tu Shuo*.

Ch'in (Qin) Dynasty (221-206 BCE)

One of Kuei Ku Tzu's students was a government minister of Ch'in Shih Huang Ti,[1] the ruler of the short lived but immensely important state of 秦 Ch'in. In fact Ch'in Shih Huang Ti became the 'First Emperor' of a united China and founder of the Ch'in dynasty who unified all of China for the first time, and standardised the written language, weights and measures of China.

The Ch'in dynasty was a defining dynasty for Chinese culture and identity, and for feng shui. It saw the unification of a number of independent states under Ch'in Shih Huang Ti, who is perhaps best known popularly for the serried rows of terracotta warriors buried near his as yet unexcavated tomb.

His still unopened grave mound is reputed to contain a fabulous split pyramid built over a huge hall. The ceiling of the hall is engraved with a chart of the heavens inset with precious stones for stars, and the floor is a map of all of China with all its rivers and seas actually filled with flowing liquid mercury. High concentrations of mercury found in the surrounding soil tend to confirm this account by the almost contemporary historian Ssu-ma Ch'ien (Sima Qian 145-86 BCE).[2] Adjacent pits outside the main burial mound contained the famous pottery warriors at Hsi-An.[3]

This dynasty also saw massive building projects such as the consolidation of the Great Wall of China and various palaces, so building rules and techniques are likely to have been also codified during this reign. By implication, the magical skills of the Ghost Valley Master may have been involved in the actual founding of this dynasty and hence of a unified China. But we are more interested here in the Ghost Valley Master's contribution to feng shui. His life has also been documented by Ssu-ma Ch'ien, the most famous Chinese historian of the Han dynasty.

It is often said that feng shui goes back six thousand years, but the first written traces of actual feng shui practice can be found in newly discovered records from the Ch'in dynasty dating from 217 BCE.[4] It is very likely that this dynasty saw the codification of the practice of feng shui, although not under that name. Also a number of stories of feng shui masters from this period are recorded in the historical 'Book of the Ch'in dynasty.'[5]

---

[1] 秦始皇帝 Qin Shi Huang Di.

[2] 司馬遷 Sima Qian (c. 145–90 BCE).

[3] 西安 Xi An or Xi'an.

[4] Almanac bamboo strips from Shui Hu Ti 睡虎地, which contain Stems, Branches and *Chien Ch'ü* 建除 (the cyclic characters used in auspicious time calculations) dated 217 BCE.

[5] *Ch'in Shu* 秦書 *Qin Shu.*

Han Dynasty (206 BCE – 220 CE)

The Han 漢 dynasty was also a defining dynasty for China, and in fact Chinese sometimes refer to themselves as the Han people. At the beginning of the Han dynasty the *Shih Chi* by Ch'u Shao Sun mentions *k'an yü chia* or diviners who use *k'an yü*[1] as an honourable profession. *K'an yü* was one facet of feng shui, concerned with tracing the forms of the earth, and the energy that passes through them. The Form School, *Luan T'ou* or *Hsing Shih P'ai*,[2] is really a method rather than a School. Although it could date from as far back as the Warring States period[3] (475 to 221 BCE), it is only certainly documented in the Han dynasty. This method was concerned with finding the *hsüeh* or 'the feng shui node' by making a detailed physical study of the land and watercourses, and concerned itself with tracing the dragon veins or *lung mai* connecting these. In one early text it was noted that the ch'i of the earth flowed in vessels comparable with those in the body of man and animals.[4]

During this dynasty many classics of *k'an yü* were written, such as the *Golden K'an yü Thesaurus* by 'Master Blue Raven' Ch'ing Wu.[5] *K'an yü* was championed by the Taoists Ch'ih Sung Tzu (who also taught Chang Liang) and Ch'ing Wu, who argued that geological bodies, particularly mountains and rivers, are repositories of ch'i. Much detailed study of the mountain ranges of China was carried out and this may have been the beginning of the use of the term *lung mai* or 'dragon veins.' The geographers of the period produced detailed maps with drawings of ridges, peaks, valleys and rivers, demonstrating a lively interest in 'dragons.'

Wang Ching[6] (d. 83 CE) also associated *k'an yü* with hydraulic engineering and water control. At this point Ching Fang (79-37 BCE)[7] probably established the *na yin*[8] system for ascribing an Element to each of the Sexagenary Combinations which had been invented in a previous dynasty, and in turn attributed a Sexagenary Combination to each (line) of the hexagrams of the *I Ching*.

The *Huai Nan Tzu*, a classical astronomical text written in 139 BCE, is very relevant to the history of feng shui. Its key chapters include: V – Nine Fields; VI – Five Planets; XIV – Purple Palace; XVII – Seven Habitations; XVIII – Solar Nodes; XIX – 12 Chronograms; XXVII – Dipper Handle and XXXIV-XLIII - Portents.

---

1 堪輿 *Kan Yu.*

2 形式派 *Xing Shi Pai* is now referred to as the Mountain Top School or *Luan T'ou P'ai* 巒頭派 *Luan Tou Pai.*

3 戰國 Zhan Guo.

4 'The Book of Master Kuan' *Kuan Tzu* 管子 *Guan Zi.*

5 青烏 Qing Wu.

6 王景 Wang Jing.

7 京房 Jing Fang.

8 納陰, meaning literally to 'accept yin.'

The Shih P'an

The *Shih*, an astronomical, magical and feng shui device,[1] which was the direct predecessor of the lo p'an, was developed in, or possibly just before, the Han dynasty. This artefact which is key to the understanding of the evolution of the lo p'an is called the *Shih p'an*.[2] This device is the direct ancestor of the lo p'an.

Only eight historic *Shih* boards have so far been found.[3] The earliest was found in tombs dating from the Early Han dynasty, which is therefore contemporary with the *Huai Nan Tzu*.[4] The *Shih* board illustrated in Figure 9 is reconstructed from fragments of one excavated from the tomb of the second Marquis of Yi,[5] in Wuwei County, Anhui Province dating from circa 165 BCE.[6] Of the eight *Shih* discovered, some examples have been found as far north as Korea, indicating that this instrument was fairly widespread, and also indicating a very early start to the practice of feng shui in Korea. It was obviously a very popular instrument as there are no less than 22 books on the various uses of the *Shih* listed in the Bibliography of the *T'ung Chih Lüeh*[7] in 1150 CE. Sadly none have survived.

The *Shih* board consists of two pieces: the top revolving disk called the Heaven Plate (or *t'ien p'an*) and the larger fixed square board called the Earth Plate (or *ti p'an*). A spindle connected the centre of both, so that the Heaven Plate can rotate on the Earth Plate, allowing various combinations of Heaven and Earth sectors to be derived. The Heaven Plate is often referred to as the 'cover,' and the Earth Plate as the 'chassis' in *k'an yü*.

The central Heaven Plate has an image of the Northern Ladle constellation inscribed upon it, and this image is the key to understanding how the *Shih* worked. This constellation or asterism was held to be sacred by Taoists, and it also performed the very important task of identifying both the time of night and the season, as it rotated in the night sky around the Pole Star. In the night sky the handle of the Northern Ladle acts as a sort of seasonal clock, which rotates a full circle every 24 hours. Where it comes to rest at midnight each night indicates the season.

---

[1] Referred to a "cosmograph" by Major in *Huai Nan Tzu* (*Huainanzi*). See Major (1993).

[2] 式盤 *Shi Pan*.

[3] All of these are described and tabulated in Appendix 9.5 of *The Complete Guide to the Feng Shui Compass*.

[4] Fragments of this device were found in two Han dynasty tombs in Korea, the tomb of Wang Hsü (died 69 CE) and the 'Painted Basket' tomb. Another six *Shih* have been found since (none of which were associated with or found near a spoon, magnetic or otherwise).

[5] 曾侯乙 Zeng Hou Yi.

[6] The original excavation report is in Kansu Provincial Museum report, *Guansu sheng bowuguan*, 1972, pages 14-15. Even today Anhui Province is one of the main centres for lo p'an manufacture.

[7] 通志略 *Tong Zhi Lue*.

To explain how it can tell *both* the clock and the seasonal time it is best to refer to Figure 6. This table is essential to understanding the *Shih*. It shows what you will see if you are standing in the Northern hemisphere and looking towards the North Pole, at various times and seasons.

You can see that, if you take a consistent time to observe the Northern Ladle (midnight was the standard observational time), the Northern Ladle's handle-pointer moves around the sky according to the season, moving from East (Spring) to South (Summer) to West (Autumn) to North (Winter). Likewise you can take different times during the same mid-Winter day and watch it move from East (dawn) to South (noon) to West (dusk) to North (midnight).

Apparent direction pointed to by the handle of the Northern Ladle →		South	West	North	East
at Spring Equinox	21 March	at dawn	at noon[1]	at dusk	midnight
at mid Summer	21 June	midnight	at dawn	at noon	at dusk
at Autumn Equinox	21 September	at dusk	midnight	at dawn	at noon
at mid Winter	21 December	at noon	at dusk	midnight	at dawn

Figure 6: The position of the Northern Ladle at different times of the year, and at different times of the day and night. This is the real key to understanding the *Shih*.

However the *Shih* plate is often associated with one of the two great 'red herrings' in the history of feng shui. We will therefore make a slight detour to examine these 'red herrings' before continuing with the *Shih P'an*.

The two major 'red herrings' relating to the Han dynasty which have been introduced into the study of the origins of feng shui, and which I would like to dispose of, are the South-pointing carriage, and the hypothetical magnetic spinning spoon. These mistaken notions have resulted in some rather confused thinking, and have helped to muddy the history of both the compass and the lo p'an.

The South-Pointing Carriage

The first 'red herring' is the South-pointing carriage or *chih nan ch'e*[2] which has often been confused with the compass. The South-pointing carriage has been known since the Han dynasty but probably existed before then. This device was a carriage, which had an elaborated system of gears by which, no matter which way it drove, its pointer would always point South. As Needham puts it:

[1] Of course neither the Northern Ladle, nor any other stars, will be visible at noon.

[2] 指南車 *Zhi Nan Che.*

puts it:

> It was in fact essentially a self-regulating device, involving a system of gear-wheels such that a pointer would maintain an originally fixed direction by continually compensating for any excursions of the vehicle from that direction.[1]

On poor roads with wheel slippage this pointer would indeed have become less accurate the further the carriage travelled or the more corners it turned, but it was an ingenious, even if clumsy, mechanical device for maintaining direction. It had nothing to do with the magnetic compass, with which it was originally confused by Jesuit missionaries. So we must be careful to eliminate any references to this device from our study of the compass or lo p'an.

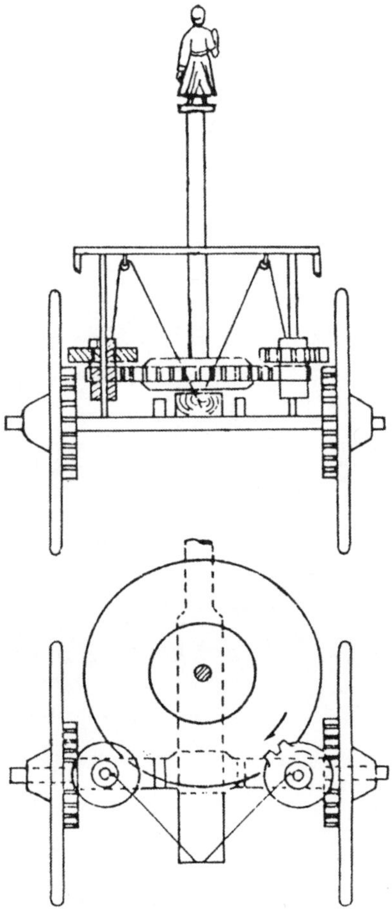

Figure 7: The self-adjusting directional mechanism of the mechanical South-pointing carriage, which works by gears and is not in any sense a compass.[2]

[1] Needham (1962), Volume 4, Part 1, page 229.
[2] Cheng (1994), page 84.

The Hypothetical Magnetic Spinning Spoon

The second 'red herring' is the interpretation of some archaeological spoon fragments as evidence that a spoon was part of a prototype lo p'an. A lot has been made of a rotating magnetic spoon in a rather dubious 'reconstruction' of an early *ssu nan* compass by Wang Chen-To[1] which is also quoted by Joseph Needham.[2] This reconstruction shows a magnetised spoon rotating on a *Shih*[3] board (see Figure 8). The *Shih* board certainly existed and was used for astrological, divinatory, magical and feng shui purposes, and was, as we will see, the forerunner of the lo p'an.

But it was never intended as a base plate for a rotating magnetic soup spoon. This misconception arose from the finding of fragments of a (non-magnetic) pottery soup spoon in the same archaeological gravesite dig as the *Shih*.

Figure 8: A model of the base *Shih* plate, with the hypothetical spinning soup spoon.

Even Needham wrote:

> It should be noted that Wang Chen-To's theory of the lodestone spoon still lacks the crucial confirmation which would be afforded by the discovery of an actual example [of a magnetic spoon] from a Han tomb.[4]

---

[1] Wang Chen-To 王振鐸 'Origin and Development of the Chinese Compass Dial, etc.' in *Chinese Journal of Archaeology*, Academia Sinica, 1948, 50, 51, Nos. 3, 4, 5.

[2] Needham (1962), Volume 4, Part I, page 253-277.

[3] 式 *Shi*.

[4] Needham (1962), Volume 4, Part I, page 263.

No such spoon has ever been found. This fallacy has become so widespread that Chinese museums even offer models of it for sale to cultural tourists.

Assuming you could magnetise a pottery spoon, or carve one out of loadstone, even a strongly magnetised spoon is going to turn very sluggishly and with considerable frictional drag, unlike a finely suspended or floating needle.[1] None of the spoons ever excavated in Han tombs were either magnetised or made of lodestone. This leap of imagination in marrying the *Shih* board with a rotating magnetic spoon was just that, imagination, and not justified by the facts.

However Joseph Needham accepted it as a convenient historical link between the *Shih* and the lo p'an, because he was very keen to prove the existence of an early Chinese dial-and-pointer device. Many other scholars have blindly followed and accepted it as gospel ever since. The text that Wang Chen-To quoted from the *Lun Heng*[2] of Wang Ch'ung[3] (written 83 CE) to justify his theory simply stated:[4]

> But when the South-pointing [or 'South-controlling'] spoon is thrown upon the ground, it comes to rest pointing to the South.[5]

Wang Chen-To jumped to the unjustified conclusion that the spoon was elegantly balanced upon a *Shih* board, rather than being just thrown upon the ground as the text very clearly states. Other basic errors appear in Wang's work, where for example he shows 180° as the compass bearing for Tzu 子 the North point in one of his illustrations, rather than 0° or 360° as it should be.[6]

Derek Walter succinctly dismisses Wang Chen-To's other supporting evidence which relied upon this misreading:

> Chinese museums, particularly those concerned with the history of science and technology frequently display a model of a diviner's [*Shih*] plate with a metallic spoon-shaped object in the centre, which is claimed to be a replica of the world's first magnetic compass... The device is pure conjecture; it never existed. The concept is based on a misreading of the description of the Diviner's *Shi*[*h*], which had at its centre a disc with a depiction of the seven stars of the Great Bear.[7]

The name of the inscribed group of seven stars was the well known *pei tou*[8] or

---

[1] Even Wang Chen-To admitted that his highly magnetised test tungsten steel spoon would not turn satisfactorily on even a highly polished wood base plate. See Needham (1962), page 267.

[2] 論衡 *Lun Heng*.

[3] 王充 Wang Chong (27-97 CE).

[4] Wang Chen-To (1948-51).

[5] *Lun Heng*, Chapter 52 (chapter 17).

[6] Wang Chen-To (1948) Figure 54, page 248.

[7] Derek Walters, *Chinese Astrology*, Watkins, London, 2002 (only in the second edition), page 352. The constellation the Great Bear is called the 'Northern Ladle' in Chinese, hence the confusion with a spoon.

[8] 北斗 *Bei Dou*.

Northern Ladle asterism, and this was mistakenly interpreted literally (by Wang Chen-To) as a physical ladle or spoon! We can therefore safely dismiss the connection made between the *Shih* board and the hypothetical magnetic spoon from the history of the compass, although the *Shih* by itself is still definitely a part of that history. Let us therefore return to considering the *Shih*.

The *Shih* base board was a square plate (or *p'an*) with many of the same marked characters as are used on the lo p'an today, but on top of it was a *non-magnetic* circular heaven plate which was turned *manually* in order to calculate certain astronomical configurations. The *Shih* was definitely the predecessor of the modern lo p'an, and it clearly shows the ring of 24 Mountains, and the base plate or *Shih* board is very much a part of the early history of feng shui.

Wang Chen-To based his theories on just the divorced bottom of one of these plates, and erroneously thought that it must be the support for a magnetised loadstone spoon. Although this theory was repeated by Joseph Needham, it is now clear that the idea of a spinning loadstone soup spoon was just a red herring. Joseph Needham describes the *Shih* as:

> ...composed of two boards or plates, the lower one being square (to symbolise the earth, hence called the *ti p'an*); and the upper one being round (to symbolise heaven, hence called the *t'ien p'an*). The latter revolved on a central pivot and had engraved upon it the 24 Mountains, composed, just as in the later traditional lo p'an, of the denary and duodenary cyclical characters, *wu* and *chi* [which are the two Earth Element Heavenly Stems] being repeated in order to make up the full number. It always bore, engraved at the centre, a representation of the Northern Ladle. The 'ground-plate' was marked all about its edge with the names of the 28 *Hsiu* [Mansions of the Moon], and the 24 Mountains were repeated along its inner gradations. Moreover, it carried [four of] the eight chief *kua* (trigrams) arranged according to the Hou T'ien [Later Heaven Sequence] system so that Ch'ien occupied the North-West and K'un the South-East.[1] This...differs from that found on all later lo p'ans where Ch'ien is the South and K'un the North [the Former Heaven Sequence].[2]

It has also been possible to determine what the board was made of, and Needham continues:

> Something is known of the wood from which the *Shih* [boards] were usually made in later times. The *T'ang Liu Tien* ('Institutions of the T'ang dynasty') from between +713 [CE] and +755 [CE] states that the round 'heaven-plate' was made of maple wood, and the square 'ground-plate' of selected jujube wood.[3]

[1] In fact, Needham is mistaken and the trigrams were *not* part of the Han dynasty *Shih*, but only appeared much later during the Six Dynasties period. They were imaginatively added by Wang Chen-To to his reconstruction.
[2] Needham (1962), Volume 4, part 1, pages 262-3.
[3] Needham (1962), Volume 4, part 1, page 265.

We now know from further discoveries that in fact *Shih* were treasured items and made from wood, lacquer, bronze, silver, copper and even ivory.[1]

Just as the Northern Ladle acts as both an astronomical clock and season-keeper in the heavens, so its image has this same function on the *Shih* board. It is not haphazardly placed on the *Shih* but points in a very specific direction. In Figure 10 its handle points to T'ien Kang,[2] one of the 12 Monthly Generals inscribed around the Heaven Plate. In Figure 9 its handle also points to the 辰 Chen Mountain which is the starting point of the 28 *Hsiu* or Mansions of the Moon on the square Earth Plate, as well as on the lo p'an.

The *Shih* was also used for a form of military tactical divination called *Liu Ren*.[3] The central circular disc could be turned by hand to 'set' the Heavens for a specific reading. It is also likely that the *Shih* had a place in the practice of early Taoist magic, because the 12 Monthly Spirit Generals appear on it. This disk may have been, in the more advanced versions, a swivelling hemisphere rather than just a flat disk (see Figure 12).

On the later lo p'ans, the K'un, Ch'ien, Hsun and Ken Mountains (the four trigram Mountains) are still referred to as the 'corner' Mountains. Obviously the concept of a 'corner' makes no sense if the lo p'an has *always* been circular, so this terminology helps to confirm that the round lo p'an was originally constructed from the square format of the early *Shih* boards.

At some point the current method of using a magnetic needle and reading the lo p'an by using cross-hairs was invented to replace the Northern Ladle pointer. Now the Earth Plate just acts as a holder for the cross hairs, rather than needing to be separately calibrated, as it was on the *Shih*.[4]

The following illustrations show the progressive unravelling of the *Shih P'an* from its original form written in seal script, through a interpretation written in modern Chinese characters, a Northern Dynasties *Shih,* to a three-dimensional film set reconstruction.

---

[1] See the Appendix 9.5 for more details. See Plate 1 for an ivory lo p'an.

[2] 天罡 *Tian Gang.*

[3] 六壬 *Liu Ren*. This means '6 *Ren*' divination, *Ren* being the yang Water Heavenly Stem (N1) position on the lo p'an. This is one of the three Heavenly Stems missing from the *Huai Nan Tzu* illustration.

[4] Don't confuse the dichotomy of square Earth base Plate surmounted by a round Heaven Plate on the S*hih*, with the later San He, Earth Plate and Heaven Plate.

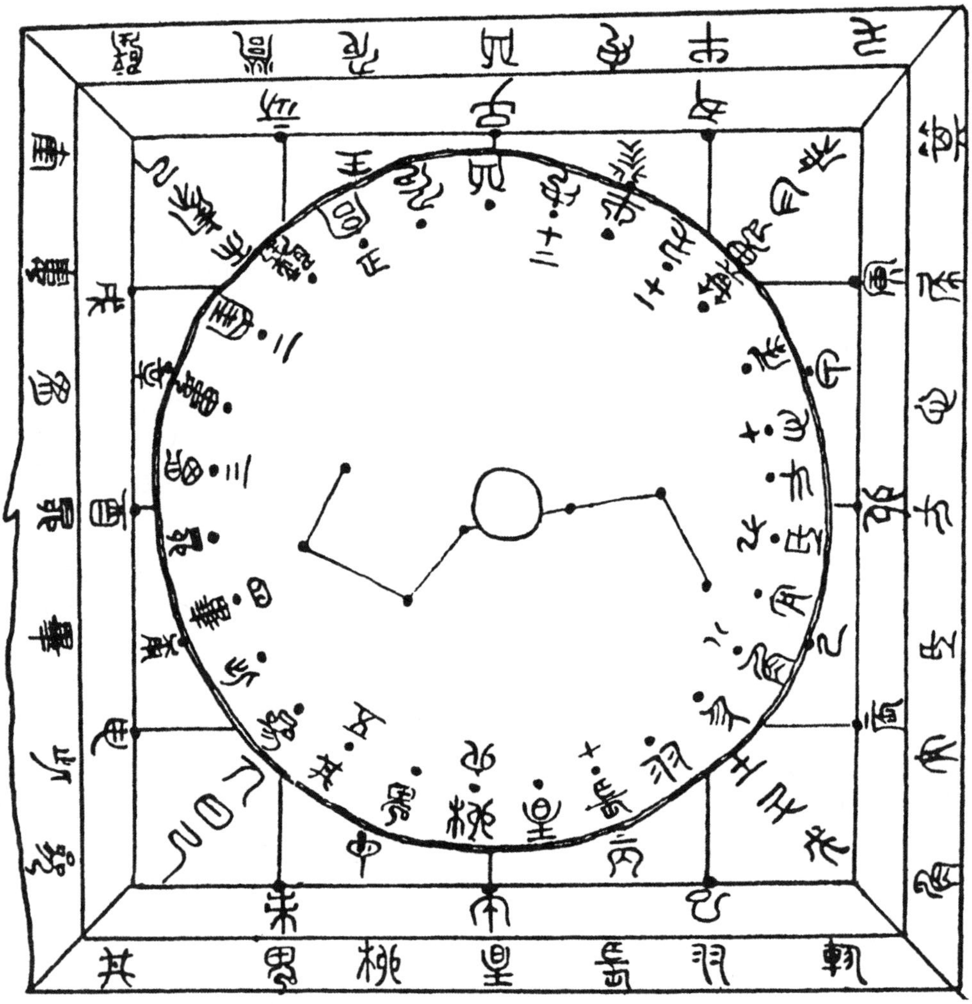

Figure 9: The *Shih* from the tomb of the second Marquis of Yi in Anhui Province (Han dynasty) dated 165 BCE. The central circular Heaven disk rotates with the Northern Ladle constellation which is inscribed upon it. The square outer is the Earth Plate. Note that this drawing shows the original seal script, and is much more accurate in its positioning of the Branches than the redrawn modern Chinese version (Figure 10). Note also that the positions which will later come to be held by the 4 corner trigrams are occupied in this period by a repeated pair of the two Earth Stems, 戊 *wu* and 己 *chi*. This means that the early *Shih* utilised all of the Earthly Branches and *all* of the Heavenly Stems (unlike the later lo p'an which only uses 8 of the 10 Stems). It also shows that the trigrams were *not* a part of the *Shih* during this early Han dynasty period. This important point indicates that the *Shih* was a forerunner of the Branches-and-Stems San He School rather than the trigram-dependant San Yuan School of feng shui. The positioning of the Northern Lade is not depicted accurately.[1]

[1] Illustration from Yan Dunjie (1985), page 451. See also *Kaogu,* 1978, Volume 5, page 340.

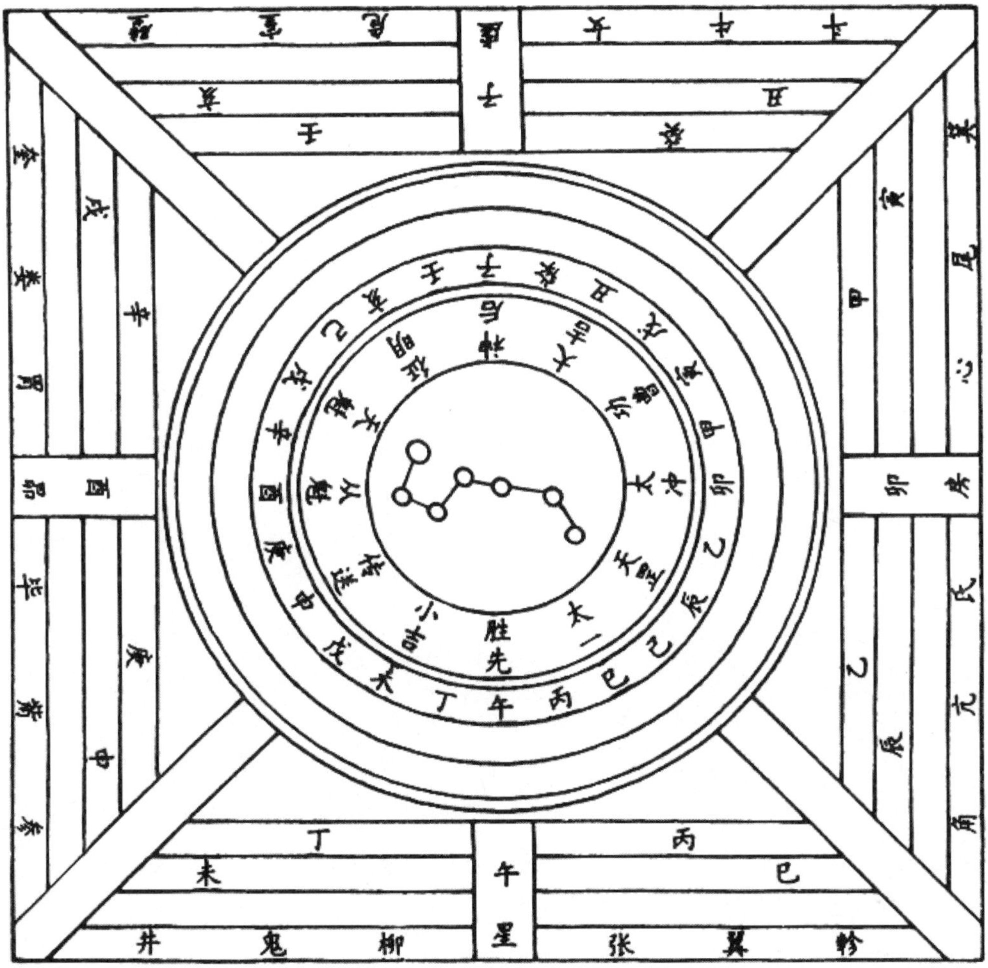

Figure 10: A reconstruction of the *Shih* board clearly showing the square Earth Plate and the circular Heaven Plate with the Northern Ladle constellation in the middle. The Northern Ladle handle points to 辰 Chen (the Earthly Branch corresponding to the Dragon, in the 24 Mountains ring) and also to the first *Hsiu*, 角 Horn, on the Earth Plate (the 4 o'clock position). The 'corner' positions of the circular Heaven Plate ring of 24 Mountains (which are the 4 'corner' trigrams on the lo p'an) are here occupied by the two Earth Heavenly Stems, 戊 *wu* and 己 *chi* repeated twice, and *not* by the trigrams.[1] Note that the original seal script has been translated into modern Chinese. The character 癸 Kuei, often missing from other reproductions, has also been here restored.[2]

[1] The 4 Cardinal trigrams do *not* occur on *any* extant *Shih*, and so have been removed from this reconstruction. The 'corner' trigrams only occur on the most recent *Shih* from the Six Dynasties period, and so have also been left out of this reconstruction.

[2] Modified illustration from Wang Chen-To (1948-1951) page 214 as reconstructed from the fragment shown on his page 216. Note that the orientation of the Northern Ladle, not shown correctly in either Needham, Wang Chen-To, or Harada and Tazawa (the original archaeologists who sketched it) has here been rectified. It is obvious by comparing it with the original archaeological photograph, that the 'bucket' of the Northern Ladle has been accidentally flipped by all three scholars, and repeated unchallenged in Needham (1962) and all later writers. Its correct orientation has been here restored.

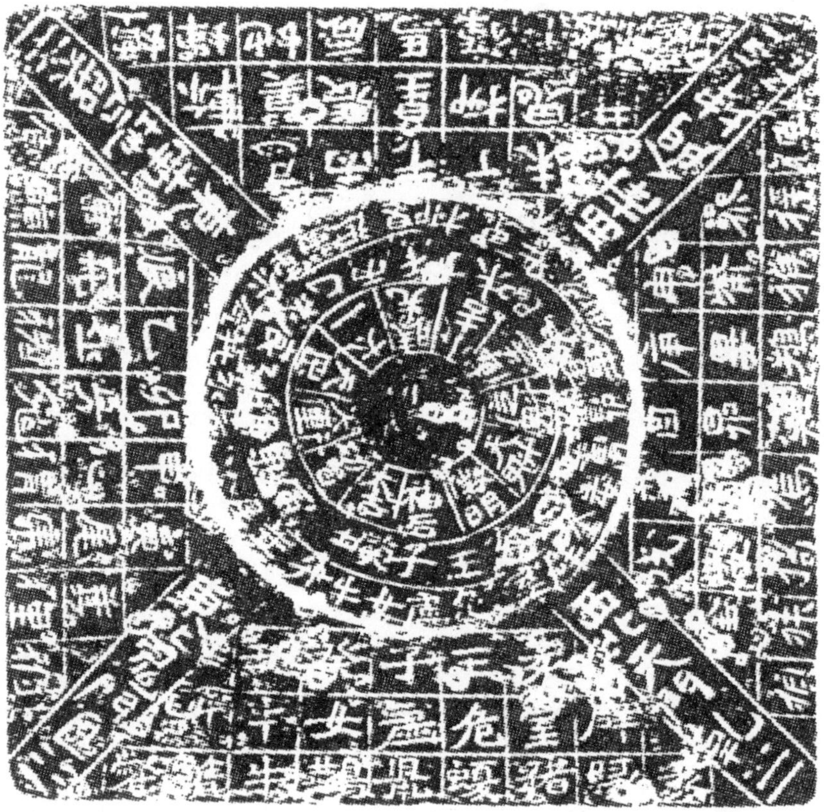

Figure 11: A later *Shih*. Note that the Ghost Gate diagonal Path is bottom left, and the Heaven Gate is the diagonal Path at bottom right. Although we are in this chapter considering the history of the Han dynasty, this particular *Shih* was made in the Southern and Northern Dynasties (386-589 CE) of copper. Only at this later point in history have the 'corner' trigrams been introduced.[1]

[1] From the Shanghai Museum. See also Cheng (1998), page 8.

Figure 12: A reconstructed three-dimensional model of the above *Shih*, with a rotating hemi-spherical Heaven Plate, also oriented the same way, with the Ghost Gate to the bottom left, and Heaven Gate to the bottom right.

The Pi Disk

The question now arises as to how the position of the actual Northern Ladle asterism in the sky could have been transferred to an exact positioning of the Northern Ladle marked on the *Shih*. I believe I have discovered the answer to this and at the same time cleared up the mystery of what the highly valued and beautiful jade *pi* (*bi*) disks were used for. These circular jade disks are often referred to by academics as "of no known use." It is worth noting that they sometimes had precision marks carved upon them around their inner edge, or many dots (stars?) or the 4 celestial animals of feng shui marking the four quarters of heaven. Some even had an irregular notch cut on the inner ring, which I believe may have been used to mark the 'handle' of the Northern Ladle.

I believe these were held up to the sky at night (particularly at midnight) and used as a sighting template to precisely determine the positioning of the Northern Ladle. This position was then reproduced by the *fang shih* practitioner on the *Shih* by turning it to the same position. Then the relationships between the circular Heaven disk and the square Earth disk could easily be read off. This is however only my hypothesis at this point in time.

It is logical that these disks are often found in aristocratic tombs near the body (as were *shih*) because they form a connection between the alignments of Heaven and those of Earth, something of relevance to the departed owner of the tomb.

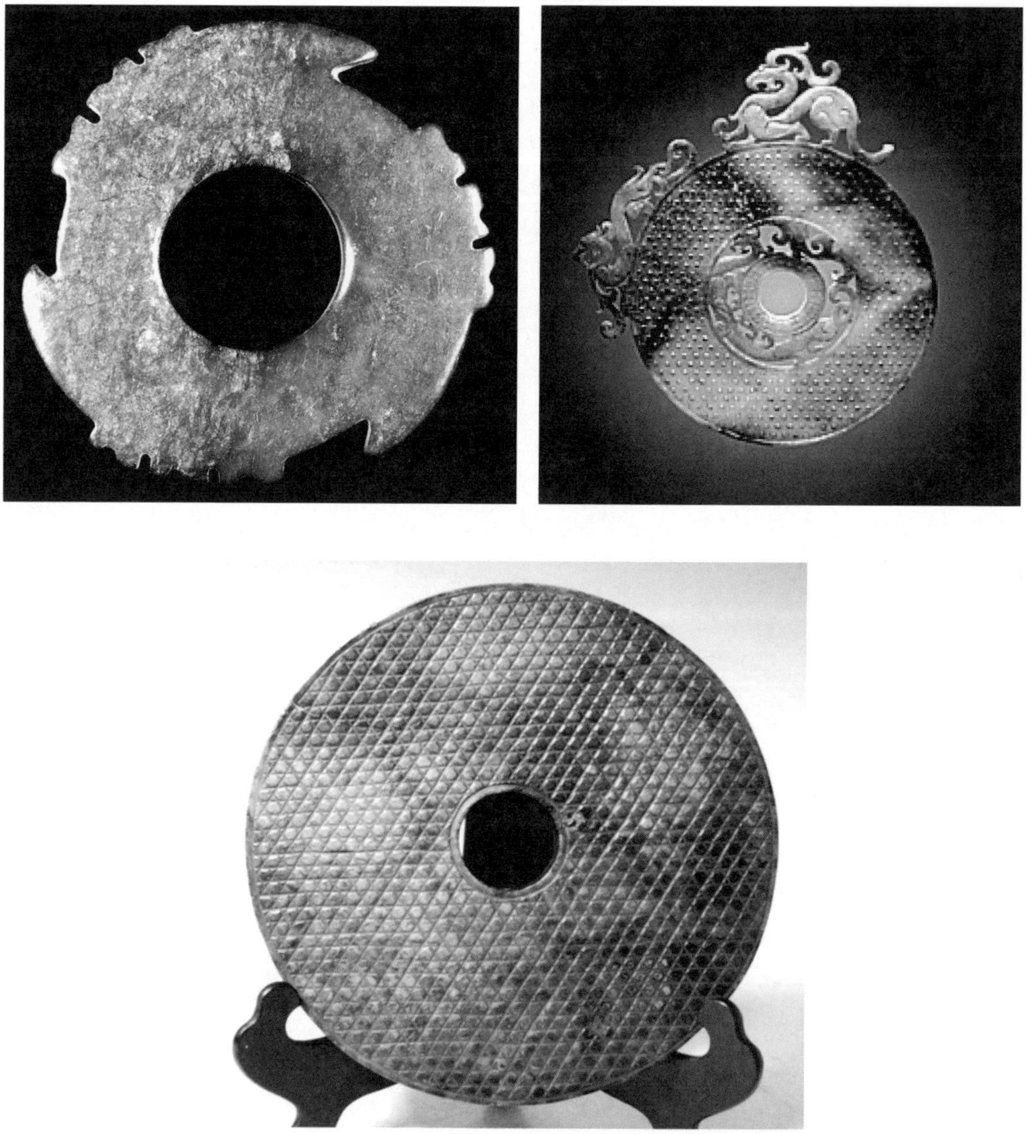

Figure 13: Three different *pi* (*bi*) disks made of jade, with different calibrations.

The 'Dipper Dial'

On the *Shih* the 28 *Hsiu* are always evenly spaced. However in the same early second century BCE tomb excavation where the *Shih* was found, there was a second instrument which has been largely ignored by scholars.[1] This instrument has two circular disks. Nobody knows what it was called but for convenience Harper refers to it as the 'Dipper Dial' and it is quite separate from the *Shih*.

[1] See Cullen (1980) page 34. Also see the original excavation report in *Wenwu* 1978, Volume 8, page 12 onwards, and the comments in *Kaogu* 1978, Volume 5, pages 334-343.

The lower disk shows the names and exact *variable* day-degree[1] measurements of the 28 *Hsiu*. This is significant as the *Shih* only shows same-size *Hsiu* extents.

This is similar to the format of the *Hsiu* ring of the modern lo p'an, but without its sector division lines. The upper disk of the 'Dipper Dial' has a representation of the Northern Ladle (or Dipper) in it centre, like the *Shih*, but it also has 365 tiny markings showing the *tu* or day-degrees[2] on its outer edge, exactly like the day-degrees ring on the modern lo p'an. This device, by showing the exact extent of degrees of each *Hsiu,* helps bridge the gap between the *Shih* (with equal length notional *Hsiu*) and the lo p'an (with real unequal length *Hsiu*). It was therefore likely to have been used in conjunction with the *Shih.* The following set of points needs some technical knowledge of the lo p'an, and may be skipped by the reader if desired.

Shih and Lo p'an

There are five key connections between the *Shih* and the lo p'an:

1. The 'Dipper Dial' contains the *Hsiu* ring and the 365.25 *tu* divisions of the day-degree ring. These two rings are the outermost, and probably the oldest rings still extant on the lo p'an.

2. On the *Shih* itself, the *Hsiu* ring falls exactly in the same position on the lo p'an as it does on the *Shih,* starting in both cases with the Horn *Hsiu* at the Chen Dragon Mountain position (SE1), and then proceeding anti-clockwise.

3. As we have seen, the 8 Heavenly Stems and 12 Earthly Branches that make up the 24 Mountains of the lo p'an are in exactly the same position on both instruments.[3]

4. The 12 Monthly *Teng Ming* Generals on the upper part of the *Shih* occur on the Outer Heaven (Man) Plate of lo p'ans extant up to the early Ch'ing dynasty.

5. Finally, and perhaps most significantly, there is a quote found in a *Ch'i Men Tun Chia*[4] text which says:

> *Tzu* and *Wu* are the warp thread[5] of Heaven and Earth. The first and seventh stars of the Northern Ladle, the Bowl-god [star][6] and Rigid [star],[7] are also the

---

[1] In fact the degree extents are closer to the old *K'ai Yüan Chan Ching* 開元占經 *Kai Yuan Zhan Jing* list than to the *Huai Nan Tzu.*

[2] 'Day-degrees' is my translation of *tu* 度 *du*, which are the 365.25 degrees into which the Chinese divided the circle, unlike the 360° used by the Babylonians, and later by Western science.

[3] The corner Earth Stems were replaced at a much later date by the 4 corner trigrams.

[4] An early form of divination.

[5] *Ching* 經 *jing.*

[6] *K'uei* 魁 *kuei.*

[7] *Kang* 剛 *gang*. This refers to the two parts of the Ladle, the 'bowl' and the handle.

warp-thread of the Northern Ladle.[1]

Thus the North point (*Tzu*) and the South point (*Wu*) of the lo p'an are clearly identified with the two ends of the Northern Ladle (or Dipper) constellation. We know from the *Shih* that the tail of the Northern Ladle is the pointer, and we also know that the *Wu* end of the lo p'an magnetic needle is the pointing end. This suggests that the magnetic needle was the natural development of and replacement for the *Shih's* Northern Ladle pointer.[2]

It is clear from the above that the lo p'an is the natural successor of the *Shih* board. At least one of the functions of the *Shih* is still in regular demand in modern day Taiwan. Taoist priests there (and in other Chinese cultural areas) use the Northern Ladle in operations of Thunder Magic. As part of this operation they need to draw up a chart showing the position of the Ladle in the sky at the time of the operation. Nowadays they use a printed 'Dipper Almanac' to find the position, rather than using the *Shih* to work it out by 'dialling,' as they did in the past.[3]

To appreciate the sequence of development of the *Shih* into the lo p'an, look at Figure 9 to Figure 12 which show the main elements of the *Shih* in a diagrammatic form and how they later develop into a lo p'an. The lo p'an contains all the same *Shih* elements but slightly rearranged, as shown in Figure 14.

Category	On the *Shih*	On the early lo p'an
The Pointer	Northern Ladle/Dipper	Magnetic Needle
12 Monthly Generals	Heaven Dial	Astronomical Rings[4]
24 Mountains	Heaven Dial	Earth/Man/Heaven Plates
10 Heavenly Stems	Earth Plate	[5]
12 Earthly Branches	Earth Plate	Earth Plate/Chiang P'an
28 *Hsiu*	Earth Plate	Astronomical Rings

Figure 14: The translation of 'rings' from the *Shih* to the early lo p'an, in broad terms.

[1] From the 'Five Elements Great Meaning' *Wu Hsing Ta I* 五行大意 *Wu Xing Da Yi*, quoted (and slightly amended) from Harper (1979), page 3. Note that *K'uei* and *Kang* are the Month Spirits corresponding to the Solar months 2 and 8, numbers which came to represent Earth.

[2] The difference being that the *Shih's* Northern Ladle related to Astronomic North, while the lo p'an's Correct needle related to Magnetic North. Note the lo p'an's Man Plate relates to Astronomic North.

[3] Saso (1978), pages 244-250.

[4] Also the Outer Heaven (Man) Plate.

[5] No longer found as an independent ring, but used to be.

The Three Kingdoms (220-265 CE)

There are a number of parallels between Chinese military strategy and feng shui, and divination systems were often used to determine directional military strategy during the Three Kingdoms 三國 period. Such connections are even recorded in the great classical novels of China. One of the earliest such stories appears in the novel *The Romance of the Three Kingdoms*. Although this was written in the 14th century, it is set in the period of the Three Kingdoms. One of the characters in it is the real Taoist *fang-shih*[1] and magician Chu Ko Liang[2] (181-234 CE), who was an advisor to Liu Pei,[3] the lord of the Liu kingdom. Chu Ko Liang used the *pa kua* to devise military traps against the army of the state of Wei. His nickname was 'Crouching Dragon.'

Figure 15: Two different drawings of Chu Ko Liang, the Master of *Ch'i Men Tun Chia* (*Qi Men Dun Jia*). The right hand one holds a *Ch'i Men P'an*. Chu Ko Liang was featured as the strategist and magician in the Chinese film *Red Cliff*.

---

[1] 方士 *fang shi*, a master of divination and magic.

[2] Or Chu Kuo Liang 諸葛亮 Zhu Ge Liang, also known as Zhuge Liang and Kung Ming 孔明 Kong Ming.

[3] 劉備 Liu Bei.

It was said that Chu Ko Liang could manipulate the wind and conjure up mists and fog. These he duly conjured when necessary to hide the movements of Liu Pei's armies from his enemies. It is said that Chu Ko Liang introduced or utilised the techniques of *Ch'i Men Tun Chia.*[1] This term has been variously translated, but perhaps the most accurately literal translation is 'Mysterious Gates of the Hidden Stems.' *Chia* is the first of the Heavenly Stems and combines with just six Earthly Branches. These six combinations occur at key points around the lo p'an. Another more revealing translation of this technique is 'Mysterious Hidden Doors for Commanding the Six *Chia* Spirits.' Supporting this translation is the fact that the original Chinese volumes about this technique contain a key Register of Spirits, not usually spoken about now.

Much of the current teaching of this technique (especially in English) focuses just on interminable tables and date selection, without getting round to the real reason for these time and space calculations, which relates to the *Chia* spirits.

Ch'i Men Tun Chia refers to the manipulations of the secret portals related to the Heavenly Stems through which energy or even things can be made to disappear or re-appear. Chu Ko Liang was reputedly able to open up these portals or caverns in the earth and swallow up troops, so the technique could be used to hide his own kingdom's troops, or to destroy those of the enemy. Only Taoist magicians like Chu Ko Liang knew the time and the place these portals could be opened. This is a very telling story portrayed in the Chinese film *Red Cliff,*[2] as it links the subtle vapours of ch'i with the Heavenly Stems of the lo p'an which, besides controlling mists, can also be used to determine water entrances and exits.

Practitioners of *Ch'i Men Tun Chia* claim to be able to bring beneficial ch'i into a site through some of these portals, which can only be opened at very limited and specific times, in very specific directions.[3] Calculation of these directions is connected with the *tun chia* rings of the lo p'an (which are now only present on older lo p'ans), and its formulae are reputed to be amongst the most powerful formulae in feng shui practice.

Master Kuan Lo[4] (209-256 CE) wrote the important classic 'Master Kuan's Ti Li Indicator'[5] which consolidated feng shui theory for the first time. The book that presently rejoices in that title may not be the original third century CE volume.

[1] 奇門遁甲 *Qi Men Dun Jia,* or nowadays just QMDJ.

[2] *Red Cliff* is a Chinese epic based on the Battle of Red Cliff (208-209 CE) at the end of the Han dynasty and immediately prior to the Three Kingdoms period. It features Chu Ko Liang (Zuge Liang) as a master strategist, with control over wind and water. The film was produced and directed by John Woo.

[3] Some of these ideas are echoed in modern science fiction where portals between different times or dimension have some of the same qualities.

[4] 管辂 Guan Luo.

[5] *Kuan Shih Ti Li Chih Meng* 管氏地理指蒙 *Guan Shi Di Li Zhi Meng* which contains 10 chapters of very systematic explanation. Many feng shui theories are derived from this work.

Chin (Jin) Dynasty (265-420 CE)

The next key point in the evolution of feng shui occurred in the Chin 晉 (Jin) dynasty with Master Kuo P'o[1] (276-324 CE) and his classic 'Book of Burial,'[2] in which the Form School principles of siting and water dragons were well established. This book contained the first definite use of the term 'feng shui.' Therefore you could say that 'feng shui' as such only dates from this period, even if it was current under other names (like *kan yu*) as far back as 221 BCE. But there is no way that anyone can claim that feng shui is 6000 years old, as is a common boast by some current feng shui aficionados.

The precise point at which the magnetic mechanism of the compass is introduced to the structure of the *Shih p'an* to create the first lo p'an is hard to pinpoint. It is tempting to date it from the time of Kuo P'o. He was aware of the lodestone, and he definitely related its action to ch'i. He wrote that:

> …the lodestone 'breathes in' iron, and amber [via electrostatic attraction] collects mustard seeds. The ch'i [of both these things] has an invisible penetratingness.[3]

There was a clear association being drawn here between the action of ch'i and the ability of the magnetic lodestone to attract iron. For Kuo P'o the location of ch'i, and its effect on a site, especially in relation to water, was the core of feng shui. Kuo's most famous classic is the 'Book of Burial.'[4] In this book he writes:

> The Earth compass measures its direction and location; the jade ruler measures its distance.[5]

Not only does he mention the Earth compass in passing but he also gives burial instructions for each of the 8 trigram directions:

> To bury in the Ch'ien direction, the aspect [landform] should be rising and falling…To bury in the K'un direction, the aspect should be a straight linking to the heavens.[6]

And so on for each of the trigram directions. Sadly this is not as conclusive as it first looks because the translator has translated 土圭 *t'u kuei* as 'Earth compass' when *kuei* strictly refers to "an elongated pointed tablet of jade held in the hands by ancient rulers." In association with 土, the character for earth, this means a gnomon, or shadow stick. Hence the 'Book of Burial' determines its compass directions astronomically by gnomon (see Figure 5), not magnetically by lo p'an. So this is a direct continuation of the Astronomical

---

[1] 郭璞 Guo Pu.

[2] *Tsang Shu* 葬書 *Zang Shu.*

[3] Needham (1962) Volume 4, part I, page 233.

[4] *Tsang Shu* 葬書 *Zang Shu.*

[5] Translation by Juwen Zhang (2004), Chapter 3.35.

[6] Juwen Zhang (2004), Chapter 3.36-37.

North orientation of the *Shih,* rather than the Magnetic North of the lo p'an.

Kuo P'o also wrote *The Book of the Blue/Green Satchel,* which has recently been translated, and which remains a great classic to this day.

At some point in this period the magnetic needle replaced the astronomic Northern Ladle as the pointer, and we should now begin to talk about the resultant instrument as a lo p'an.[1]

Southern & Northern dynasties (420-589 CE)

During the period of the Southern and Northern 南北 dynasties there was widespread use of feng shui amongst the ruling class and there was much interest in the detailed mapping of the waterways of China. In this dynasty four of the trigrams first appeared on the corners of the *Shih* plate.

The Emperor's Dwelling Classic and the Chai Ching boards

The *Chai Ching* Earth Board is a pair of diagrams found in the 'Yellow Emperor's Dwelling Classic'[2] supposedly written by Wang Wei (415-443 CE). These diagrams are obviously related to both the *Shih* and the lo p'an. I have called them *Chai Ching* Earth Boards for convenience, although this is not how they are referred to in Wang Wei's text. Some modern writers refer to them as *'Wei-ch'i'* boards. The 'Yellow Emperor's Dwelling Classic' contains a lot of very detailed feng shui. The *Chai Ching* Earth Board shows the 24 Mountains clearly. These will later form the most important ring on the lo p'an.

The *Chai Ching* Earth Board which was certainly used for feng shui, came in two flavours, one yang version for the houses of the living (homes), one yin version for the houses of the dead (graves). This division into *yin chai* and *yang chai* versions makes it very probable that the *Chai Ching* Earth Boards were used as a kind of lo p'an diagram for evaluating the types of ch'i affecting these two types of dwelling. Figure 16 (and its translation in Figure 17) shows what was contained in a yang *Chai Ching* Earth Board. Working from the centre of the yang diagram outwards, each square 'rings' contain:

1. the 8 trigrams of the directions in Later Heaven Sequence
2. the 24 Mountains
3. various auspices plus the 4 Celestial Animals
4. the position of the 9 bodily parts of the Dragon
5. in the East and North are the fates (*ming*) of various members of the household.

[1] *Lo p'an* 羅盤 *Luo Pan* or *Lo Ching* 羅經 *Luo Jing. Lo Ching* is the more ancient term.

[2] *Huang Ti Chai Ching* 黃帝宅經 *Huang Di Zhai Jing.* Obviously this is not written by the Yellow Emperor, but his name was used by the real author. It has been suggested that it may even have been written as late as the Ming dynasty, but I don't think so.

The 4 corner Gates are the usual Heaven, Earth, Man and Ghost Gates with details of the month and days ruled by each of them. This is quite interesting as it suggests key dates on which these Gates may be 'opened.' The four Corners were the four Gates for both the yin and the yang world. But there is an additional Gate of Peace on both Boards.

Sui Dynasty (589-618 CE)

To demonstrate how the literature of feng shui swelled during this period, it is only necessary to note that in the Sui 隋 dynasty the official Catalogue of the literature only gives a dozen or so titles on the subject. But in the next dynasty, the official Catalogue of the T'ang dynasty contains a much larger number, rising to more than a hundred books on feng shui in the dynasty following the T'ang.

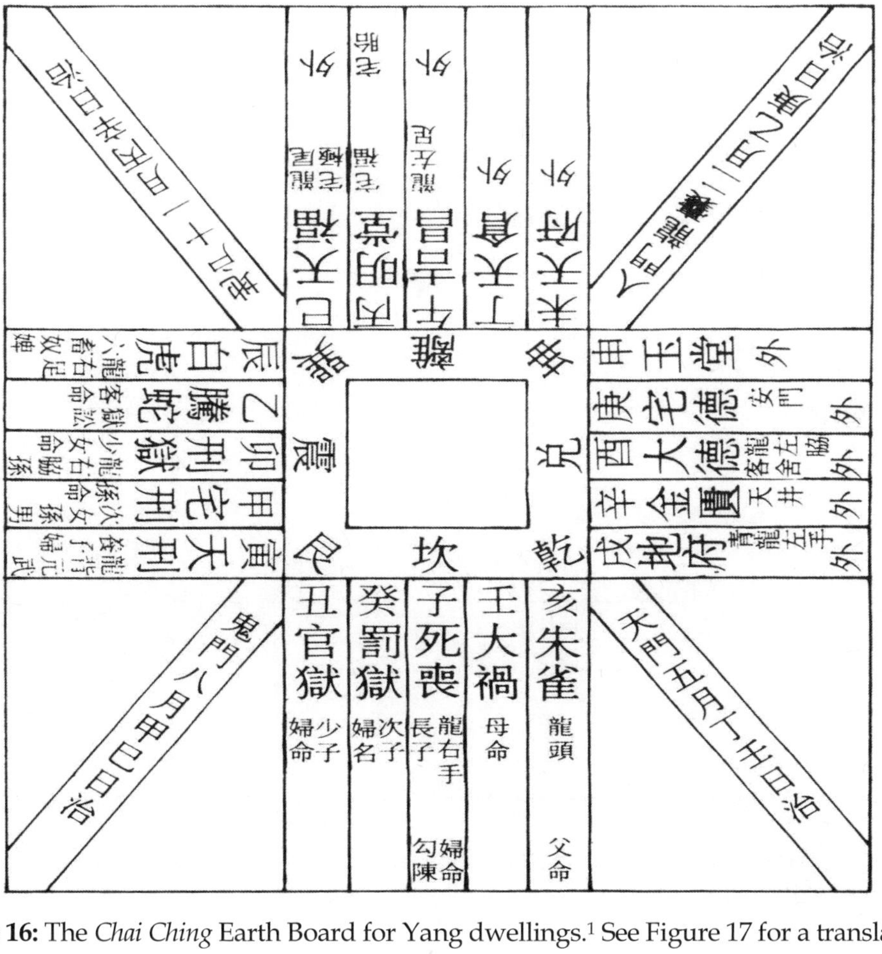

Figure 16: The *Chai Ching* Earth Board for Yang dwellings.[1] See Figure 17 for a translation.

[1] From the 'Yellow Emperor's Dwelling Classic' or *Huang Ti Chai Ching*. This is supposedly by Wang Wei and is therefore usually dated from the 5th century CE.

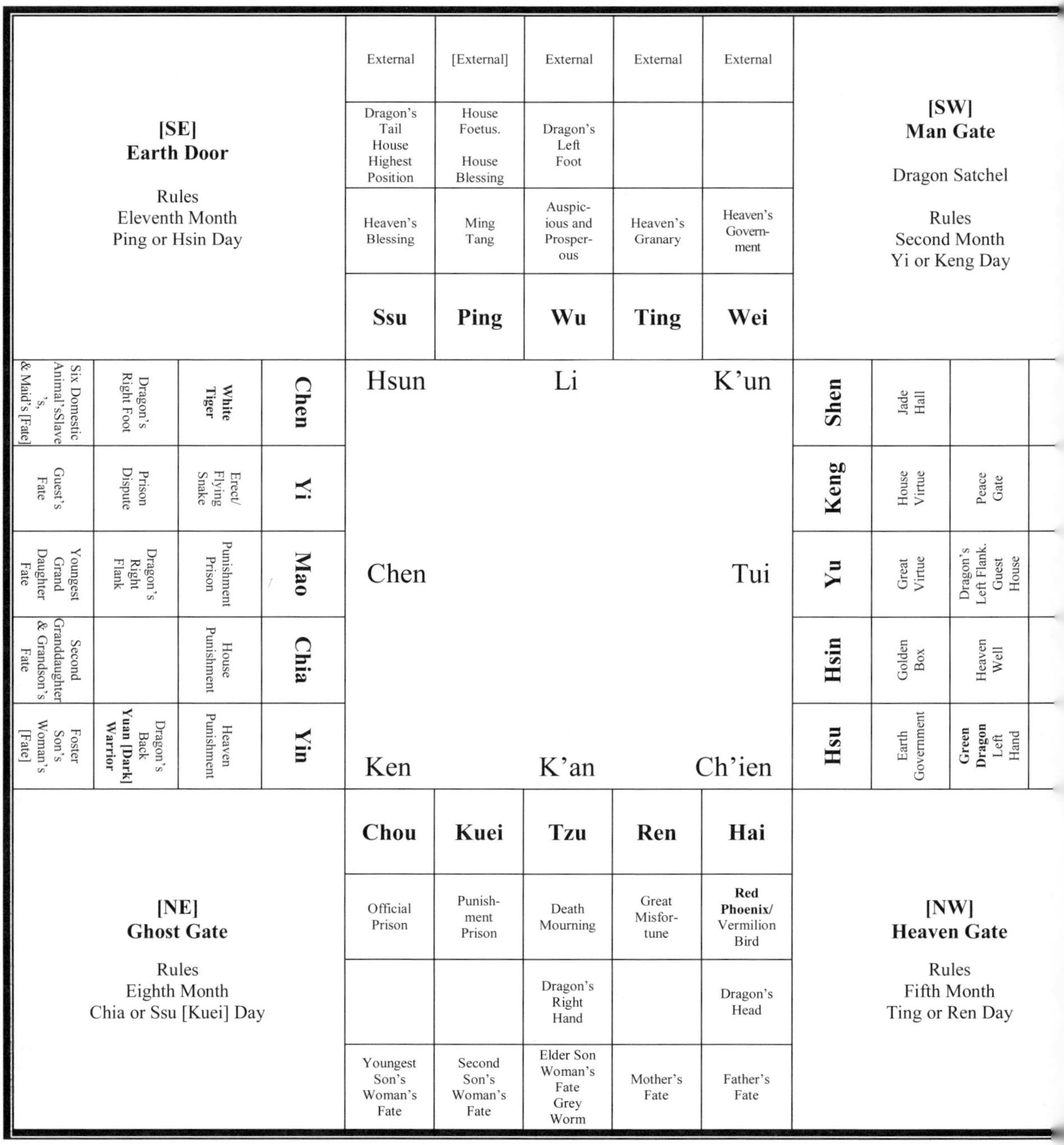

Figure 17: Translation of the *Chai Ching* Earth Board for yang dwellings shown in Figure 16. Note that the diagonal paths at each corner are shown as Gates to and from the various worlds. The East and North directions are marked with the fates of various members of the family. The Dragon's body is sprawled over the whole diagram with his head in Hai and his tail in Ssu. Its left and right flank are marked by the West and East points respectively. 'Chia or Ssu Day' is incorrect in the original Chinese, and should be labelled 'Chia or Kuei day.'

T'ang Dynasty (618-906 CE)

The T'ang dynasty 唐 was a high point in both general Chinese culture, and in the annals of feng shui. Feng shui became sufficiently important to the ruling classes for the Emperor to get involved in its regulation.

> In the 7th century, the emperor T'ai Tsung[1] (who reigned 626-649 CE) of the T'ang dynasty appointed a commission of more than ten scholars, with orders to sift, under the presidency of Lü Ts'ai,[2] a famous man of letters, the existing literature on divination and geomancy, and to glean from it everything orthodox and of real practical value. The result of their labours was a work in one hundred chapters, which was published by order of the emperor. They passed a sweeping sentence on the then existing literature on the subjects in question, flatly condemning all such selection of auspicious graves and lucky times for burial as is not sanctioned by antecedents from antiquity. An ample account of the way in which those scholars acquitted themselves of their task is given in the two Standard Histories of the T'ang dynasty.
>
> This imperial effort to check the boundless expansion of unauthentic geomantic theory and superstition was entirely without effect, and the literature on the subject has continued to swell from age to age.[3]

The lo p'an is however well established by the early T'ang dynasty, as it is recorded that Ch'iu Yen Han[4] who flourished in the early T'ang used a lo p'an featuring the Earth Plate 12 Mountains in 730 CE. It is said that this *k'an yü* master Ch'iu Yen Han[5] also wrote the 'Heaven's Secrets Pure Book.'[6]

During the T'ang dynasty, the divisions used in the lo p'an rings had become so much a part of Chinese life and culture these were even used as decoration for dining plates (see Figure 18) and mirrors (see Figure 19). The mirror also featured the 8 trigrams, 12 Branches and 28 *Hsiu* from the ancient *Shih,* with their associated planets/Elements in the outer ring.

These divisions of the lo p'an rings were also repeated in T'ang tomb decoration, such as the grave slab shown in Figure 21. This includes the 8 trigrams (in the Later Heaven Sequence, with the addition of Sun and Moon), 12 Earthly Branches, and the 28 *Hsiu* or Mansions of the Moon, just as they appear in the outer 'ring' of the *Shih*. Finally, the 4 Celestial Animals appear on the sloping sides, and orient the gravestone Cardinal directions. We can therefore deduce that *all* these rings were also present on T'ang dynasty lo p'ans (see Figure 22).

---

[1] 太宗 Tai Zong.

[2] 吕才 Lu Cai.

[3] De Groot, *The Religious System in China,* Vol. 3, Book 1, page 1006. Another attempt at Imperial standardisation of feng shui was to take place almost exactly 1100 years later in 1740.

[4] 丘延翰 Qiu Yan Han.

[5] 丘延翰 Qiu Yan Han.

[6] *T'ien Chi Su Shu* 天機素書 *Tian Ji Su Shu*. See also Needham (1964), page 299 footnote.

Figure 18: A ninth century T'ang dynasty plate clearly showing the main rings of an early T'ang lo p'an embodied in its design. This plate could even function as a rough lo p'an with a wet needle in the central hollow. The rings show (from the innermost):

1. The 4 Celestial Animals, although they are positioned one position clockwise from where you might expect to see them
2. The 8 trigrams in Later Heaven Sequence
3. Depictions of the 12 'Zodiacal' Animals, with the Horse to the South (top) and the Rat to the North (bottom) marking the 12 Earthly Branches
4. An ancient script version of the 24 Divisions
5. A clockwise ring of animals which correspond with the 28 *Hsiu* or Mansions of the Moon. The sequence begins near the bottom left with the worm-like scaly dragon which represents the first *Hsiu* or Horn
6. The outer ring contains 84 attributions of the 28 *Hsiu*, evenly distributed. Each of the 28 *Hsiu* has precisely three characters allocated: its name; the Planet attributed to it and the name of the animal depicted in ring 5.

Figure 19: T'ang dynasty bronze mirror back showing cosmological symbols and typical feng shui structure. These same sequences are also found on lo p'ans of that period.[1] The rings show, from inside:

1. The four Celestial Animals with the snake-wrapped tortoise of North at the top
2. The 12 Earthly Branches shown as the 12 'Zodiacal' animals
3. The 8 trigrams in the Later Heaven Sequence[2]
4. Very clear sigils for the 28 *Hsiu* constellations[3]
5. A seal script poem praising the mirror for its ability to confront or control the spirits.[4] The poem says that the mirror's virtue comes from the Evening Star (Venus) and the essence of the White Tiger (of the West), both appropriately yin. The poem starts near the top between the Ch'ien and K'an trigrams.

---

[1] American Museum of Natural History, New York, Berthold Laufer Collection. Note North is at the top.

[2] Above the Chen trigram are the characters *ts'ao p'u* 曹舖 *cao pu*, which is probably the workshop mark.

[3] These are very much like the shape of the *Hsiu* as seen in the early Han dynasty.

[4] *Ling* 靈.

Yang Yun Sung

The most prominent master in this dynasty, or any dynasty, was the Imperial librarian and *ti li* Master Yang Yun Sung[1] (834-906 CE), who is usually credited with inventing the Heaven Plate and the 72 Dragon ring on the lo p'an. Many current masters claim a lineage from Yang Yun Sung, and at least five books have been attributed to him, including:

'Heavenly Jade Classic'[2]
'Jade Ruler Classic'[3]
'Secret Meanings of the Universe'[4]
'Classic of the Moving Dragon'[5]
'Doubtful Dragon Classic'[6]
'Twelve Stave Method'[7]

Yang Yun Sung's importance to the evolution of the lo p'an is that he is credited with inventing the Heaven Plate around 900 CE. The Heaven Plate contained the same 24 Mountains, but was orientated 7.5° clockwise from the Earth Plate.[8]

The point of this Plate is that Yang Yun Sung would have oriented it to Astronomic North, because at this period Astronomic North (the Pole Star) was to the right (or clockwise) of Magnetic North.[9] This Plate is sometimes called the Inner Heaven Plate, or the Yang Kung Plate in his honour. To the Earth Plate, Master Yang added the ring of 72 Mountain-Piercing Dragons, which he designated for 'riding the ch'i.'

An example of a wet needle lo p'an showing the 72 dragons which could well have existed as far back as the T'ang is shown in Figure 20.

Yang Yun Sung finally settled in Kanchow (Ganzhou) which is a city in Kiangsi (Jiangxi) Province. A modern movement headed by Master Li Ding

---

[1] 楊筠松 Yang Yun Song, sometimes referred to as Yang Kung, Master Yang, Shuh Meu or Yang Jiu Ping, 'the savoir of the poor' (owing to his supposed ability to use feng shui to improve even the lot of the poor).

[2] *T'ien Yu Ching* 天玉經 *Tian Yu Jing*.

[3] *Yu Chê Ching* 玉尺經 *Yu Chi Jing*.

[4] *Ch'ing Nang Ao Chih* 青囊奧旨 *Qing Nang Ao Zhi*. See also *Ch'ing Nang Ao Yu* 青囊奧語 *Qing Nang Ao Yu*.

[5] *Han Lung Ching* 撼龍經 *Han Long Jing*. Sometimes translated as 'The Classic of the Jolting the Dragon.'

[6] *Yi Lung Ching* 疑龍經 *Yi Long Jing*. Maybe a better translation would be 'Testing the Dragon Classic.'

[7] *Shih Erh Chang Fa* 十二仗法 *Shi Er Zhang Fa*. It is sometimes said that only the first three of these titles are actually by Yang Yun Sung.

[8] It is appropriate that this Heaven Plate is used to measure water and river flows, as all water in the hydrological cycle originates from precipitation from Heaven.

[9] As we shall see, this angular relationship did not last for long, as Magnetic North 'wanders' so that roughly 200 years later the positions are reversed.

Xin, based in that city claims to have rediscovered Yang Yun Sung's secrets in his texts, especially the 'Heavenly Jade Classic.' This knowledge is being promoted as Yang Gong feng shui. Master Li has, in addition, written one of the most comprehensive books (in two volumes) in Chinese on the *lo p'an,* which covers in detail 52 of the 75 possible rings of the lo p'an.

The tomb engraving (Figure 21) contained almost the same 'rings' as the plate shown in Figure 18. It is therefore fairly easy to reconstruct a late T'ang dynasty lo p'an, by simply including the various *Shih* and lo p'an rings that had been discovered up to 900 CE, and which also persisted into the Sung dynasty. Added to that are the 'rings' appearing on T'ang plates, mirror backs, in tombs, and other cultural artefacts, which are also retained as lo p'an rings in later dynasties. The result of this reconstruction work is shown in Figure 22.

Tsêng Wên Ch'an

Yang Yun Sung's main disciple Tsêng Wên Ch'an[1] (854–916 CE) is said to have written a further two titles, 'A Treatise on Searching for Dragons'[2] and 'Queries and Answers about the two Breaths of Nature' or more succinctly 'Yin Yang Questions and Answers.'[3] He also wrote a famous preface to the *Ch'ing Nang Ao Chih Ching.*

Tsêng Wên Ch'an is often listed as one of the five greatest feng shui masters along with Kuo P'o, Yang Yun Sung, Liao Yü and Lai Pu Yi. Lai was also reputed to be a great swordsman. These disciples all lived in or near Kanchow (Ganzhou) in Kiangsi (Jiangxi) Province. They were the so called 'Gentlemen of Kanchow.' It is this tradition that Yang Gong feng shui (based in the same city and headed by Master Li Ding Xin) claims to perpetuate today.

---

1 曾文辿 Zeng Wen Chan.

2 *Hsun Lung Chi* 尋龍記 *Xun Long Ji.*

3 *Yin Yang Wen Ta* 陰陽問答 *Yin Yang Wen Da.*

Figure 20: A T'ang dynasty San He bronze wet needle lo p'an, designed circa 900 CE. This item is usually identified by scholars as Ming, but if that is so, then it uses a T'ang dynasty design. This lo p'an could easily be dated to the T'ang, because its rings are limited to those that Yang Yun Sung would have been familiar with, and wet needle lo p'ans were uncommon by the Ming dynasty. Its rings are:

1. The 8 trigrams. Note that they are in Later Heaven Sequence
2. The 24 Mountains (with San He yin/yang spots)
3. The 5 Elements of the 24 Mountains[1]
4. The 72 Mountain-Piercing Dragons (here represented by just their Stems)
5. The yin/yang of the 72 Dragons.

[1] The 5 Element attributions are according to the Hung Fan 洪範 Hong Fan arrangement.

Figure 21: A rubbing of the stone Wang family tablet, found within a tomb near the Yan River in Kiangsu (Jiangsu) Province, dating from 946 CE (just immediately after the T'ang dynasty).[1] It shows typical feng shui symbolism. The central square contains 9 characters in seal script, giving the name of the grave occupants. Around this are three square 'rings' and outer apron containing:

1. The 8 trigrams in the Later Heaven Sequence, and star glyphs for the Sun and Moon
2. The next square 'ring' contains the 12 Animals corresponding with the 12 Earthly Branches, with the Rat (North) at the bottom, and a decorative flower at the corners
3. The outer 'ring' contains the 28 *Hsiu* or Mansions of the Moon, commencing with *Chiao* (Horn) towards the top left hand corner
4. On the sloping sides are the 4 Celestial Animals: the White Tiger on the right (West); the Green Dragon on the left (East); the Black Tortoise encircled by the snake at the bottom (North), and the Red Bird displaying its plumage at the top (South).

[1] 風水趣談 *Feng Shui Qu Tan* by 完顏紹元 Wan Yan Shao Yuan, 2005, page 93.

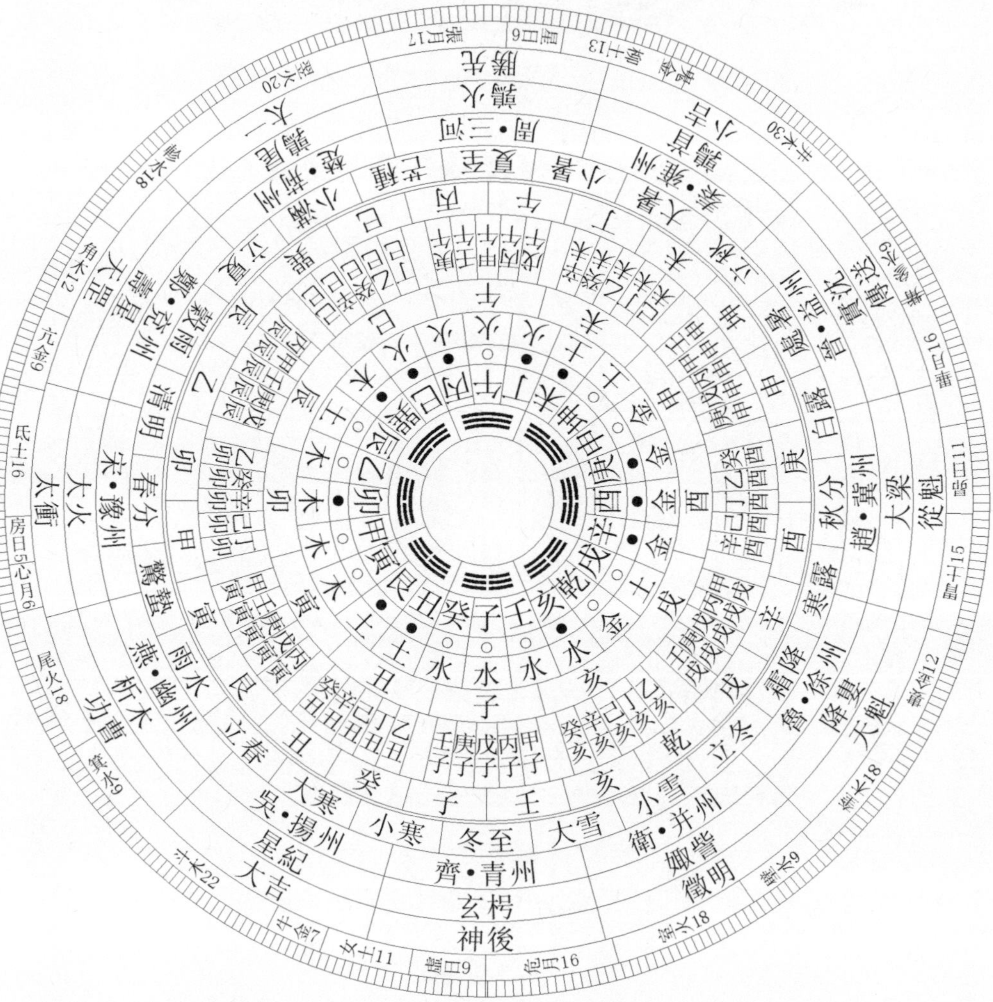

Figure 22: A reconstruction of a late T'ang dynasty lo p'an from circa 900 CE. Note the Heaven Plate and 72 Dragon ring just recently introduced by Yang Yun Sung.

1. The 8 trigrams in Former Heaven Sequence (from before the Han dynasty)
2. **Earth Plate 12** Mountains (since 730 CE Ch'iu Yen Han, or earlier)
3. Pure yin/Pure yang for the 24 Mountains (dark spot = yin) (from Chou dynasty)
4. The 24 Mountains 5 Elements attributions (from Han dynasty)
5. The 12 Earthly Branches ring (from the *Shih*, and also seen on mirror backs)
6. The 72 Mountain-Piercing Dragons (added by Yang Yun Sung c. 900 CE)
7. **Heaven Plate 12** Mountains (added by Yang Yun Sung c. 900 CE)
8. **Astronomical Plate 12** Mini-Seasons, known since Han dynasty)
9. The *fen yeh* (Provinces) ring (known since Chou dynasty)
10. The 12 Jupiter Stations *shen* ring (Chou dynasty, also related to the *Shih*)
11. The 12 Monthly *Teng Ming* Generals ring (from the Han dynasty *Shih*)
12. The 28 *Hsiu* ring with Elements (from the Han dynasty *Shih*)
13. The 365.25 day-degrees of the *Hsiu* (known from the Han 'Dipper Dial').

Five Dynasties and Ten Kingdoms Period (906-960 CE)

During the next dynasty, in the 10th century CE, Ts'ai Shen Yü[1] divided the Earth Plate into 60 Dragons, which he formed from the 60 Sexagenary Combinations of the 10 Heavenly Stems combined with the 12 Earthly Branches. This in turn rapidly led to the generation of the rings of 240, and then the 120 *fen-chin*. These additions obviously worked well in practice, as Ts'ai and his son went on to plan their own graves so effectively that almost all their sons and grandsons became famous, rich and Imperial Officials.

Sung Dynasty (960-1271 CE)

In 1027 CE the Tibetans adopted the *chia-tzu* cycle as a way of counting the years, using 1024 CE as its Epoch or starting point, with the *chia-tzu* combination being the Wood-Rat. This later developed into the 5 Element Tibetan divination system.[2]

Wang Chi

In about 1030 CE Wang Chi[3] (990-c.1060 CE) established the lo p'an in its modern form, with exactly 17 rings, at least two of which were the 24 Mountains ring, and of course another contained the 28 *Hsiu*.

It is useful at this point to be able to see what a Sung dynasty lo p'an would have looked like (see Figure 23 for a reconstruction of this lo p'an). We can be sure that the lo p'an had Earth, Heaven and Astronomical Plates, and by a careful process of deduction we can be certain that its rings would have included all those shown in Figure 23.[4]

Wang Chi wrote extensively about magnetised needles, clearly associating them with the configuration of ch'i.

> The ch'i influence of the lodestone is truly as if it were a living [thing]. It has a head and a tail. Its head points towards the North and its tail towards the South.[5] The force of the head is superior to that of the tail. If it [the lo p'an needle] is broken into pieces, all of them have [their own] heads and tails…If it is heated in the fire, it 'dies' and can no longer point to the South.[6]

The important association here reinforced is that of the needle with ch'i, a theme that dates back to Kuo P'o. The ch'i of compass needles was sometimes

---

[1] 蔡神與 Cai Shen Yu. Don't confuse him with his son Ts'ai Yüen Ting 蔡元定 Cai Yuan Ding (1135-1198).

[2] See my *Tibetan Oracle Pack,* Carroll & Brown, London, 2005.

[3] Often written as Wang Chi 王伋 Wang Ji. His courtesy name was 肇卿 Chao Ch'ing.

[4] This reconstruction has been arrived at by adding those rings present on the ancient *Shih* (which still survived on Ch'ing dynasty lo p'ans) to the rings known to have been introduced during 900-1030 CE.

[5] Maybe where a fish shaped needle was used.

[6] Needham (1962) Volume 4, Part 1, page 275.

said to be 'nourished' by laying them in a box with a lodestone floor, which would indeed increase their magnetic strength.

Wang Chi's pupil Yeh Shu Liang[1] published his 'Heart Classic'[2] and 'Questions and Answers on Received Passages.'[3]

In China the use of the compass for maritime navigation was delayed till at least 850-1050 CE. So for a long period the compass was used *primarily* if not entirely for land-based feng shui orientation using the 24 Mountain divisions, rather than for maritime navigation.[4] Once introduced to its use at sea, Chinese navigators remained faithful to floating compasses of one kind or another until the last part of the sixteenth century when the dry-pivoted compass was ironically re-introduced to East Asia by Dutch or Portuguese ships. The other improvement made by those sailors was the attachment of a directional compass card, but showing European rather than Chinese directions.

The founding of the Sung 宋 dynasty in 960 CE was later used as the epoch (or date starting point) for the 28 *Hsiu* on the lo p'an which still endures as their starting point on many lo p'an till today.[5]

Flying Stars

Some of the earliest physical evidence of the practical use of Flying Stars comes from a calendar found in the caves at Tun Huang[6] which can be dated exactly to 982 CE.[7] In the manuscript, the Flying Stars are marked in colour and a full set of month stars are shown as well as the annual stars. It is interesting that here the star names are not used, just the colours and numbers. Anyway, the point is that the 9 Flying Stars shown in the familiar Lo Shu[8] squares were obviously in common use more than a thousand years ago, and that a system of 'flying the stars' was by then well developed, although it might not have been in exactly the same form as is currently understood. The Flying Stars were also personified as shown on the cover of this book, the seven main stars on the right followed by the two Assistant (Left & Right) Stars.

---

[1] 葉叔亮 Ye Shu Liang.

[2] *Hsin Ching* 心經 *Xin Jing*.

[3] *Wen T'a Yü Lu* 問答語錄 *Wen Da Yu Lu*.

[4] The Chinese use of the compass for navigation was long retarded by the fact that for much of their history, coastal, canal and river traffic (which do not require a compass) predominated over long ocean voyages.

[5] This means that a number of modern lo p'ans are still showing the sky as it was in 960 CE. This is not just a case of extremely conservative behaviour, but one of not understanding the function of the *Hsiu* on the lo p'an, and hence not attempting to update it.

[6] 敦煌 Dunhuang.

[7] The dynasty is mentioned in the manuscript, and the Flying Star chart shown is marked as *Ren Wu* (or the 9th Heavenly Stem and 7th Earthly Branch). This combination is one of the 60 Sexagenary Combinations used for dating. This gives two possible dates separated by 60 years: 922 and 982, with the second being most likely.

[8] 洛書 *Luo Shu*.

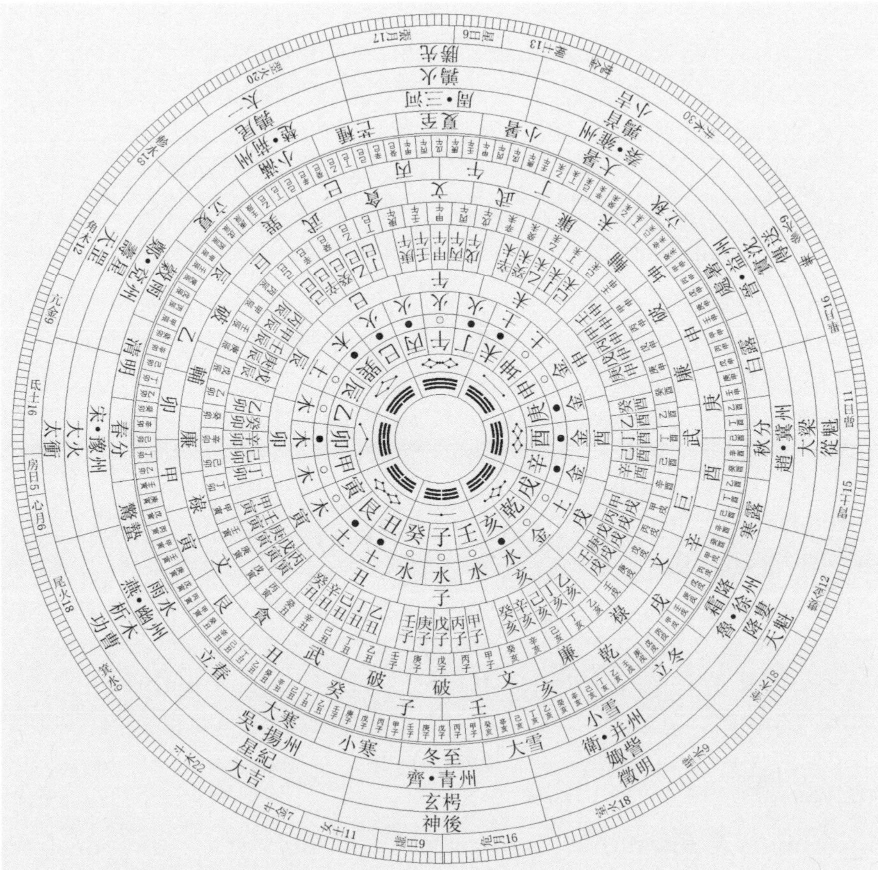

Figure 23: A reconstruction of a Sung dynasty lo p'an as used by Wang Chi circa 1030 CE.

1. The 8 trigrams in Former Heaven Sequence (seen on T'ang mirrors and graves)
2. Lo Shu numbers (Later Heaven Sequence)
3. The 24 Mountains (**Earth Plate** Correct Needle, known since 730 CE and *Shih*)
4. Pure yin/Pure yang of the 24 Mountains (dark spot = yin) (from Chou dynasty)
5. The 24 Mountains 5 Element attributions (from Han dynasty)
6. The 12 Earthly Branches ring (from the *Shih*, and also seen on mirror backs)
7. The 72 Mountain-Piercing Dragons (added by Yang Yun Sung 900 CE)
8. The 60 Earth-Penetrating Dragons (Earth Plate) (added by Ts'ai Shen Yü 10th century)
9. The *T'an Lang* Nine Stars (present at least by 982 CE)[1]
10. 24 Mountains (**Heaven Plate**) (added by Yang Yun Sung 900 CE)
11. The 120/240 *fen chin* (Heaven Plate) (added c. 906-960 CE)
12. **Astronomical Plate 12** Mini-Seasons (known since Han dynasty)
13. The *fen yeh* (Provinces) ring (Astronomical known since Ch'in dynasty)
14. The 12 Jupiter Stations *shen* ring (from the *Shih*)
15. The 12 Monthly *Teng Ming* Generals ring (from the *Shih*)
16. The 28 *Hsiu* ring with Elements and planets (from the *Shih*)
17. The 365.25 day-degrees of the *Hsiu* (from the Han 'Dipper Dial').

[1] See Walters (2002), pages 240-243.

The Early Division of Feng Shui into two 'Schools'

Also about this time there was a division of feng shui into two Schools. This Schools division was a product of geography and of the two main masters who were prominent 900-1000 CE. Both these Schools practiced San He feng shui. It was only much later (circa 1827 as we shall see) that San Yuan feng shui proper arose and split from the older San He style. The two Schools were:

a) The gentlemen of Kanchow,[1] or *Kan-chou hsien-sheng* who originated from Kiangsi Province,[2] and followed the Imperial Librarian and feng shui Master Yang Yun Sung and his main disciple Master Tsêng Wên Ch'an. They subscribed to the principles of landform, utilising the shape of mountains and the courses of rivers to determine the flow of ch'i. Nineteenth century writers therefore described Master Yang's School as 'Form School,' but this is a slightly misleading description, as every classical feng shui analysis must take both landform and lo p'an into account.[3]

b) The gentlemen of Fukien,[4] a coastal Province of China, who followed Master Wang Chi and his disciple Yeh Shu Liang. They regarded the lo p'an as all-important for determining the movement of ch'i through the land. Accordingly nineteenth century writers described Master Wang Chi's School as 'Compass School,' but this is also a misleading description, as every feng shui analysis also involves the lo p'an.[5]

Both methods are used by all masters, although the study of feng shui conveniently divides in this way. Modern masters still use this conceptual division, for example Pai He Ming,[6] a well known Hong Kong feng shui master, after enumerating the eleven main schools of feng shui, says that:

> though the above may be classified as the most common kinds of feng shui practice used now, in reality, feng shui can really only be divided into two main types, namely *luan t'ou*…and *li chi*.[7]

Luan t'ou and *li chi* are effectively *methods* or ways of looking at the feng shui rather than Schools, or in Chinese, they are 法 *fa* (methods) rather than 派 *p'ai* (Schools).

---

[1] 贛州 Gan Zhou.

[2] 江西 Jiang Xi.

[3] As has been pointed out by Master Joey Yap.

[4] 福建 Fujian.

[5] Sometimes the 'Form School' has been identified as San He and 'Compass School' as San Yuan. This is a mistaken identification, because both the gentlemen of Kanchow and Fukien practised San He feng shui. It is only much later that San Yuan split off from San He.

[6] 白鶴鳴 Bai He Ming or Pak Hok Ming.

[7] 巒頭 *Luan Tou* and 理氣 *Li Chi*. See Pa He Ming 風水羅盤逐層詳解, 1997, pages 26-28.

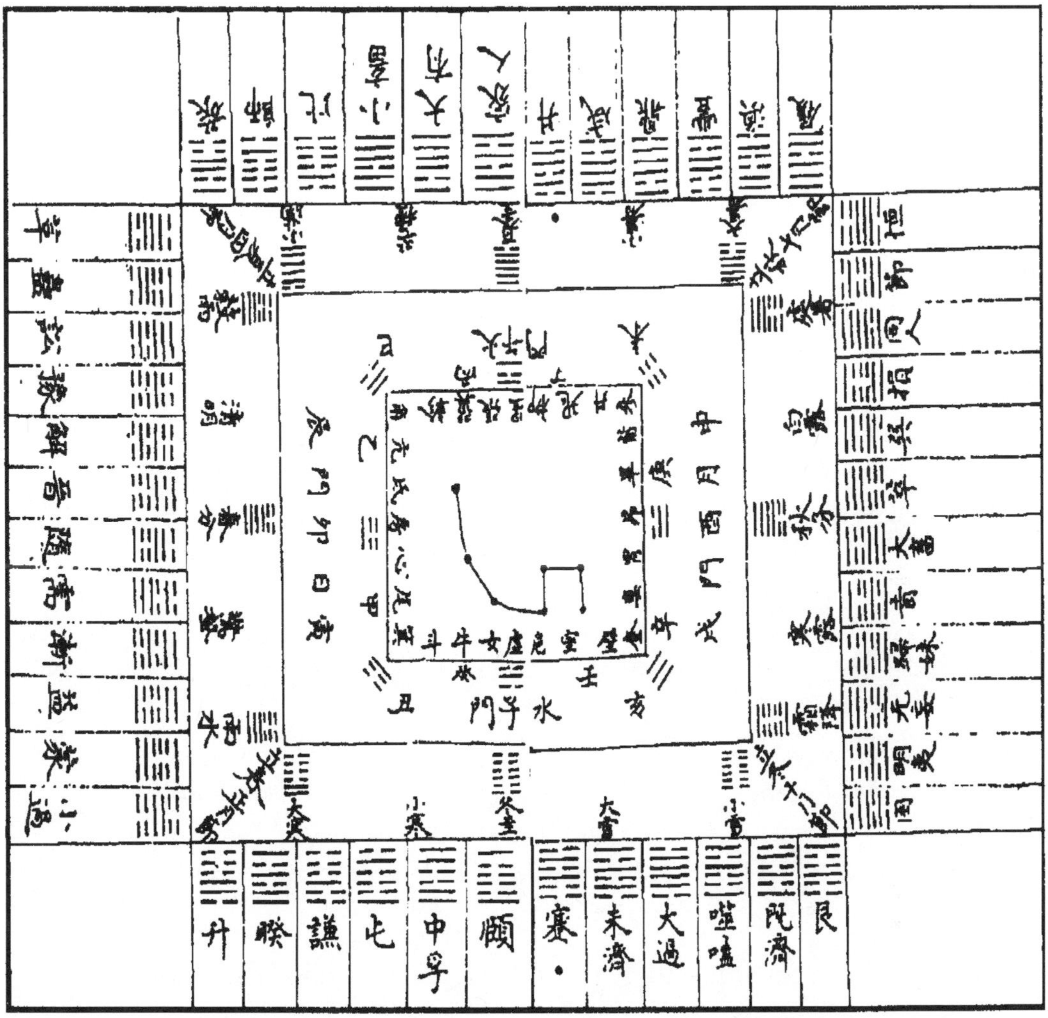

Figure 24: The key diagram (first printed in 1019 CE) which connects the *Shih* with the lo p'an, the 24 Mini-Seasons and the 60 hexagrams. It contains the Northern Ladle diagram and the 28 Hsiu (in the centre square); with the Later Heaven Sequence 8 trigrams, 8 Stems, 12 Branches and 4 Gates (in the first square 'ring'); the 12 Sovereign hexagrams and the 24 Mini-Seasons (second square 'ring'); and the remaining 48 hexagrams, making 60 in all (in the outer 'ring').[1] The figure therefore reconciles the arrangement of the early *Shih* plate with the 24 Mountains and the 60 hexagrams of the San He School.[2] This system does not yet qualify as San Yuan, as the full 64 hexagrams are not yet used together in one ring.

[1] From the 'Cloud Bookcase of the 7 (Bamboo) Divination Slips' *Yün Chi Ch'i Ch'ien* 云笈七籤 *Yun Ji Qi Qian* Sung dynasty 1019.

[2] Although this sounds like a strange association, it is in fact correct. It is only when all 64 hexagrams are used that it can be referred to as a San Yuan diagram.

Shao Yung and the I Ching

San Yuan feng shui was actually developed in the Ch'ing dynasty, but had its much earlier *theoretical* roots with Shao Yung in the Sung dynasty.

Shao Yung[1] (1011–1077) was a Northern Sung dynasty Chinese philosopher, poet, cosmologist and historian based in Luoyang, who was seminal to the development of Neo-Confucianism and the re-ignition of interest in the trigrams and hexagrams of the *I Ching*. Instead of just studying the *texts* of the *I Ching*, as so many before him had done, Shao took the 'number and image' approach to the hexagrams.[2] He was also interested in cycles of time, including *yuan* (Cycles), *hui* (Epochs), and *yün* (Revolutions).[3]

With the waxing and waning of these *kua,* and of the Elements, he attempted to trace the rise and fall of dynasties.[4] Shao was also greatly interested in cycles of time, including *yuan* (Cycles), and *yün* (Revolutions). The *kua* and the time cycles form the basis for the San Yuan School of feng shui.

You can easily see that taken together these three interests underpin the whole San Yuan approach to feng shui. It therefore seems plausible that Shao Yung, whilst maybe not directly involved in feng shui, might be seen as the inceptor or intellectual patron of San Yuan feng shui.

Shao Yung favoured the Early Heaven Sequence of the hexagrams, based on Fu Hsi's arrangement of the *kua*. Shao Yung's diagram of the evolution of the hexagrams, by the combination and re-combination of yang and yin, leads automatically to the order of the hexagrams used on San Yuan lo p'ans today. He separated out 12 'Sovereign' hexagrams and correlated them with the 12 months of the year, the 12 Earthly Branches and the phases of the Moon. Soon after these Sovereign hexagrams appeared as a ring on the San He lo p'an.

Shao Yung took Fu Hsi's square arrangement of the hexagrams and translated it into a circular arrangement. These two arrangements are complimentary and transform easily one into the other. His circular arrangement (see Figure 25) is the key to understanding the hexagram ring on the San Yuan lo p'an.

---

[1] 邵雍 Shao Yong, also known as Shao K'ang Chieh 邵康節 Shao Kang Jie, his courtesy name was Yao Fu 堯夫. His most famous book was the *Huang Chi Ching Shi Shu* 皇極經世書 *Huang Ji Jing Shi Shu.* See Huang (2000).

[2] The best book in English on this approach is Huang (2000) which is a worthwhile primer before getting involved at any depth with the hexagrams of the San Yuan School of feng shui.

[3] According to Shao Yung these periods related to each other as follows: 1 Cycle (元 *yuan*) = 12 Epochs (會 *hui*); 1 Epoch = 30 Revolutions (運 *yün*); 1 Revolution = 12 Generations (世 *shih*); 1 Generation = 30 years; 1 year = 12 months; 1 month = 30 days; 1 day = 12 double hours. Note the alternation of 12 and 30 which when multiplied together give 360. Also note that this arrangement is not exactly the same as modern San Yuan periods, for which see Skinner (2003), page 23.

[4] The theory was that the Element of each dynasty destroyed the Element of the dynasty it replaced.

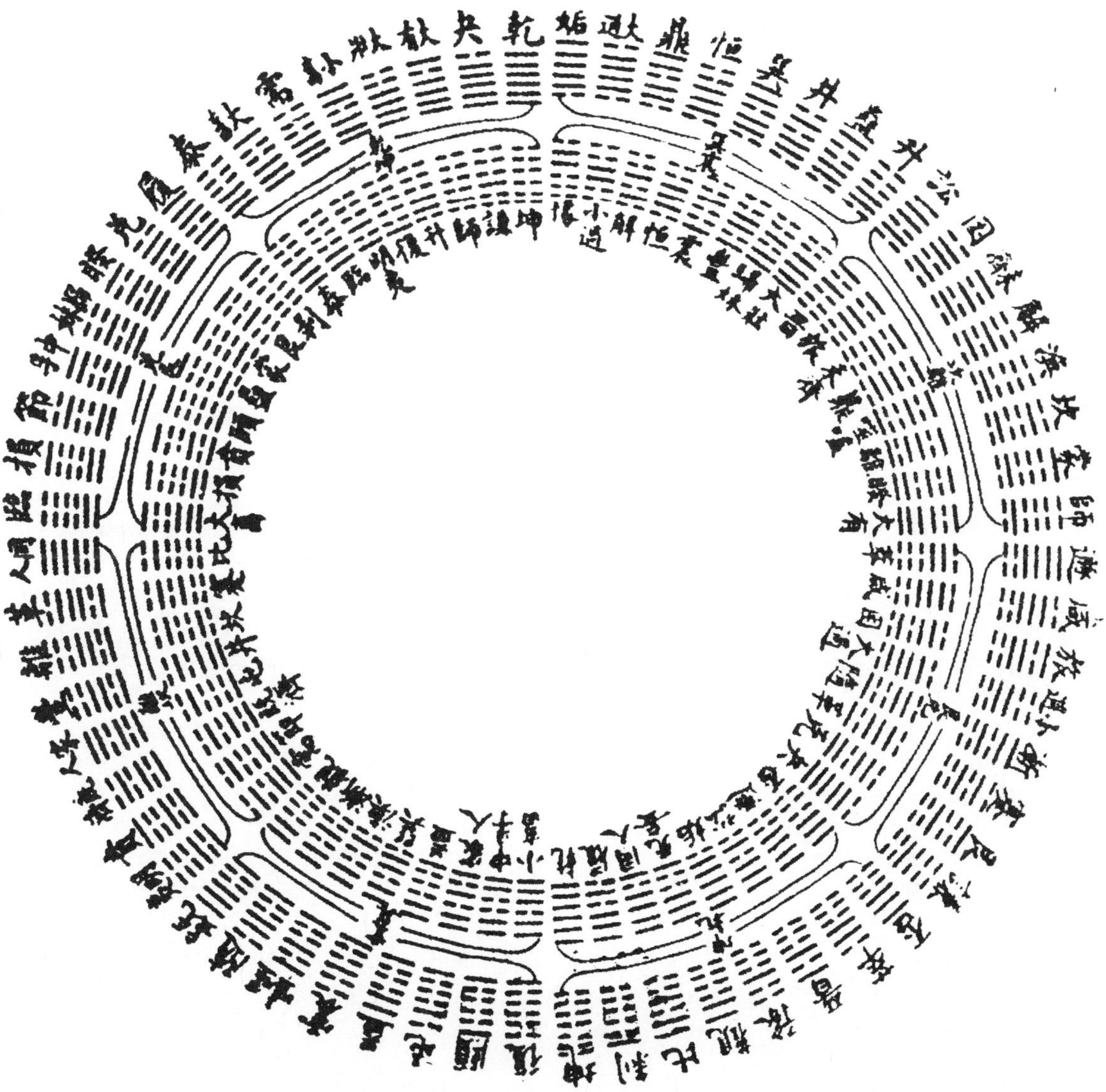

Figure 25: Shao Yung's arrangement of the 64 hexagrams. The two arrangements correspond with the two Plates (Inner and Outer Plate) of a complete San Yuan lo p'an. The names of the 64 hexagrams are shown around the outer and inner edges. The inner ring is Fu Hsi's 'square' arrangement of the hexagrams transformed into a circular format. The outer circle is Shao Yung's arrangement. The curved brackets mark out the Palaces, each of 8 hexagrams, which contain the same common base trigram.

Neo-Confucians

In this dynasty the Neo-Confucians, especially Shao Yung, popularised the arithmetic behind the hexagrams of the *I Ching*. The circular form provided the basis for the early San He rings of 60 Root hexagrams, which later in the Ch'ing dynasty transmuted into the San Yuan School with it rings of 64 hexagrams.

Yet another neo-Confucian important to the history of San Yuan feng shui was Chou Tun-I [1] (1017-1073 CE). In the same period, the Emperor Ren Tsung,[2] who reigned 1023-1063 CE, reintroduced the study of the 'Three Cosmic Boards,' which are divinatory systems derived from the *Shih*, into the Imperial examination curriculum.

Hsüan K'ung School

Hsü Ren Wang[3] who flourished from 1023-1063 CE is regarded by many as the founder of the Hsüan K'ung School of feng shui. He is supposed to have accurately predicted the fall of the Northern Sung dynasty, after having his advice rejected by the Emperor. Hsü transmitted his *k'an yü* teachings orally, leaving no books, and so it is often said that only in the early Ch'ing dynasty the secrets of Hsüan K'ung were 'revealed' by Chiang Ta Hung.

Hsüan K'ung,[4] which means 'Dark or Mysterious Void,' is the branch of feng shui that includes Hsüan K'ung Fei Hsing (Flying Star feng shui) and Hsüan K'ung Ta Kua (which utilises the 64 hexagrams).

These methods are more likely to have been first propagated and taught by Wu Ching Luan[5] from Kiangsu (flourished 1041-1064 CE), who was the head of the Imperial Astronomy Bureau, and who had suspiciously similar dates to Hsü Ren Wang. Also the same stories were told about him as about Hsü Ren Wang. He is said for example to have accurately predicted his own death date. His main books were:

'Hsüan K'ung Secret Decree'[6]
'San Yuan First Revision'[7]

The fact that he reputedly wrote books on both San Yuan and Hsüan K'ung

[1] 周敦頤 Zhou Dun Yi.

[2] 仁宗 Ren Zong.

[3] 徐仁旺 Xu Reng Wang.

[4] 玄空 *Xuan Kong*. This is sometimes misleadingly translated as 'time and space,' but that is a rather broad brush generalisation about its methods, rather than an exact translation of the characters.

[5] 吳景鸞 Wu Jing Luan.

[6] *Hsüan K'ung Mi Chih* 玄空秘旨 *Xuan Kong Mi Zhi*.

[7] *San Yuan Yi Chi* 三元一機 *San Yuan Yi Ji*.

suggests that they were similar, if not the same system of feng shui.

Incidentally, the *Tzu Wei Tou Shu*[1] astrology system also arose in this dynasty, having reputedly been devised by a Taoist named Lü Ch'un Yang[2] and developed by Chen Hsi-I[3] (who was a pupil of Tsêng Wên Ch'an, in turn the disciple of Yang Yun Sung).

Feng Shui Meets the I Ching

After Shao Yung, in the Southern Sung dynasty, there was an attempt to fit the circular arrangement of the *I Ching* hexagrams to the existing San He feng shui rings, possibly by Hsü Ren Wang. First of all the 12 Sovereign hexagrams of Shao Yung were matched with the 12 Earthly Branches, and made into a ring of their own.[4] Then 60 'Root Hexagrams' were matched with the 60 Sexagenary combinations. These rings have now mostly been lost from feng shui practice.[5]

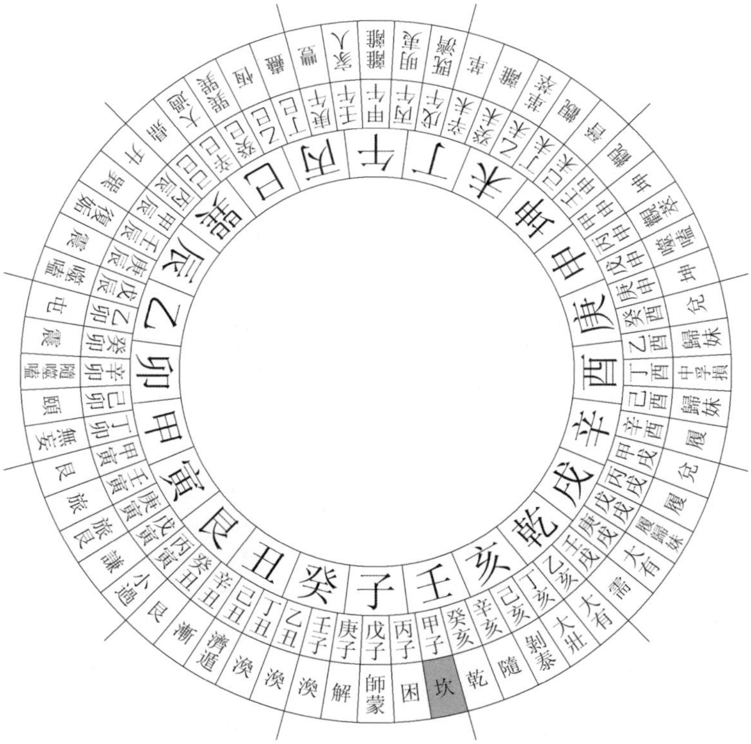

Figure 26: The 60 Sexagenary combinations matched with just 60 of the hexagrams.

[1] 紫微斗數 *Zi Wei Dou Shu.*

[2] 呂純陽 Lu Chun Yang.

[3] 陳希夷 Chen Xi Yi (871-989 CE).

[4] The 18th ring of the lo p'an described in the Ming dynasty *Lo Ching Chieh*.

[5] See page 115 for more details of this development and what became of it.

Magnetising the Needle

Apart from simply rubbing with a lodestone, the needle can be magnetised by thermo-remanence, a technique known to Tsêng Kung Liang[1] who as early as 1044 CE wrote about it in conjunction with a wet suspension needle.

> A thin leaf of iron is cut into the shape of a fish [hollowed so it will float] two inches long and half an inch broad, having a pointed head and tail.[2] This is then heated in a charcoal fire, and when it has become thoroughly red-hot, it is taken out by the head with iron tongs and placed so that its tail points due North towards *tzu*.[3] In this position it is quenched with water in a basin, so that its tail is submerged for seven tenths of an inch.[4]

This procedure of rapid cooling whilst holding the 'fish' aligned North-South will magnetise a needle just as surely as rubbing it with a lodestone. So here you have the use of water and of North-South orientation, two of the key elements of feng shui, involved in the magnetisation of the needle.

Tsêng also seems to have a great attachment to the fish symbol, for in 1072 CE he is reputed to have attached a large bronze fish to the southern gate of the capital, to indicate its South facing direction. Perhaps the fish might then have been an alternate symbol for the South instead of the currently accepted Vermilion Sparrow or Red Bird. If this were so, then this symbol seems a lot more appropriate, as houses and cities were often orientated with a river or a pool to their southern facing side.

There are also contemporary records of turtle shaped carvings containing a loadstone, designed to pivot to face North. The traditional animal symbol for the North is of course the turtle, and so the use of a South-facing fish is not altogether improbable. This then makes a hill at the back (turtle shell) with water at the front (the fish) the archetypal feng shui configuration.

Compass Mechanics and Maritime Use

Before we examine the further evolution of the lo p'an we need to look at the mechanics of the compass. In brief, early compasses first used floating wet needles, and then silk-suspended needles (which required a draught-proof location). This later developed into the dry pivoted needle which is used in compasses and lo p'ans to this day. More solid suspension leads to much greater precision in readings. This precision enabled further subdivision than the 24 Mountains, a process of division that began around 900 CE with Yang Yun Sung's addition of a ring of 72 dragon divisions to the standard 24 divisions.

---

[1] 曾公亮 Zeng Gong Liang.

[2] The fish shape surfaces again hundreds of years later in Arab compasses.

[3] *Tzu*, the due north sector of the 24 Mountains division of the lo p'an.

[4] Needham (1962), Volume 4, Part I, page 252.

In the *Shih Lin Kuang Chi*[1] the Sung Encyclopaedia edited by Ch'en Yüen Ching[2] probably compiled after 1135 CE, but not printed till 1325, the author describes the activities of Taoist immortals in relation to early versions of the compass. The first passage describes a wet-mounted compass or *shui lo ching*:[3]

> They cut a piece of wood into the shape of a fish, as big as one's thumb, and make a hole in its belly, into which they neatly fit a piece of lodestone, filling up the cavity with wax. Into this wax a needle bent like a hook is fixed. Then when the fish is put in the water it will of its nature point to the South, and if it is moved with the finger it will return again to its original position.

A second passage describes a dry-mounted compass or *han lo ching*:[4]

> They also cut a piece of wood into the shape of a turtle, and arrange it in the same way as before, only that the needle is fixed at the tail end. A bamboo pin about as thick as the end of a chopstick is set up on a small board, and sustains the turtle by the concave under-surface of its body, where there is a small hole. Then when the turtle is rotated, it will always point to the North, which must be due to the needle at the tail.

See Figure 27 for a reconstruction of the turtle-shaped dry-mounted compass.

This demonstrates that both wet and dry pivoting were well established by 1135 CE, and also that the construction of such devices was under the control of Taoist *fang-shih,* or magicians and feng shui masters, rather than mariners.

The early compass is most likely to have been iron and shaped like a fish floating on the surface of water, much as a present day 'wet' compass. In modern feng shui parlance the needle housing is still referred to as the 'Heaven Pool.' This is important because it helps confirm that the central depression was originally water-filled, and more importantly, that maybe the forces that moved the needle were thought to be from Heaven rather than Earth.

---

[1] 事林廣記 *Shi Lin Guang Ji.*

[2] 陳元靚 Chen Yuan Jing. Quoted in Needham (1962) Volume 4, I, page 255.

[3] 水羅經 *shui luo jing.*

[4] 旱羅經 *han luo jing.*

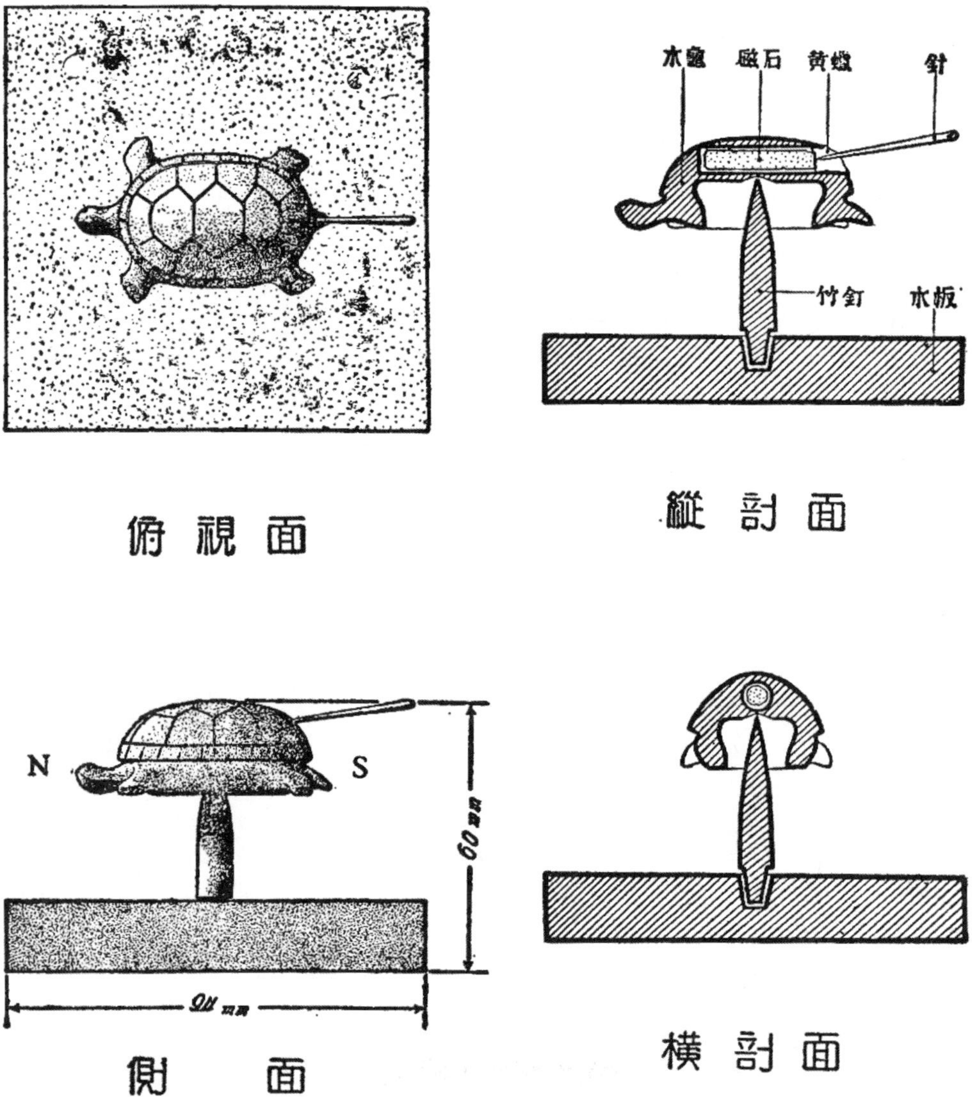

Figure 27: An early wooden dry-pivoted compass made in the shape of a turtle with an embedded magnetised needle, as described in the *Shih Lin Kuang Chi*.[1]

Compass Mounting & Shen Kuo

Following on from wet-mounted compasses, with their fish and water associations, came experiments in other forms of mounting. A full century before the first European mention of the compass, in about 1086 CE, the amazing Shen Kuo (1030-1093 CE), the head of the Imperial Astronomy Bureau, wrote a very explicit and practical passage about magnetism, in his delightfully titled *Dream Pool Essays*:

[1] From Needham (1962), Volume IV, Part 1, page 257, after Wang Chen-To.

> Magicians rub the point of a needle with the loadstone; then it is able to point to the South… [The magnetised needle may be made to] float on the surface of water, but it is then rather unsteady. It may be balanced on the finger-nail, or on the rim of a cup, where it can be made to turn more easily, but these supports being hard and smooth, it is liable to fall off.[1]

His list of the various early means of needle suspension is later quoted by Wang Chen-To and Professor Cheng Jian Jun[2] to confirm that wet suspension came first. The four forms of needle suspension suggested by Shen Kuo are therefore:

a. the 'wet' compass floating in water
b. balancing the needle on a fingernail
c. balancing the needle on the rim of a cup
d. dry mounting from a silk thread

Cup rim and finger-nail suspension are of course not real alternatives, just mentioned for the sake of completeness. Shen Kuo continues with the preferred dry method of suspension:

> It is best to suspend it [the needle] by a single cocoon fibre of new silk attached to the centre of the needle by a piece of wax the size of a mustard seed – then, by hanging it in a windless place, it will always point to the South. Among such needles there are some which, after being rubbed, point to the North. I have needles of both kinds by me.

The last comment is of particular interest, because it shows that the Chinese well understood that all needles point both North and South (in fact in line with the magnetic lines of force of the Earth's magnetic field). They also knew that this direction simply depends upon the direction the lodestone is stroked along the needle when it is being magnetised.[3]

Even more to the point, it depends upon which end is considered the 'point.' It has become a cultural convenience that Europeans conventionally mount compass needles with the arrow point at the North-pointing end, whilst Chinese consider this (the end with a bulge on a Chinese compass) to be the 'tail' of the needle. The needle performs exactly the same function regardless of which end you consider to be the point. Shen Kuo also wrote about Liu Ren (*Liuren*) divination which is one of these three methods, which uses a modified form of the *Shih,* so he was well acquainted with that instrument as well.

---

[1] *Meng Hsi Pi T'an* 夢溪筆談 *Meng Xi Bi Tan*. Quoted by Needham (1962), Vol. 4, part 1, page 249-250.

[2] See Cheng (1998), page 10.

[3] More than a century later Michael Scott (1175-1236 CE), a magician and astrologer to Emperor Frederick II of Sicily, wrote in his *Liber Particularis* that there are two kinds of lodestones, one of which points north and the other south.

Lai Pu Yi and the Outer Heaven Plate

The next major event in the evolution of feng shui came soon after 1100 CE with Master Lai Pu Yi (fl. 1082-1135 CE). He saw that the relationship between Astronomic North and Magnetic North in the real world had changed in the two centuries since Yang Yun Sung had introduced the Heaven Plate. Lai Pu Yi was aware of Shen Kuo's astronomic work on the relationship between Magnetic North and Astronomic North, and the corrections that he had made as a result of close observation. He therefore introduced a Plate which he called the 'Outer Heaven Plate,' which he added outside the existing Heaven Plate of Yang Yun Sung, without disturbing it. It is clear that *at this point in time* this Plate was supposed to perform the same function as the 'Inner Heaven Plate,' and was created as a response to the actual change in the relative positions of Astronomic North and Magnetic North. Master Lai also aligned his Plate with the outer Astronomical rings, as their point of reference was also the Pole Star.

Master Lai wrote:

> 'Li Ch'i *Hsüeh* Method'[1]
> 'Chapters on the Bringing Forth of Officials.'[2]

Figure 28: Lai Pu Yi who created the Outer Heaven (Man) Plate to take into account the change in magnetic declination.[3] If he were alive today he would undoubtedly see the need for another such adjustment.[4]

Unfortunately, by the Ch'ing dynasty the relationship between Astronomic North and Magnetic North had changed yet again, and the Plate had lost its real world significance. As a result, in the Ch'ing Dynasty, the 'Outer Heaven Plate' was re-named the 'Man Plate,' and adjusted in position to fall between the Earth Plate and the Heaven Plate, because its true function was not remembered. Because this Plate no longer aligned with Astronomic North it

---

[1] *Li Ch'i Hsüeh Fa* 理氣穴法 *Li Qi Xue Fa*.
[2] *Ts'ui Kuan Pien* 催官篇 *Cui Guan Pian*. To increase the chances of family members becoming Mandarins.
[3] See Appendix IV for declination.
[4] Drawing by Chong Yi Ming 鐘義明 Zhong Yi Ming.

had ceased to perform its function, and was therefore given a new function, a function unrelated to what Master Lai had originally intended for it. As a result, many of the Man Plate formulas were abandoned as they no longer worked.

It is time that the 'Man Plate' again reassumed its role as the 'Outer Heaven Plate' centred upon Astronomic North. It has also become obvious that with feng shui being practiced in many places around the world, where there is a wide range of different declinations, that the Man Plate needs further adjustment.[1] When this is done, the old 'Outer Heaven Plate' (and Astronomic ring) formulas work again.

It cannot be emphasised too much that although much reliance is placed nowadays on directions recorded by the Earth Plate using Magnetic North, feng shui is just as reliant on directions recorded by the Man Plate and the astronomical rings which are based on Astronomic (or True) North. Calculations need to take into account magnetic orientation as well as stellar (astronomic) orientation. In fact Astronomic North was initially much more important as it governed time and the seasons, and the fixed position of the mountains.

Lai Pu Yi completes the four great Grand Masters of San He feng shui, who lived in or near Kanchow:[2] Yang Yun Sung, Tsêng Wên Ch'an, Liao Yü and Lai Pu Yi.

By the end of the Sung dynasty, San He feng shui was well established and Hsüan K'ung may have just launched, although the latter doesn't appear to have got into its stride till the early Ch'ing dynasty. Figure 29 summarises the history of the introduction of the three Plates.

Date	Dynasty	Master	Plate introduced	Needle name
c. 730 CE	T'ang	Ch'iu Yen Han	Earth Plate	Correct Needle
c. 900 CE	T'ang	Yang Yun Sung	Heaven Plate	Seam Needle
c. 1150 CE	Southern Sung	Lai Pu Yi [*aka* Lai Wên Chün]	Outer Heaven Plate [Man Plate]	Central Needle

Figure 29: Summary of the history of the evolution of the 3 Plates of the San He lo p'an. The Plates are in chronological order, and in the order they occurred on ancient lo p'ans. However on modern lo p'ans they are in the order Earth-Man-Heaven Plates.

[1] The present author teaches a class on how this is done.

[2] 贛州 Ganzhou in Jiangxi Province.

Rings, Plates and Needles

Perhaps the most important ring on any lo p'an of whatever School is the 24 Mountain ring. This ring is fairly prominent, and is usually found close to the centre, often the 3rd, 4th or 5th ring from the centre. It is divided into 24 sectors or 'Mountains.' The term 'Mountain' is a technical term (hence the initial capital letter) and does not mean the same as a physical or geographic mountain.

Let us now look at the structure of the first kind of lo p'an, the San He lo p'an. This type of lo p'an is distinguishable by 3 repetitions of this most important ring, the 24 Mountain ring. Each repetition (with its allied rings) is referred to as a 'Plate.' The 3 Plates are only relevant to San He and Combined Tsung He lo p'ans, and not to San Yuan lo p'ans.

You should notice that the 3 rings all carry the same characters, in the same order, but the two outer rings are turned by 7.5° to the left or the right of the innermost ring. Look at Figure 30. Find one Chinese character on the inner ring, and check its position on the other two repetitions of the 24 Mountain ring. For example, take 子 Tzu (at the bottom). You can see it repeated near the bottom in two other rings. Taken together, over all the three Plates, Tzu extends over a 30° span. But this is not the correct way to look at it. You must look at each Plate in turn where Tzu holds sway over just 15° at a time, albeit a different 15°.

The inner 24 Mountain ring is called the 'Earth Plate.' The second similar 24 Mountain ring is called the 'Outer Heaven (or Man) Plate,' and it is turned 7.5° anticlockwise. The third of 24 Mountains is the 'Heaven Plate,' and it is turned 7.5° clockwise by comparison with the inner Earth Plate.

Although the inner 24 Mountain ring was established at the time of Ch'iu Yen Han in 730 CE, its constituents and arrangement date back to the *Huai Nan Tzu* over 1000 years before. It is aligned to the magnetic North-South axis and forms the inner or Earth Plate of the lo p'an. The Chinese maritime compass, which was derived from the feng shui lo p'an, has to this day got just that one simple ring.

In about 900 CE the great feng shui patriarch Yang Yun Sung added the Heaven Plate. This Plate is deflected by 7.5° clockwise (outer ring in Figure 30).

In about 1100 CE Master Lai Pu Yi introduced the third Plate, the Outer Heaven Plate which is now rather confusingly placed in the middle between the other two Plates, and was renamed the Man Plate. This Plate is deflected 7.5° anti-clockwise from the Earth Plate.

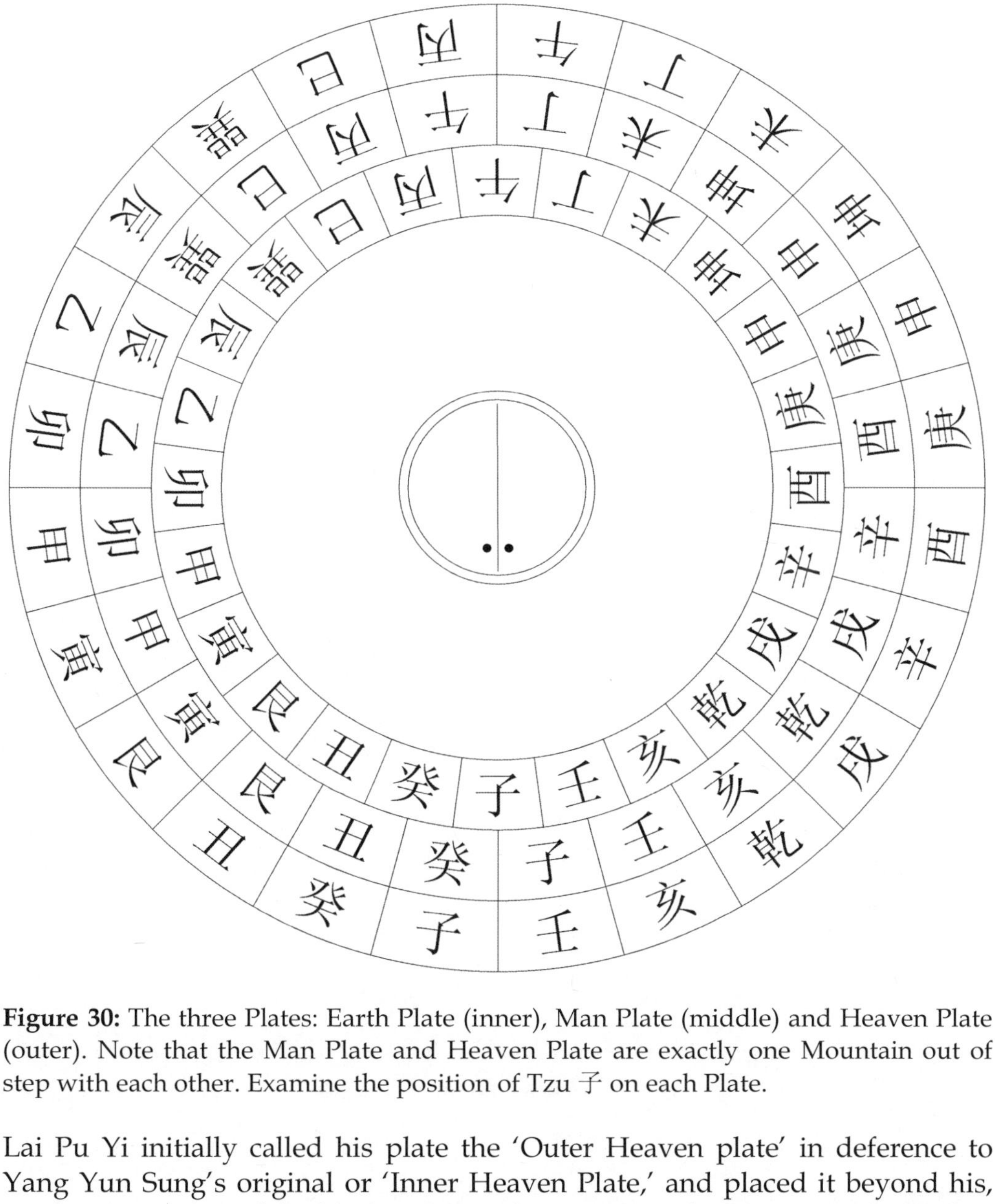

Figure 30: The three Plates: Earth Plate (inner), Man Plate (middle) and Heaven Plate (outer). Note that the Man Plate and Heaven Plate are exactly one Mountain out of step with each other. Examine the position of Tzu 子 on each Plate.

Lai Pu Yi initially called his plate the 'Outer Heaven plate' in deference to Yang Yun Sung's original or 'Inner Heaven Plate,' and placed it beyond his, on the outer edge of the lo p'an. Later its position and name were changed to the arrangement shown above, which is what you see on modern lo p'ans.

The first step in analysing any San He lo p'an is to identify the three Plates. Use Figure 30 to get orientated, and then take a look at Figure 48 to see if you can find the same Plates in the layout of a real lo p'an.

Initially this looks very complex. The trick is to pick out the three main rings using just one character, and then the rest will just fall into place.

Figure 48 is a typical Ch'ing dynasty San He lo p'an, with no trace of San Yuan rings. Even the innermost ring, which contains the Former Heaven Sequence trigrams, is engraved with their Chinese characters rather than the trigrams themselves. At first sight such a lo p'an looks immensely complex. It just takes a little practice to isolate the three rings in order to make sense of its structure. Figure 31 does just this. Using it we can look at the way the different rings relate to each other. You can see that this complex lo p'an breaks down into sets of rings grouped into 3 Plates (Earth, Man, Heaven). A further two Plates, the Sha Plate (introduced in the Ming dynasty) and the Astronomical Plate make up the rest of every San He lo p'an.

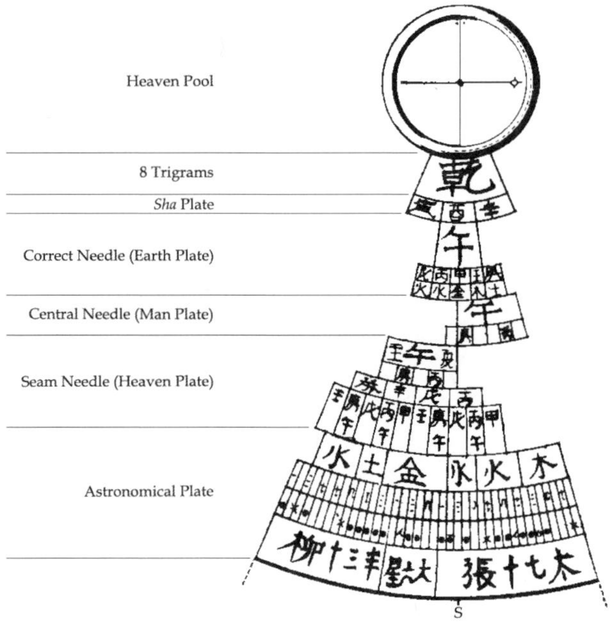

Figure 31: The relative positions of one of the 24 Mountains on each of the three Plates. In this example the character *wu* 午 the South point, has been chosen to illustrate the angular divergence of the three Plates.[1]

It is worth mentioning that early lo p'ans (T'ang to Ming dynasties) spaced the Plates in the order they were discovered or invented, Earth-Heaven-Man. It is only after some time that these were 'corrected' into the usual modern order of Earth-Man-Heaven, which is seen on most Ch'ing dynasty and all modern lo p'ans.[2]

---

[1] From Skinner (2006), page 127 modified.

[2] Feuchtwang (1974), page 26, working from the *Lo Ching Chieh* of Wu Wang Kang, calls the Heaven Plate the 'Inner Heaven Plate' and calls the Man Plate the 'Outer Heaven Plate.' This is at first sight confusing, until you realise that the Plates didn't change, but their order did.

Chu Hsi

Another philosopher of the same period who had a hand in fashioning Neo-Confucianism and feng shui was Chu Hsi[1] (1130-1200 CE) from Fukien and Kiangsi.[2] He was instrumental in defining the concepts of li and ch'i which are so important to feng shui. His student was the son of Ts'ai Shen Yü, the man who devised the 60 Dragon ring. Chu Hsi helped define the relationship between *li* (natural laws) and ch'i, a definition which helped define feng shui itself.

It is worth looking back over the feng shui achievements of this dynasty. The Sung dynasty was a very fertile time for feng shui, and the following elements came together in the century between 1030 and 1150 CE:

Summary of Sung dynasty Achievements	Scholar
Establishment of the lo p'an in its modern form with 17 rings	Wang Chi
Revival of the Three Cosmic Boards, including *Liu Ren*	Emperor Ren Tsung
Revival of *I Ching: kua,* number, image and circular arrangement	Shao Yung
Historical *yuan* and *yün* time cycles proposed	Shao Yung
Neo-Confucian ideas about *li* and *ch'i*	Chu Hsi
Research into declination and the relationship between Magnetic and Astronomic North	Shen Kuo
Spherical trigonometry; calendar reform	Shen Kuo
Possible roots of Hsüan K'ung School planted	Hsü Ren Wang or Wu Ching Luan
The Outer Heaven (Man) Plate of 24 Mountains invented	Lai Pu Yi
Tzu Wei Tou Shu astrology system invented	Lü Ch'un Yang and Chen Hsi-I

[1] 朱熹 Zhu Xi.

[2] Chu Hsi 朱熹 Zhu Xi. Chu Hsi is quoted extensively in Eitel (1873) on the concepts of 理 *li* and 氣 *ch'i*.

The Compass in Europe

While both wet and dry mounted compasses were being used in China, the compass made its way to Europe. Li Shu Hua very succinctly sums up the arrival of the compass in Europe.

> One can remark that, in the work of Bailak [al-Qabajaqi],[1] the south or 'noon' [*wu*] is mentioned before the north [*tzu*] in practical use, both in the sea of Syria [the eastern Mediterranean Sea] and in the Indian Ocean. This detail leaves hardly any doubt that the Arabs had adopted the practical method used in China. The aquatic [wet] compass or needle floating on water, which Bailak encountered in 1242 in the Syrian Sea [the eastern Mediterranean Sea], and which served the French navigators during the reign of Saint Louis (1226-1270), is exactly of the same type described in the [*Pên Tshou Yen I*] by [Khou Tsung-Shih] around 1116. Likewise, the iron fish, used in the Indian Ocean, of which Bailak speaks in 1282, is exactly of the same type that was described in 1040 in the [*Wu Ching Tsung Yao*]. [2]

Europeans acquired the compass directly from the Chinese, rather than via the usual cultural route of the silk road and the Arab world. In fact Europeans seem to have had a compass several decades before Arab mariners were using one. The dating of the first written record of a compass in Europe is precisely 1190 CE, when Alexander Neckam (in *De Naturis Rerum*) wrote that:

> …sailors, moreover, as they sail over the sea, when in cloudy weather they can no longer profit by the light of the sun, or when the world is wrapped up in the darkness of the shades of night, and they are ignorant to what point of the compass their ship's course is directed, they touch the magnet with a needle. This [needle] then whirls around in a circle until, when its motion ceases, its point looks direct to the Pole star.[3]

Interestingly, Alexander also mentions silkworms in the same book, suggesting a Chinese source for both pieces of information, and that therefore suggests the possibility that maybe the silk-suspended compass was the one Alexander Neckam was familiar with.

The earliest Arabic reference to the compass I have been able to discover is in a collection of stories by Muhammad al-Awfi who, in 1232 CE, mentioned sailors finding their way by means of a fish-shaped piece of iron rubbed with a magnet.

---

[1] He wrote about 1282, and was the first Arab writer to mention the compass.

[2] Li Shu Hua (1954) as quoted by Amir Aczel (2001) pages 120-121. Aczel is keen on promoting the idea that Flavio Gioia/Gioja invented the compass, but Flavio's contribution was probably just to unite the wind rose card with the magnetic needle, thereby just replacing the 24 Mountains with European compass points as directional indicators.

[3] Of course, because of magnetic declination, it very seldom pointed exactly to the Pole Star, often being some degrees one side or the other of Astronomical North. The Pole Star was of navigational importance to both Europeans and Chinese, but it was also of Taoist religious significance to the Chinese who therefore had an additional reason for revering the compass.

Yuan Dynasty (1271-1368 CE)

Kuo Shou Ching

Kuo Shou Ching (1231-1316) [1] was a Chinese astronomer, engineer, and mathematician born in Hsing Tai in Hupeh Province[2] just before the Yuan 元 dynasty began. Kuo was brought up by his grandfather Kuo Yung, who was an expert in the Five Confucian Classics, mathematics and hydraulics. By the age of 16 Kuo Shou Ching had obtained from his grandfather a blueprint for a water clock, and soon understood its operating principles. He worked on improving the Chinese *gnomon*[3] at Kublai Khan's Kao Cheng Astronomical Observatory. [4] There he formulated the *Shou Shih* calendar,[5] and calculated the length of the tropical year to be exactly 365.2425 days or 365 days 5 hours 49 minutes and 20 seconds, a value very similar to the value used to construct the Western Gregorian calendar, but discovered by Kuo some 300 years earlier than the European calculation.

His calendar was successfully used from 1281 till 1644, when it was finally replaced at the start of the Ch'ing dynasty. This is important for us as it helps to date pre-Ch'ing lo p'ans, and confirms that the *Lo Ching Chieh* (which includes a ring specifically using this calendar) must have been written before 1644. Kuo also used mathematical functions in his work relating to spherical trigonometry, following upon the earlier work of Shen Kuo. This was the most important work on trigonometry written in China and not surpassed till 1607. Kuo also devised a number of astronomical instruments, and conducted large-scale geodetic surveys and celestial observations at a number of observatories across China.

He made superb astronomical observatory instruments cast in 1270 CE, copies of which now reside (at the wrong latitude) in the Purple Mountain Observatory in Nanking (Nanjing). His *torquetum* was supported by amazingly beautiful bronze dragons, and weighed several tons, a masterpiece of casting for the thirteenth century, and certainly not easy to make even today. Star maps produced by these devices relate to the lo p'an's outer *Hsiu* ring.

---

[1] 郭守敬 Gou Shou Jing, courtesy name Ruosi.

[2] 邢台 Xingtai in 河北 Hebei Province.

[3] A pole used to cast shadows at key times of the year for Chinese astronomers to precisely fix the Sun's movements, and the position of Astronomic North. See Figure 4 and Figure 5.

[4] 藁城 Gao Cheng in Hebei Province.

[5] 授時曆 Shou Shi Li.

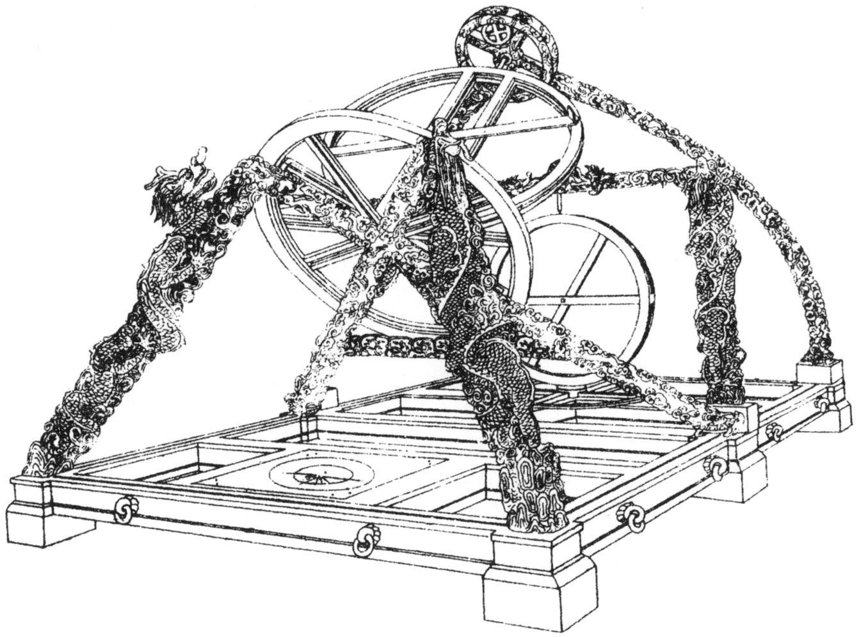

Figure 32: The equatorial *torquetum*, based on Kuo Shou Ching's 1270 CE design, with a Pole star determining circle at the top. It acts like a dissected armillary sphere, and is designed to take readings on three planes: the horizon, equatorial and ecliptic planes. Such exquisitely built Chinese astronomical equipment enabled very precise mapping of the stars.

Chao P'ang

Chao P'ang (1319-1369),[1] who lived in Hsiuning in Anhui Province (the then centre of lo p'an manufacture), wrote 'General K'an Yü Discussion'[2] about the lo p'an, specifically declaring that its practitioners originated from Fukien Province, which agrees with my conclusions that Fukien (and Anhui) were centres of Compass School feng shui. Chao P'ang first used the words *'lo ching'* to describe the lo p'an.

It was possibly that in this dynasty the stars of Flying Star feng shui, which were previously identified only by colour and number, acquired their bizarre names. For example 1-white was called the Greedy Wolf star, and 2-black became the Great Gate star. The Mongols are one speculative source for the origin of these Flying Star names. It would be appropriate if the number one Flying Star, which is called the Greedy Wolf, came from the Mongols, whose number one leader, Genghis Khan, recognised the wolf as his ancestral totem animal.

I hypothesise that it may also have been in the Yuan dynasty that one School

---

[1] 趙汸 Zhao Pang (not Fang).

[2] *K'an Yü Tsung Lun* 堪輿總論 *Kan Yu Zong Lun.*

of feng shui may have changed its name from Yuan K'ung 元空 to Hsüan K'ung 玄空 (Xuan Kong) because the use of the actual reign name (元 Yuan) was always forbidden to other organisations when it became a dynasty name.

It is not surprising to see that Chinese battle formations were described in the same terms as were used in feng shui, as location and direction are as important in feng shui as in warfare strategy. One of the greatest Chinese novels is *Outlaws of the Marshes* (sometimes called *The Water Margin*)[1] about a band of 108 loyal heroes (supposedly incarnations of 108 spirits) who held out against the corrupt forces of the Emperor's court. It was written by Shih Nai An[2] (c.1290-1365 CE). In one battle scene the outlaw commander arranges his troops according to the *pa kua*, with banners coloured according to the 5 Elements.

Another key feng shui text from this era is the 'Agreeable K'an Yü Aphorisms' by the mathematician Liu Chi (1311-1375 CE).[3]

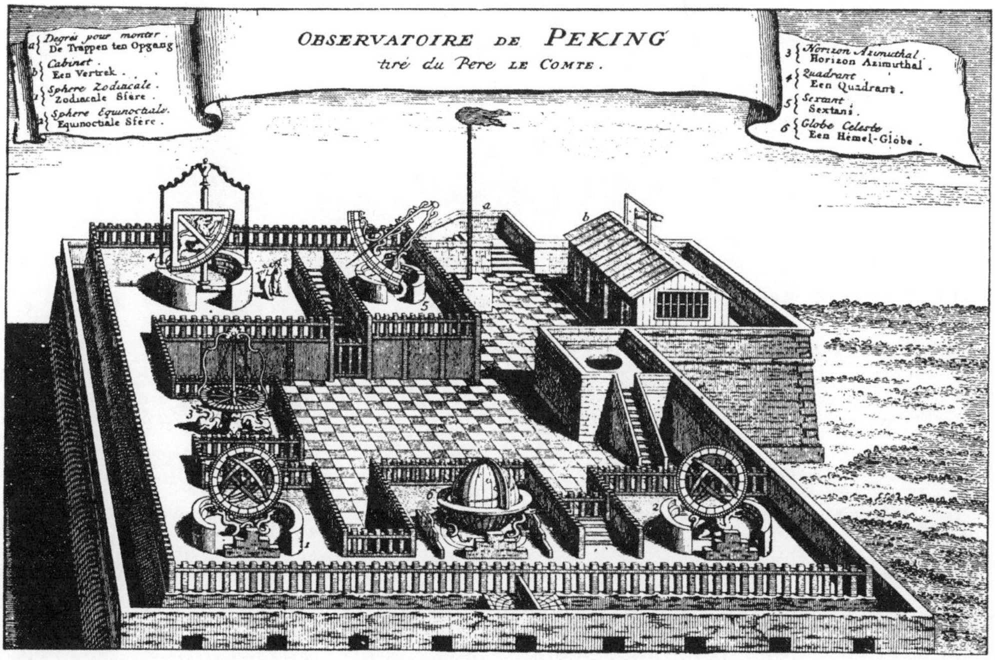

Figure 33: An engraving of the elaborate Ancient Beijing Observatory. It contains armillary spheres, quadrants and celestial globes probably originally designed by Shen Kuo in the late 11th century. It was re-equipped by Ferdinand Verbiest (1623-1688), a Flemish Jesuit missionary in Beijing in the late 1660s, working with Chinese craftsmen from designs he found in Tycho Brahe's book *Mechanica*.[4]

---

[1] 水滸傳 *Shui Hu Zhuan*.

[2] 施耐庵 Shi Nai An.

[3] *K'an Yü Man Hsing* 堪輿漫興 *Kan Yu Man Xing* by Liu Chi 劉基 Liu Ji.

[4] The *Mechanica* was published in 1598 and 1602, so it was already quite old by the time Verbiest used its guidelines. Engraving by Père le Comte, Paris 1750.

Ming Dynasty (1368 - 1644 CE)

Before considering feng shui in the Ming dynasty, we should just examine what happened to the maritime compass. One of the first Chinese sailors recorded to have used the compass as a major navigational aid was Cheng Ho (1371-1435),[1] from Yunnan province in China. He made seven long distance ocean voyages between 1405 and 1433, during which he discovered most of the countries bordering the Indian Ocean and the South China Sea, and possibly even the Pacific coast of America.[2] Without the aid of the compass, and a detailed knowledge of navigational astronomy, these voyages would simply have been impossible.

Figure 34: Cheng Ho's huge ships, like this one, used a compass with 24 Mountains for his seven lengthy voyages of discovery between 1405 and 1433.[3]

A navigational text of the period states that sailors "depended upon the 24 positions of the compass Earth Plate or *ti lo ching*." By calling it the Earth Plate the author implicitly acknowledges that there were more rings on the much more complicated lo p'an than on a maritime compass.

[1] 鄭和 Zheng He.

[2] For these speculations, see Gavin Menzies, *1421: the Year China Discovered the World*, Bantam, London, 2002.

[3] From an early 17th century woodblock print.

Figure 35: A typical Chinese dry mounted maritime compass from the early Ch'ing dynasty, showing one ring of the 24 Mountains plus the four cardinal points.[1]

In an introduction written by Li Yü Heng[2] in 1570 for the classic by Ch'ing-Wu Tzu, he confirmed the maritime change from floating to dry-pivoted lo p'an, and the change to mounting the written direction points. This meant they turned with the needle, rather than being printed around the compass, so that directions could be directly read off, without turning the compass:

> The needle floating on water and giving the North and South directions, is ordinarily called the Wet Compass (*shui lo ching*). In the Chia-Ch'ing reign-period [1522-66] there were attacks of Japanese pirates (on the coast), so from that time onwards Japanese methods began to be used. Thus the needle was placed in the compass box, and a paper was stuck on to it carrying all the directions, so that no matter what direction is taken the *tzu* (North) and *wu* (South) signs are always situated at the North and South. This is called the Dry Compass (*han lo ching*).[3]

---

[1] From Needham (1962), Volume 4, Part I, Plate CXVII.

[2] 李豫亨 Li You Heng.

[3] Needham (1962), Volume 4, part I, page 289.

There are very few Indian mentions of the compass, although it is faintly possible that a reference to the *maccha-yantra* (or sacred fish design) might refer to a fish-shaped piece of magnetised metal floating on oil. At about the same time, Michael Scot, in his *Liber Particularis,* identified polarity by saying that there are two kinds of lodestone, one of which points North and the other South, two hundred years after the equivalent Chinese statement.

In fact in Europe the Earth's magnetic field was not described in detail till precisely 1600 CE when William Gilbert published *De Magnete*. Gilbert, who got most of his navigational knowledge from Dr John Dee (1527-1604), and who was much better informed about magnetism than many 20th century writers, unequivocally attributed the invention of the compass to China.

Half a century later, in 1657, Robert Turner published a book of magical prayers called *Ars Notoria*, which was published

> Together with a rare Natural secret, necessary to be learn'd by all persons; especially Sea-men, Merchants, and Travellers. An excellent Invention, done by the Magnetick Vertue of the Load-stone.

The fact that this information about the magnetic compass was appended to a book of magical arts indicates that in England at least the use of the compass was still being treated as a 'rare Natural secret' or even magic, as it had been in the time of Dr John Dee, who helped assemble the navigational aids used by the great Elizabethan explorers like Drake and Raleigh. It is clear who in this period was treating the compass scientifically (the Chinese), and who was still regarding it superstitiously (the English).

Building Beijing

But to return to Chinese feng shui. During the Ming 明 dynasty feng shui was popular amongst the *literati* class. The founding emperor of the Ming dynasty, Chu Yuan Chang,[1] probably sought feng shui advice for the building of his new capital city in Beijing. The construction of the Imperial compound or Gugong (1406-1420 CE) and its water layout definitely adhered to feng shui principles, as was the building of Coal Hill behind the Forbidden city, to support it. Although many theories have been put forward about the specific feng shui formulas used in the Forbidden City, the easiest to recognise is enshrined in the river which passes from the NW to the South. This passes in front and is crossed by five bridges symbolic of the 5 Elements, before draining away SE.

During this dynasty the Emperor appointed an official called the Kuan Tai Fu to regulate the correct practice of feng shui and the production of accurate lo p'ans. He was also responsible for grading and registering the different levels of *ti li* masters. The production of lo p'an needles was brought to a new level

[1] 朱元璋 Zhu Yuan Zhang (reigned 1368-1398).

of efficiency in this dynasty (see Figure 52).

During the Ming dynasty, the most authoritative text on the lo p'an was the *Lo Ching Chieh* by Wu Wang Kang. Although it described 38 rings in detail, it rather frustratingly has only a few illustrations.[1]

During the late Ming and into the Ch'ing dynasty a number of Christian missionaries sent back accounts of China to Europe. One Jesuit, the Reverend Father Martin Martini, describes a lo p'an of the period in some detail in 1654 as follows:

> Here, I will conveniently report on an elegant Chinese compass. It has a round form, and is made of wood, covered with varnish. Its circumference measures about 2 feet. Its diameter is about four thumbs and a half [about 7.5 inches], and has a cover of the same kind of wood. In its centre is a hole, of nearly one thumb large. On the bottom (of this hole) is the very small style of a see [sea?] needle; this is circumferenced by a large perforated sliver plate, fitted to contain this cup-shaped vessel. In one of its extremities, that which is directed to the South, the needle itself is tinged with red colour. A very transparent glass closes the entire hole in which the needle is contained. Through that glass, one can easily observe the movements of the needle. In the circumference (of the compass) one can see circles, signed [inscribed] with black Chinese characters. The most exterior circle contains 24 parts, and so also the second and third one. The fourth circle has eight small compartments with notes in such a way as one can discern, expressed in this figure.[2]

This lo p'an obviously included three rings of 24 Mountains. There is a ring of the basic directions, North, South, East and West, and a ring of hexagrams. Because it has three rings of 24 Mountains it is likely to be a San He lo p'an, and so that ring will have had just 60 hexagrams.

During the early Ch'ing dynasty, San He was still the most popular School of feng shui practice. The largest lo p'an from this period (1658 to be exact) in the author's collection appears on the endpapers his *Complete Guide to the Feng Shui Compass,* and its rings are analysed in Appendix 10 of that book. On this 42 ring lo p'an divisions by 24 and 72 are common. The 24 Mountains date back to the Han dynasty, but divisions by 72 sectors only originated with Yang Yun Sung's 72 Dragon ring.

---

[1] All 38 of the lo p'an rings in the *Lo Ching Chieh* (plus many more) are listed in Appendix 9.7 of my *Guide to the Feng Shui Compass.*

[2] He wrote about this lo p'an in his letter sent from Brussels dated 27 Feb. 1654 to Father Wilhelm Van Aelst. Martini returned to China in 1658 with Ferdinand Verbiest, a Jesuit missionary who taught Emperor K'ang Hsi Western astronomy, and who was therefore indirectly responsible for ring 32.

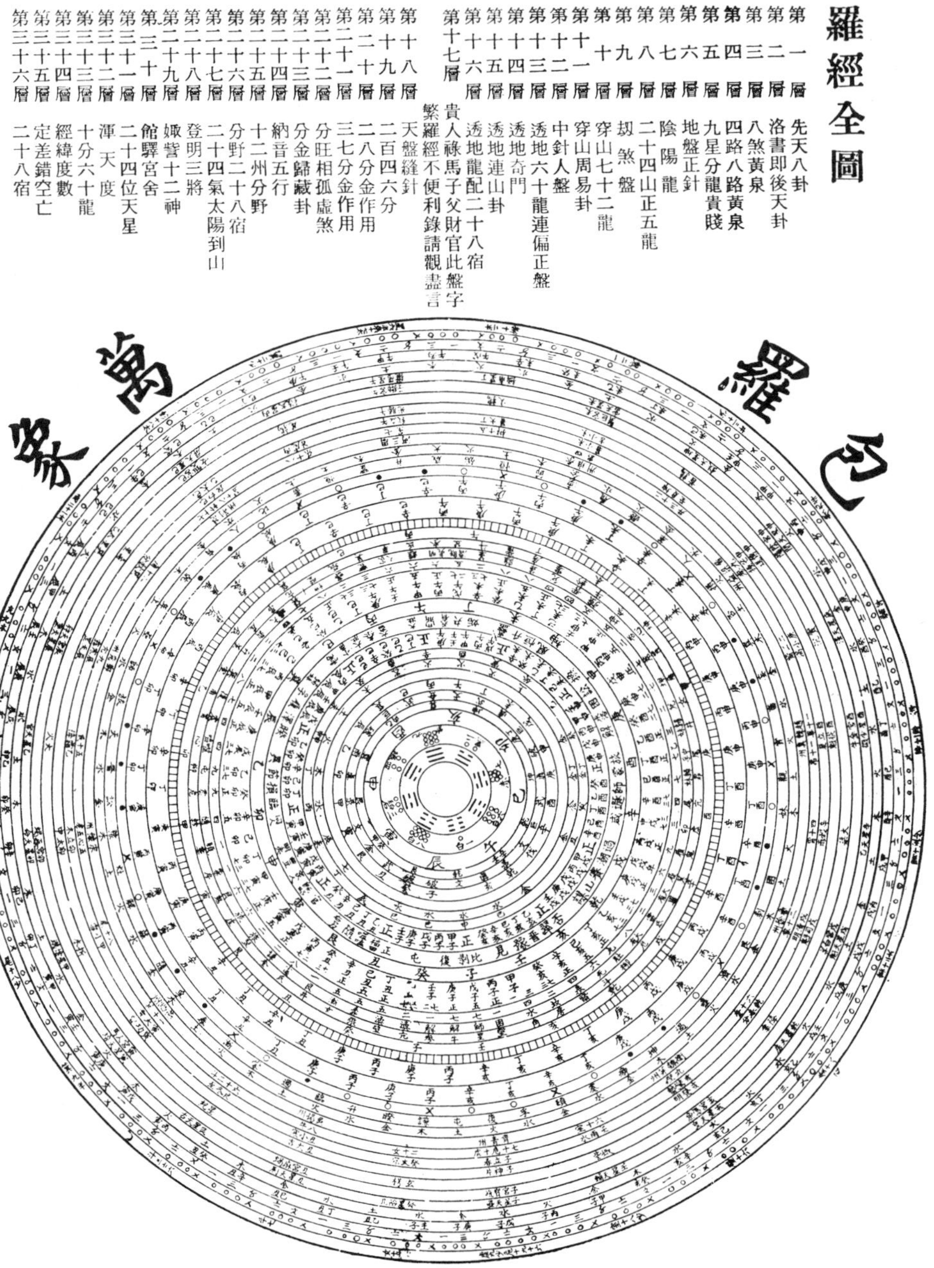

Figure 36: The 38 classical Ming lo p'an rings from Wu Wang Kang's classic *Lo Ching Chieh* were never illustrated. However this diagram from the Ch'ing dynasty *Lo Ching T'ou Chieh* is based on that Ming classic, and shows 35 of the 38 rings, albeit without precise sector divisions. It therefore shows the maximum set of lo p'an rings as they might have been around 1600.[1]

---

[1] 王道亨 Wang Dao Heng *Lo Ching T'ou Chieh* 羅經透解 *Luo Jing Tou Jie,* 1823. In fact the original text has 38 rings, but two (including the Ming calendar) are omitted. Ring 17 is too complex to be shown.

Figure 37: Hsü Shih K'o (c.1550-c.1630 CE) teaching *ti li* and the lo p'an. Hsü was the author of probably the second Ming dynasty book detailing the rings of the lo p'an.[1]

[1] From 中國堪輿名人小傳記, page 170.

Ch'ing Dynasty (1644 - 1911 CE)

Chiang Ta Hung

Although he was born in the last decades of the Ming dynasty, Chiang Ta Hung (Jiang Da Hong) (1620-1714) was very much a Ch'ing dynasty master.[1] He is often referred to as the grandmaster of Hsüan K'ung Ti Li.[2] In fact some credit him with founding Hsüan K'ung, but this is not so likely as his works are most often in the form of a commentary on a previous master's texts. Chiang Ta Hung wrote a number of books about *ti li*[3] including:[4]

'Ti Li Distinguishing the Correct'[5]
'Heaven Period Five Poems'[6]
'Heaven Period Remaining Principles'[7]
'Profound Converging Records'[8]
'Ancient Mirror Poem'[9]
'[Commentary on] the Water Dragon Classic'[10]

In his old age Chiang lived at Shao Hsing near Hangchow in Chekiang. Chiang considered Hsüan K'ung feng shui to be a 'heavenly secret,' and therefore not one to be taught lightly. Or to look at it another way, Chiang was afraid of passing on such powerful knowledge to the 'ethically ignorant' as he saw it. The late Ch'ing dynasty master Shen Chu Reng explained that sadly Master Chiang Ta Hung "did not understand the principle of the need for the wise to write, teach and pass on their tenets."

---

[1] Jiang Da Hong. He is often called Chiang P'ing Chieh and styled 'Ta Hung' or the 'Big Goose' 蔣平階 (大鴻) Jiang Ping Jie (Da Hong). Some authorities suggest 1616 as his birth date.

[2] 玄空地理 Xuan Kong Di Li.

[3] The term *ti li* as we have seen was still used in preference to the term feng shui, as it meant 'principles of earth,' although today it describes the more limited study of geography.

[4] As mentioned earlier both Hsü Ren Wang and Wu Ching Luan are credited with the founding of Hsüan K'ung. Wu is probably the most likely candidate.

[5] *Ti Li Pien Cheng* 地理辨正 *Di Li Bian Zheng*. This is a commentary on the *Green Satchel Classic* (by Huang Shih Kung) and the *Green Satchel Profound Sayings* and *Heavenly Jade Classic* by Yang Yun Sung. It has been recently translated as *Earth Study Discern Truth Volume One*, a *translation of the Feng Shui Classic Di Li Bian Zheng,* foreword by Master Joey Yap, translated by Zeng Yong Xing, JY Books, Kuala Lumpur, 2006. This book is part of the trend of the last few years towards the publication of Chinese Classics of feng shui in English.

[6] *T'ien Yuan Wu K'o* 天元五歌 *Tian Yuan Wu Ge*. These 'songs' or 'poems' are in fact tightly packed mnemonic rhymes summarising feng shui formulae.

[7] *T'ien Yuan Yu I* 天元余義 *Tian Yuan Yu Yi.*

[8] *Kuei Hou Lu* 歸厚錄 *Gui Hou Lu.*

[9] *Ku Ching K'o* 古鏡歌 *Gu Jing Ge.*

[10] *Shui Lung Ching* 水龍經 *Shui Long Jing*. This is a commentary on the *Water Dragon Classic.*

The Simplified Chiang P'an

Chiang Ta Hung's Chiang P'an[1] is popularly thought to be the same as a Hsüan K'ung Ta Kua lo p'an. This is not so. The original Chiang P'an did not have a 64 hexagram ring,[2] but was a very simple design compared with either the San He lo p'ans of his time, or modern San Yuan lo p'ans. It seems as if Chiang originally aimed at simplicity, discarding many of the complexities of the San He lo p'an, especially its Heaven, Man and Astronomical Plates.

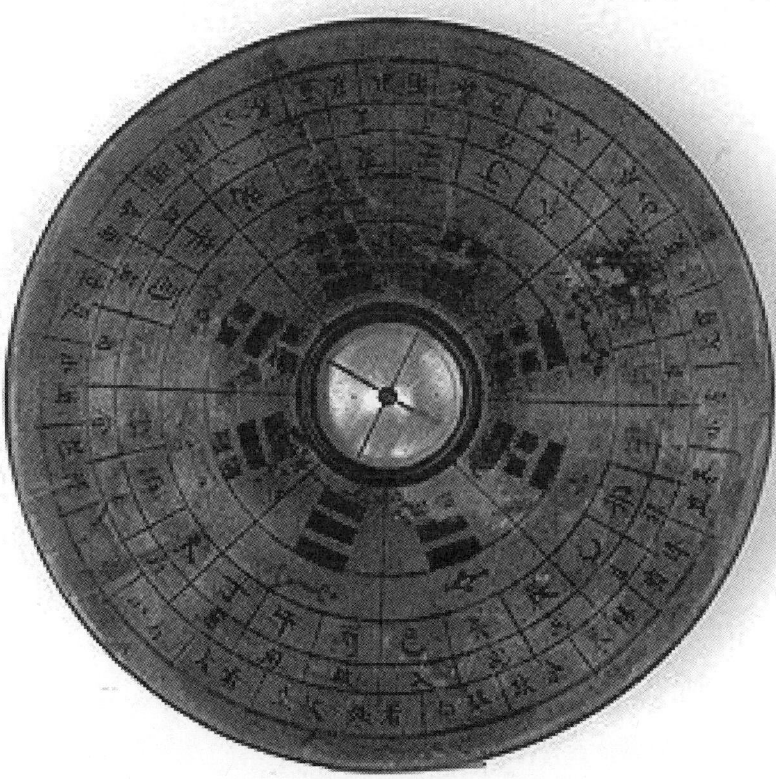

Figure 38: A simple 5 ring 'Chiang p'an' possibly dating back to the early Ch'ing dynasty. Its rings are: the 8 trigrams in Former Heaven sequence; the Lo Shu numbers; Earth Plate 12 Mountains; the 9 Stars; the 24 Mini-Seasons, but not the 64 hexagrams.[3]

---

[1] 蔣盤 Jiang Pan. A Chiang P'an is a lo p'an made according to the doctrines of Chiang Ta Hung (Jiang Da Hong). These are much simpler than any other lo p'ans of the same period.

[2] Tai Wen Hsin (2003), page 19.

[3] This lo p'an was originally owned by a maternal ancestor of mine, Robert Newall of Avon Cottage and Littleborough, and possibly acquired by him through the family fur trading post in Archangel in Russia. Courtesy of the Whipple Museum of the History of Science, Cambridge University [cat. 2351]. Another lo p'an which is specifically marked with Chiang's name on the back (and made by Fang Hsiu Shui) can be seen in the Peabody Museum [item E.1.124 E8772] confirming the same basic simplicity of the original Chiang P'ans. It also has an extra ring of 12 Earthly Branches.

It was only in the late Ch'ing dynasty that San Yuan feng shui became really popular and the 64 hexagram ring was introduced. The contrast with the other lo p'ans in this chapter, is best shown by looking forward to Shen Chu Reng's design for his ideal compass, version of a 'corrected Chiang P'an.' The Chinese title on Shen's lo p'an (see Figure 45) refers to it as a 'simple *Shih,*' which is interesting, but not strictly correct. But the fact that Shen refers to his lo p'an as a *Shih* helps to prove that lo p'ans were still seen as the lineal descendants of the ancient *Shih*.

Shen initially followed Chiang Ta Hung's simple design, but circa 1900 he added rings like the 64 hexagrams and the 120 *fen chin,* which Chiang did not use on his lo p'ans (see Figure 45). The double line between the fourth and fifth rings of this lo p'an shows that Shen (and his contemporaries) saw the San Yuan part of the lo p'an as quite separate from the older San He inner rings. Such useful graphical hints are often absent from twentieth century lo p'ans.

Note that on this lo p'an there is only one 24 Mountain ring, whose yin/yang markings are in evenly spaced groups of three, and are therefore San Yuan. The next ring is the Substitute Star ring devised by Chiang. There is another major ring further out which has just the 12 Earthly Branches. Beyond this is a ring with 120 *fen chin,* which are aligned with the 12 Earthly Branches ring. The outermost ring contains the 5 Element attributions of these 120 *fen chin.*

Another example of the transition from the simple 5 ring Chiang P'an to the more complex San Yuan p'an is shown in Plate 9. Note that it is clearly divided into three Plates, divided by double lines:

1. an Earth Plate with no Man or Heaven Plate.
2. the 12 Earthly Branches.
3. the Astronomical rings (including the 24 Mini-Seasons).

You can see that there is no hexagram ring on this lo p'an, and the inner plate is very similar to a San He Earth Plate. The 12 Earthly Branches are still very prominent, as they are in Shen Chu Reng's version of the Chiang P'an.

Modern lo p'ans tend to be more complex than Ch'ing lo p'ans. This is a function of two things. First the tendency to try to include as many rings as possible, in order to be 'complete' rather than discriminating. Secondly the fact that with computer aided design much more can be accurately crammed into the same space than was practical with hand painting methods. Strangely it is the San Yuan lo p'ans which now look the most complex, in direct opposition to the tenets of their patron Chiang Ta Hung, who tried to get rid of superfluous rings and reduce the lo p'an to simplicity.

In the Ch'ing 清 dynasty many buildings were built according to feng shui rules, with gates to the courtyard houses predominately located on the front left corner of the courtyard (facing outwards), the Green Dragon door.

The classic source for the details of 38 of the main Ch'ing rings is to be found in Wu Wang Kang (1810). See the list of 36 rings from it shown in Figure 36. Although this diagram lacks readability and sector divisions, it is a useful reference list. Many Ch'ing lo p'ans were made with a list of their rings written on the back.

In the case of the Whipple lo p'an (Figure 46) the list of rings drawn up by the person who actually designed the lo p'an is shown. In many Ch'ing dynasty San He lo p'ans there is no trigram ring, not even to show the basic 8 directions. Later in the Ch'ing dynasty the design of the lo p'an became standardized, by inclusion in the *Imperial Encyclopaedia* as shown in Figure 40.

An interesting early Ch'ing lo p'an was owned by Sir Hans Sloane (1660-1753) (see Figure 39). It was much simpler than the 1658 lo p'an, as it only had 15 rings, but the basic three Plate, plus *sha* Plate and Astronomical Plate structure is clearly visible.

Sloane was the man who, more than any other, helped preserve the works of the English Elizabethan magician and mathematician Dr John Dee,[1] and whose manuscripts and curiosities formed the basis of the collections of both the present day British Library and British Museum. For Sloane the lo p'an was no more than a curiosity, but he certainly would not have used the term 'geomancy' to describe its usage, because he was very familiar with divination by Western geomancy, which he himself used and which he knew had nothing to do with feng shui.[2]

[1] See Skinner *Dr John Dee's Spiritual Diaries (1583-1608)*, 2011, Singapore.

[2] See Skinner *Geomancy in Theory and Practice* (1980) for a full description of Western divinatory geomancy.

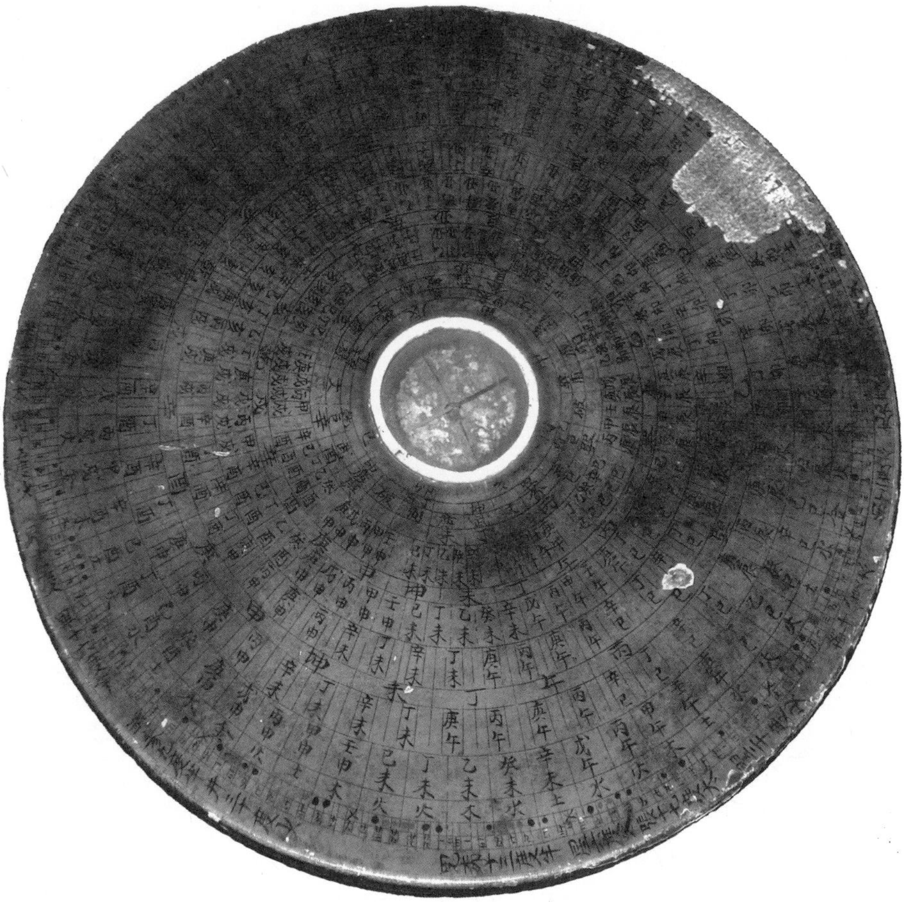

Figure 39: Sir Hans Sloane's lo p'an dating from between 1685 and 1753, early Ch'ing dynasty. The arrangement of rings is typical of the whole dynasty:

1. *Yao sha*
2. Yellow Springs
3. **Earth Plate 12** Mountains
4. 72 Dragons
5. Outer Heaven or **Man Plate 12** Mountains
6. 60 Dragons
7. Earth Plate 90 *fen chin*
8. **Heaven Plate 12** Mountains
9. Heaven Plate 90 *fen chin*
10. **Astronomic Plate** 60 *ying so* Expanding/Contracting Dragons
11. 61 Elements for the *ying so*
12. 365.25 *Hsiu* auspiciousness indicators
13. Odd degree numbers for each *Hsiu*
14. 28 *Hsiu* with their extent and Element.[1]

[1] Copyright © Trustees of the British Museum, London (Sloane Misc. 1760). Significantly, there is no trigram ring. It has been incorrectly repaired, as the line on the bottom of the Heaven Pool is mis-aligned.

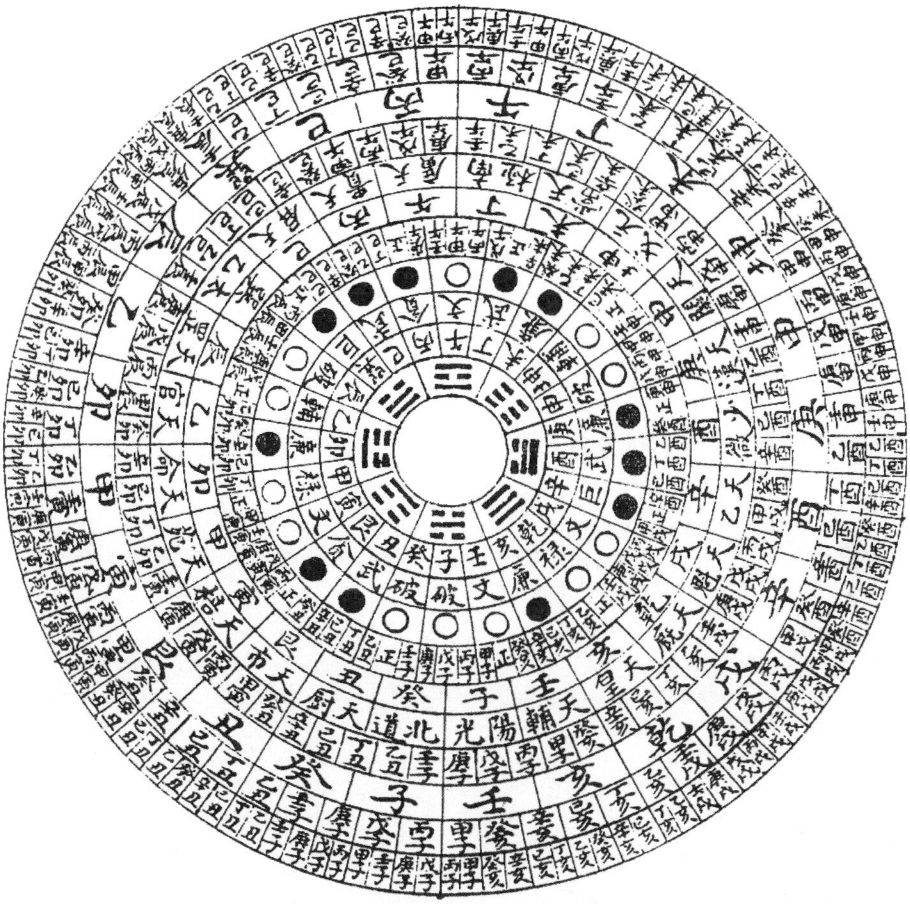

Figure 40: A standard Imperial Ch'ing dynasty lo p'an design from the 1736 Ch'ing *Imperial Encyclopaedia*.[1] Rings also mentioned in the text, but not illustrated, relate to *kua, sha* and the *Hsiu*. The rings actually illustrated above from the *Encyclopaedia* are:

1. 8 trigrams in Later Heaven Sequence
2. **Earth Plate** Correct Needle 24 Mountains
3. Sitting Mountain Nine Star flipping *kua*
4. Pure Yin Pure Yang, for the 24 Mountains
5. 72 Mountain-Piercing Dragons
6. Outer Heaven or **Man Plate** Central Needle 24 Mountains
7. 24 Fixed Heaven Stars
8. 60 Dragons belonging to the Central Needle
9. **Heaven Plate** Seam Needle 24 Mountains
10. 60 Dragons belonging to the Seam Needle
11. 120 *fen chin* belonging to Seam Needle, used to manage *sha* and accept water.

[1] 欽定協紀辨方書 *Chüan* (roll) 33, page 45.

During the Ch'ing dynasty the Ming *ti li* master grading practice was retained until the Emperor Yung Cheng (1723-35)[1] instituted a separate system of *ti li* examinations.[2] You can see that not only were the doctrines of feng shui well established by then, but that also quality control of practitioners was seen as essential. These exams might not necessarily have been sat by wandering *fang-shih*[3] who gave feng shui advice to non-Imperial families. The examinations were held by the office of the Ch'in T'ien Chian,[4] which was also the rank of the highest *ti li* master in the country. One of the best known Ch'in T'ien Chian of the late Ch'ing dynasty was Hung Ch'ao He,[5] who was also responsible for producing the official Imperial Almanacs.

Emperor Ch'ien Lung's Feng Shui Reformation

Perhaps the most resplendent of the Ch'ing Emperors was Emperor Ch'ien Lung[6] who reigned 1736-1796. He was intensely interested in feng shui and Chinese astrology and was particularly interested in separating the true from the false. Accordingly he gathered around himself the best feng shui masters of the period. If the splendour of his reign was anything to go by, then the feng shui they applied must have been very good indeed. During his reign Beijing became the largest and possibly the most splendid city in the world.

In 1740 he commissioned a manual which would record and analyse all of the key feng shui and calendaric methods, separating out the bogus and incorrect methods that had sprung up over the previous 1000 years. This volume of Imperial feng shui was called the 'Treatise on Harmonising Times and Distinguishing Directions,' as the essence of feng shui is time and direction.[7]

The first two chapters of this treatise have been translated recently by Thomas Aylward, and published as *The Imperial Guide to Feng Shui & Chinese Astrology*.[8] The translation is especially refreshing as the translator has put a lot of thought into the translation of feng shui technical terms, and has not been content to simply use the rather worn English approximations of the Chinese, that have been used by other translators. The translator also displays a detailed knowledge of the subject, so that his explanatory glosses are very helpful. It is a pity that the subsequent chapters have not yet been published.

---

[1] 雍正 Yong Zheng.

[2] There had been an Imperial examination system governing entrance into the Chinese imperial civil service since the T'ang dynasty till its closure in 1904, but this may be the first time that feng shui was officially included in that examination.

[3] 方士 *fang shi.*

[4] 欽天監 Qin Tian Jian.

[5] 洪潮和 Hong Chao He.

[6] 乾隆 Qian Long.

[7] See Aylward (2007) and Yün Lu (1741).

[8] Watkins, London, 2007.

Chang Ping Lin

Just one year earlier in 1739, under the same Emperor, one of the main feng shui masters of this period, Chang Ping Lin[1] wrote a very clear and practical exposition of four of the main methods then current, stripped of their theoretical accretions.[2]

Figure 41: Chang Ping Lin (1739) from a contemporary woodcut. His name in Chinese characters is to be seen almost hidden by the tree on the middle right of the picture.[3]

[1] 張丙琳 Zhang Bing Lin.

[2] These have also recently been translated and published as the first four books of the Feng Shui Classics series: *The Water Dragon; The Original Eight Mansions Formula; The Key San He Feng Shui Formulas* and *The Mountain Dragon*, all translated by Er Choon Haw and edited with commentary by Stephen Skinner, Golden Hoard Press, Singapore, 2006 & 2007. Available direct from www.GoldenHoard.com.

[3] From *Ti Li Ch'uan Ch'eng Lien Huan Chi* 地理全成連環記 *Di Li Quan Cheng Lian Huan Ji*.

Eight Mansion Formula

The monk Jo Kuan Tao Ren[1] is reputed to have written the classic of the Eight Mansions School, the 'Eight Mansions Bright Mirror.'[2] The earliest known copy of this has a preface which dates from 1790, and this is often said to be the origin of the Eight Mansions School. But as a lot of this material can be found in the 1741 'Treatise on Harmonising Times and Distinguishing Directions,' and also in the even earlier 1609 *Ming Imperial Encyclopaedia,* so it would seem that the monk did not originate the system. We can say for sure that Eight Mansion theory pre-dates 1609. The *Pa chai* (Eight Mansions) School has become very popular in the later half of the 20th century, particularly as it has been extensively promoted in various popular manuals in English. It deals only with the feng shui of residences and not with *yin chai.*

兑	坤	离	巽	震	艮	坎	乾
生	天	六	天	延	六	五	六
祸	延	五	五	生	绝	天	天
延	绝	绝	六	祸	祸	生	五
绝	生	延	祸	绝	生	延	祸
六	祸	祸	生	五	延	绝	绝
五	五	生	绝	天	天	祸	延
天	六	天	延	六	五	六	生

Figure 42: The Bright Mirror Table found on the backs of older traditional lo p'ans. This is like a spreadsheet. Each column represents a type of house whose sitting position is indicated by the trigram at the top of the column.

[1] Also called Jo Kuan Tao Shih 箬冠道师 Ruo Guan Dao Shi.

[2] *Pa Chai Ming Ching* 八宅明镜 *Ba Zhai Ming Ching.*

Figure 43: An early San Yuan lo p'an possibly dating from 1804-1824 (as suggested by the Changing Heaven Star alignment in Ring 3), just a few years before the first textual reference to the change from 60 to 64 hexagrams. Note that this in an early example of the use of the 64 hexagrams (as distinct from 60 hexagrams) in rings 7, 9, and 10. This is probably contemporaneous with the lo p'an shown in Plate 9, which does not show the 64 hexagrams. Hence, 1824 is probably very close to the cusp between the use of 60 and 64 hexagrams. The dating of both lo p'ans having been deduced by the position of the Lung Lou[1] Changing Heavenly Star.[2]

[1] 龍婁 *Long Lou* adjacent to Ch'ien Mountain.

[2] Museé de l'Homme, Paris, as reproduced in Martel (1972) Fig. 1, page 128. Note that Fig 2 in the same source which shows the back of a lo p'an, is probably a different lo p'an, although that is not made clear by Martel. The second item 43.27.118 is made by the Fang Hsiu Shui workshop in Hsin An town, Hsiu Yi region in Anhui.

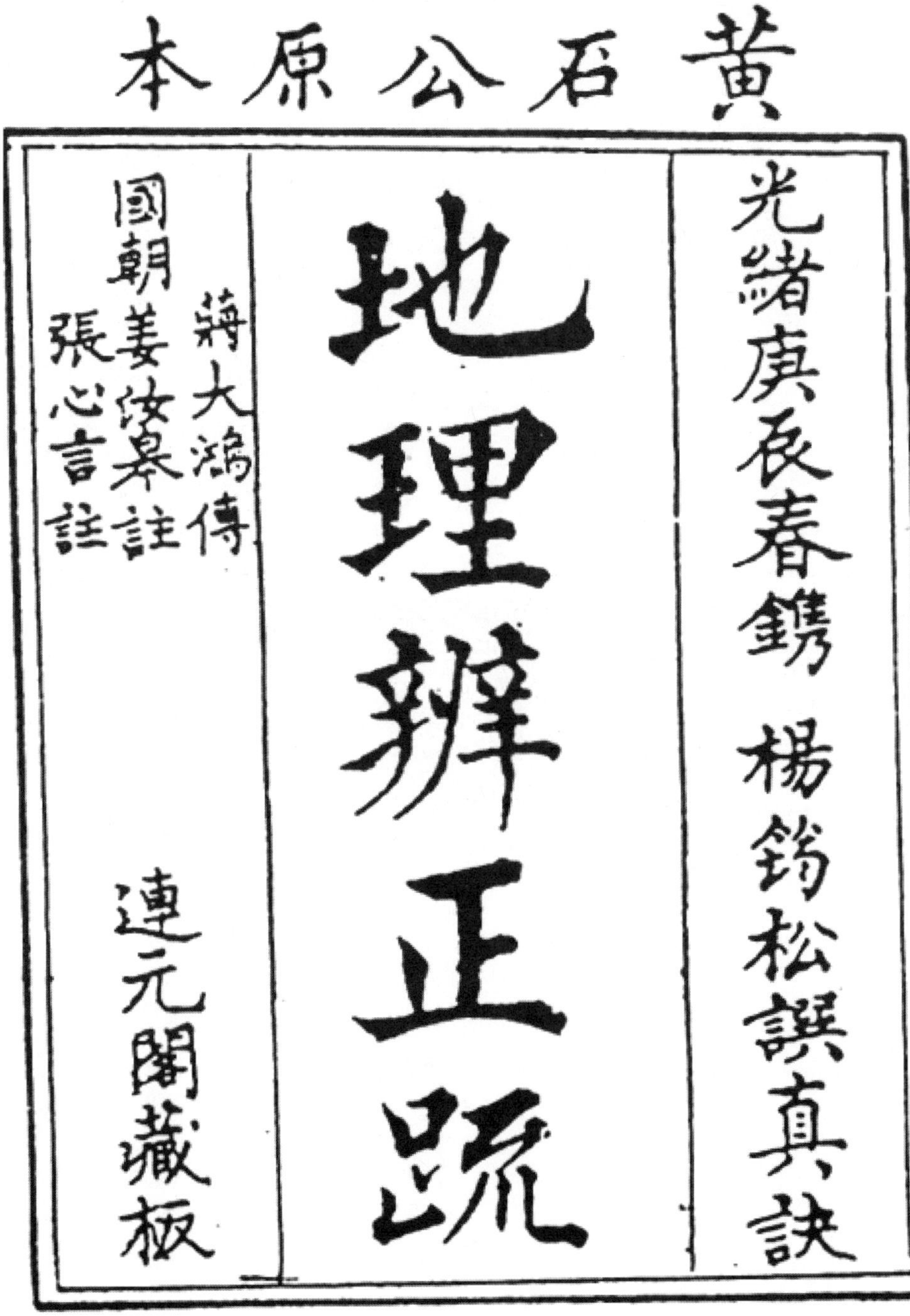

Figure 44: The cover of an 1880 edition of the important book by Chang Hsin Yen which in 1827 first outlined the change from 60 *chia-tzu* related hexagrams to the 64 hexagram ring.

Moving from 60 to 64 Hexagrams on the Lo p'an

In 1827 Chang Hsin Yen[1] published his commentary *'Jottings on "Ti Li Distinguishing the Correct."'*[2] This suggested the alternative arrangement featuring all 64 hexagrams, which has become the familiar 64 hexagram ring on San Yuan lo p'ans today. Although Chang lists a number of classical *ti li* masters like Yang Yun Sung and Chiang Ta Hung as his mentors on the cover of his book (see Figure 44), none of these had ever suggested that the full 64 hexagrams should appear on the lo p'an. Therefore the arrival of the full 64 hexagrams on to the lo p'an probably occurred not more than a few years before 1827, probably around 1804-1824 (see also the evidence of Figure 43).

At this point in time San Yuan masters replaced the 60 Root hexagram ring with a full 64 hexagram ring. The result of this was a more exact correlation with the *I Ching*, but the correlation with the 60 Dragon *chia-tzu* and the rest of the San He lo p'an rings was then completely lost, and the two Schools thereafter began to grow irrevocably apart.

The result was that the San Yuan lo p'ans fell completely out of sync with the original San He lo p'ans. The two purely San He kua rings (the 12 Sovereign kua and the 60 Root kua) disappeared from common usage by the late Ch'ing dynasty. Since then the full 64 hexagrams have held sway on the San Yuan lo p'an, and this change marks the parting of the way between these two Schools. This is because 64 hexagrams are not at all geometrically or arithmetically compatible with the original San He rings which depended upon combinations of 5, 10, 12 and 60, and not upon multiples of 8.

The change from the standard San He ring of 60 hexagrams to 64 hexagrams was achieved by duplicating the Sexagenary combinations *chia-tzu, keng-yin, chia-wu* and *keng-shen*, and adding the 4 Cardinal hexagrams to these duplicates. The distinction is made in this book between Chiang Ta Hung's 'San Yuan Hsüan K'ung School' and Chang Hsin Yen's 'San Yuan 9 Yün 64 Kua Method.' Chiang Ta Hung's lo p'an is said by this book to have had only 60 hexagrams, but Hsin Yen's theory demanded 64 hexagrams.[3]

It is interesting that the caption on Shen Chu Reng's lo p'an (Figure 45) also states that he 'corrected' Chiang Ta Hung's original lo p'an (Figure 38). There are earlier references, but it seems that the change from 60 to 64 hexagrams only solidified around 1827, relatively recently in terms of the history of feng shui.

---

[1] 張心言 Zhang Xin Yan.

[2] 張心言 Zhang Xin Yan, *Ti Li Pien Cheng Shu* 地理辨正疏 *Dili Bian Zheng Shu.*

[3] According to Tai Wen Hsin 戴文鑫 Dai Wen Xin.

式簡盤蔣正更礽竹沈唐錢

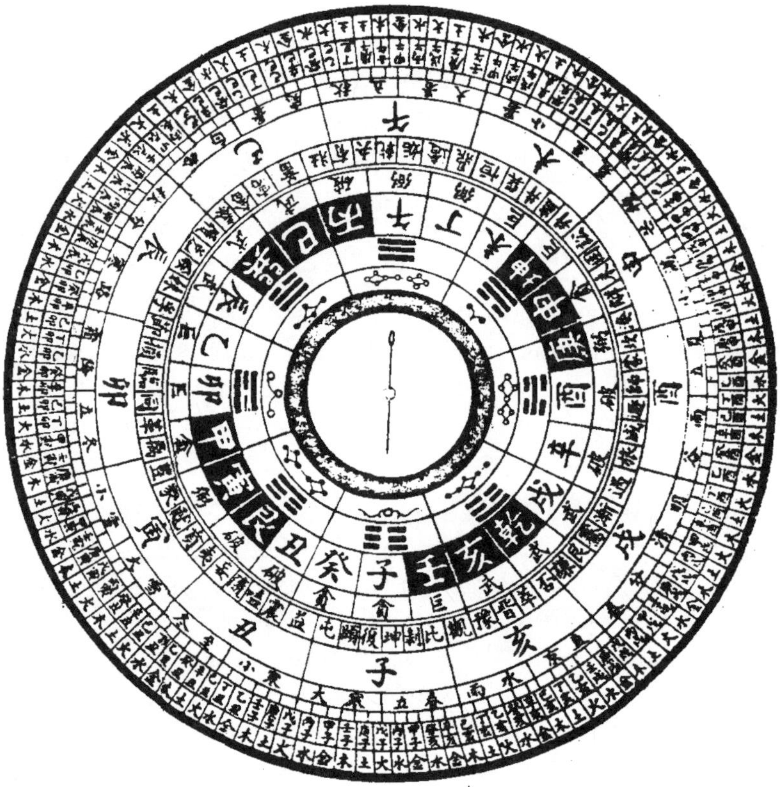

Figure 45: The revised Chiang Ta Hung p'an designed by Shen Chu Reng, showing a continuance of the simple Chiang P'an circa 1900.[1] Compare it with the San He lo p'an of the same period. It contains the following rings:

1. Lo Shu numbers of the Later Heaven Sequence
2. Trigrams of the Former Heaven Sequence as direction indicators
3. The 24 Mountains [Earth Plate]
4. The Substitute or Replacement Stars (1, 2, 6, 7 and 9)
5. The 64 hexagram names[2]
6. The 12 Earthly Branches.
7. The 24 Mini-Seasons (anti-clockwise starting at *Tzu*)
8. The 144 empty divisions
9. The 120 *fen chin*
10. The *na yin* 5 Elements of the 120 *fen chin.*

---

[1] From Shen (1996) Volume I, page 235 in the unpunctuated first edition. His title for it is: "At Chien Tang, Shen Chu Reng corrected this Chiang p'an simple *Shih.*" Chien Tang is the river that significantly flows between the two main feng shui related Provinces of Anhui and Kiangsi, near to Hsin An.

[2] Only ring 5 can actually be considered as a San Yuan ring, and this ring did not appear on early Chiang p'ans. Compare with Plate 9.

From San He to San Yuan

To summarise the overall development of San Yuan feng shui: after Shao Yung in the Sung dynasty there was an attempt to fit the circular arrangement of the *I Ching* hexagrams to the existing San He feng shui rings, possibly by Hsü Ren Wang. To this end, first the 12 Sovereign hexagrams of Shao Yung were easily matched with the 12 Earthly Branches, and made into a ring of their own.[1]

Then just 60 of the hexagrams were matched with the 60 Sexagenary Combinations (with the four pure Cardinal hexagrams being given 'guardian' positions at the four quarters). This ring became known as the Root 60 hexagram ring (see Figure 26). Such rings of just 60 Root hexagrams were common in the Ming dynasty.[2] The advantage of a ring of 60 hexagrams is that it still matches exactly with the 60 *chia-tzu* Dragons. It was therefore still possible for proto-San Yuan practitioners to reconcile their work segment by segment with that of San He practitioners.[3]

The four 'suppressed' hexagrams were the ones located exactly at the cardinal directions. Which four were suppressed depends upon which version of the Root *kua* ring you are looking at. For rings reliant on the Former Heaven Sequence, the *kua* of the Cardinal Directions are Ch'ien (S); K'un (N); Li (E) and K'an (W). For the Later Heaven Sequence, the *kua* of the Cardinal Directions are Li (S); K'an (N); Chen (E), and Tui (W).

Development of the San Yuan Plate

For their inner rings, San Yuan lo p'ans still borrowed a number of rings originally found on San He lo p'ans, such as the Sha Plate; Earth Plate 24 Mountains; 24 Mini-Seasons; 60 Dragons; 72 Dragons and the 120 *fen chin*. San Yuan lo p'ans also incorporate the outermost Astronomical rings of the 28 *Hsiu* with its division into 365.25 day-degrees.[4] This borrowing is clearly visible. On our 'standard' San Yuan lo p'an (see Plate 11 and Plate 12) rings 1-6 and 23-30 are all inherited from the San He lo p'an. The remaining rings 7-22 are purely San Yuan.[5]

The purely San Yuan rings are not at all reliant upon the 12 Earthly Branches and the 10 Heavenly Stems (as are the San He rings) but now instead derive

[1] The 18th ring of the lo p'an described in the Ming dynasty *Lo Ching Chieh*.

[2] See also Feuchtwang (1974), pages 71, 75-77.

[3] It is instructive to examine the practical results of using a 60 Root hexagram ring against the modern 64 hexagram ring. The difference in the extent of each hexagram is the difference between 6.000° and 5.625° or just 0.375°, so in practice many results are the same, but those that are not are most instructive.

[4] In the later case, some San Yuan lo p'ans attempt to 'update' this ring to the 360 Jesuit-inspired 'new' degrees, thereby missing the whole point of this ring, which is its connection of direction with the time element of the 365.25 days of the year.

[5] Ring 13 works with both, but was originally San He.

from the 8 trigrams, 64 hexagrams, and their 384 constituent lines or *yao*.

Despite the fact that the *I Ching* is one of the most ancient books in Chinese culture, when feng shui was first invented it was strictly San He feng shui and it relied upon the 5 Elements, 10 Heavenly Stems, 12 Earthly Branches, and later the 60 Dragons, and not on the *kua* or the *I Ching*.[1]

San Yuan practitioners took a leaf out of San He practice and generated two hexagram Plates, the Inner Plate and the Outer Plate, using the two different arrangements of the 64 hexagrams as shown in Figure 25. The current convention is that the Inner Plate is used for yin house (grave) feng shui and the Outer Plate relates to yang house feng shui. Look carefully at Figure 25 and you will see these two rings of hexagrams, separated by a ring of brackets.

Every hexagram is made up of two trigrams. Look on the Outer hexagram ring in Figure 25, and you will notice that the inner trigram of this ring remains fixed for 8 hexagrams, whilst the outer trigram rotates through a sequence of 8 different trigrams. The trigram that is fixed is usually called the 'controlling trigram.' Each group of 8 fixed 'controlling' trigrams is marked by a bracket. Each of these 8 bracketed groups is called a Palace.

Numbers of Rings

How many rings did a typical early Ch'ing dynasty lo p'an have? Working lo p'ans of 42 rings existed quite early in this dynasty. In Emperor Ch'ien Lung's standard work on feng shui 'Treatise on Harmonising Times and Distinguishing Directions'[2] published in 1741 the 'official' number of rings was just 13. Beyond this Ch'ing makers of lo p'ans were using their own initiative and including older less 'canonical' rings up to more than 30 rings.

By the end of the Ch'ing dynasty San He lo p'ans, especially those from famous workshops had settled down to a fixed pattern. Figure 50 and Plate 3 show a classical hand made San He Ch'ing dynasty lo p'an from the best known Fang Hsiu Shui workshop, a famous Anhui workshop (from the author's collection), which is typical of the hand-made lo p'ans of this period. This concentrates on just presenting the most important San He rings. The key to that lo p'an is shown in Figure 50, but its rings divide very clearly into:

1. The inner rings including *yao sha*, Yellow Springs, and the Nine Stars[3]
2. The three San He Plates: Earth, Man and Heaven
3. The *Hsiu*, and related Astronomical rings such as the 60 Uneven *ying so* Dragons and 365.25 day-degrees.

---

[1] This is also supported by analysis of the *Shih*, the predecessor of the lo p'an.
[2] Yün Lu (1741) but not in Aylward (2007).
[3] These rings will be explained in Chapters 6.6, 6.7 and 6.8. Here however the Nine Stars still have the old San He meanings, and are not used like modern San Yuan Flying Stars.

This is a pattern which holds true for most San He lo p'ans of the late Ch'ing. The trigrams do not make an appearance, but the *sha* Plate and the most important rings of the three Earth, Man and Heaven Plates plus the Astronomical Plate are present.

There is of course no such thing as a 'standard' lo p'an ring list for either San He or San Yuan lo p'ans which applies to every lo p'an. I have however chosen two relatively modern and similar Taiwanese produced lo p'ans as 'standard,' simply because they are clear and readable, as well as carrying almost all of the most of the important rings of their respective Schools, see Plate 6 and Plate 11.[1]

Chang Chung Shan and the Wu Ch'ang School

Chiang Ta Hung's later theory successor was Chang Chung Shan[2] who flourished around 1825 and wrote many books, especially commentaries on Chiang Ta Hung's work. A few of these commentaries include:

> 'A Straight Explanation of [Chiang's] "Ti Li Distinguishing the Correct" '[3]
> 'Intelligently Indicating the Important'[4]
> 'Heaven Yuan: explaining the Meaning of Five [Mnemonic] Poems'[5]
> '"Hsüan K'ung's Secret Decree" Annotated and Commented Upon'[6]
> 'Yin Yang Both Houses: A Record of Experiments'[7]
> 'Two House Hsüan [K'ung] Key Points'[8]
> 'Guide to Arriving at the Hsüeh'[9]

Chang was the founder of the Wu Ch'ang School.[10] This School's name could be translated as the 'School of Impermanence' in the Buddhist sense of the word. He is sometimes credited with originating the Flying Star School as it is now practised. However Chang also observed secrecy in the same way as Chiang Ta Hung, and kept the true secrets to himself, so this origin is difficult to determine. This endemic secrecy led to a rise in the propagation of false feng shui theories, and perhaps a loss of standards, which is a great pity. It is

---

[1] The 'standard' San He lo p'an is shown in Plate 6 and Plate 7. The 'standard' San Yuan lo p'an is shown in Plate 12 and Plate 11.

[2] 章仲山 Zhang Zhong Shan.

[3] *Ti Li Pien Cheng Chih Chieh* 地理辨正直解 *Di Li Bian Zheng Zhi Jie.*

[4] *Hsin Yen Chih Yao* 心眼指要 *Xin Yan Zhi Yao.* 'Intelligently' is literally 'heart-eye.'

[5] *T'ien Yuan Wu K'o Ch'an Yi* 天元五歌闡義 *Tian Yuan Wu Ge Chan Yi.*

[6] *Hsüan K'ung Mi Chih P'i Chu* 玄空秘旨批注 *Xuan Kong Mi Zhi Pi Zhu.*

[7] *Yin Yang Erh Chai Lu Yen* 陰陽二宅錄驗 *Yin Yang Er Zhai Lu Yan.* The 'two houses' of course refer to *yin chai* and *yang chai* feng shui.

[8] *Erh Chai Hsüan Chi* 二宅玄機 *Er Zhai Xuan Ji.*

[9] *Lin Hsüeh Chih Nan* 臨穴指南 *Lin Xue Zhi Nan.*

[10] 無常派 Wu Chang Pai. Literally the 'changing School' because of the stress on luck changing with period.

understandable that such Masters may wish to keep the trade secrets of their livelihood safe, as these are like the commercial patents of today, but by not publishing them clearly, they encourage all sorts of false theories to circulate.

The Wu Ch'ang School had its origin in the town of Wushi, Chang Chou, also within the Kiangsu Province in China.[1] Wushi is a well populated and resourceful water-town that has produced many famous feng shui masters, apart from Chang Chung Shan, including Shen Chu Ying; T'an Yang Wu; Yu Hsi Yin; Yung Po Yun and many others.[2]

This School is still active in Malaysia, and we will look at its development in a later chapter, although it may have disappeared from the People's Republic of China.

One well-known lo p'an from this period is the one upon which Joseph Needham based some of his description of lo p'an rings, the John Couch Adams lo p'an in the Whipple Museum of the History of Science, University of Cambridge (see Figure 46). The great advantage of this particular lo p'an, from an analysis point of view is twofold. First, it has a succinct description of all its rings written on its base by the artisan that made it (Figure 47). Secondly, it contains two *Hsiu* rings which clearly demonstrate the precession of the *Hsiu* over time. Of these, the outer is aligned with the K'ai Hsi Sung dynasty standard epoch, and the inner with a Ch'ing dynasty epoch.

Shen Chu Reng

One of the most important Masters at the end of the Ch'ing dynasty was Shen Chu Reng[3] (1849-1906), who in Cantonese is sometimes referred to as 'Master Sam.' Shen received both a classical Chinese and an English education. He is sometimes referred to as an 'outsider' by other feng shui Masters because he put his knowledge together from books and experiments, rather than being part of a direct lineage. Nevertheless his Flying Star feng shui has had a big impact on the practice of feng shui in the twentieth century, both in the Chinese context and in the West, thereby demonstrating that a scientific approach to feng shui is sometimes every bit as good as a lineage approach. Shen was born near Hangchow,[4] but spent much of his later life in Shanghai.

In 1862 Shen was caught up in the Taiping Rebellion, and was eventually employed by Captain Charles Gordon (1833-1885), the notorious 'Gordon of Khartoum,' to translate Western military strategy texts into Chinese, and to help train his Chinese soldiers.

---

[1] 無錫 Wuxi, Changzhou region, Jiangsu Province. This was a centre of Hsüan K'ung activity.

[2] Shen Zhu Ying, Tan Yang Wu, Yu Xi Yin, and Yong Bo Yun.

[3] More correctly Shen Chu Jêng 沈竹礽 Shen Zhu Reng.

[4] 杭州 Hangzhou.

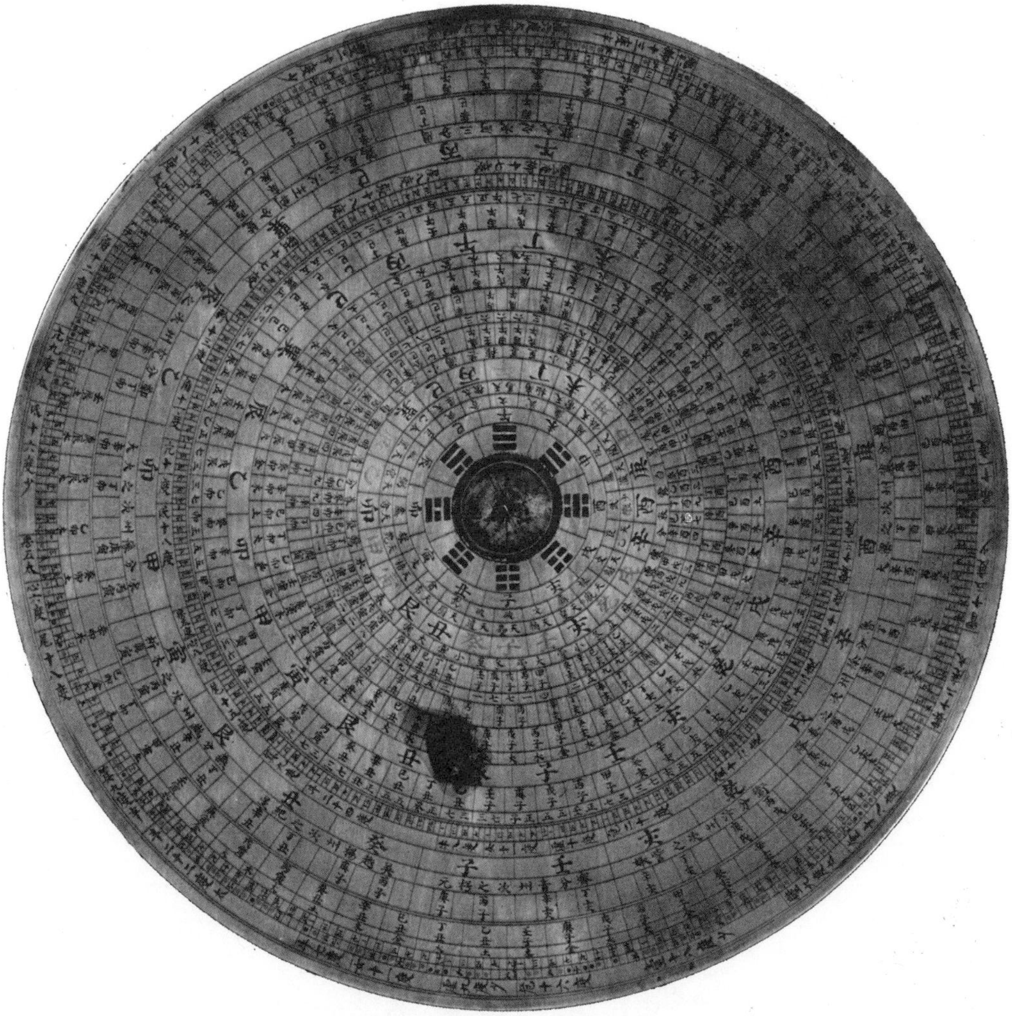

Figure 46: John Couch Adams Whipple Museum Ch'ing dynasty 24 ring San He lo p'an made circa 1860.[1] This is the lo p'an used by Joseph Needham[2] as his main source of information about the rings.[3] The date of this lo p'an must fall after the adoption of the 'New Degrees' of the Jesuits, as indicated by ring number 16. This ring starts at 113.5° (Western degrees). Therefore this ring is based on the *Shih Hsien* calendar of 1644, as it is 12.5° anti-clockwise (ahead) of the standard outer *Hsiu* ring. The extents of each *Hsiu* are also somewhat different from the standard K'ai Hsi extents. We can therefore date this lo p'an to 1860 using the start point of its 16th ring, despite some incorrect modern suggestions of a 'late 1700s' date.

---

[1] Made by Wang Yang His 汪仰溪 (courtesy name Yuan Shan 元善) (not Hsi Yang San 溪元善 as recorded by the Museum) at the Yün-I workshop 蘊易齋 at Hai Yang 海陽 near Hsin An 新安 town in Anhui Province (not in Kwangtung as stated by Needham). Courtesy of the Whipple Museum of the History of Science, University of Cambridge [1123].

[2] Needham (1962), Vol. IV, Part 1, pages 294-295.

[3] Previously owned by John Couch Adams (1819-1892) the astronomer who discovered Neptune. This is also reproduced in Needham (1962), Volume 4, Part I, Figure 350, pages 294-295.

Figure 47: The reverse of the John Couch Adams Whipple lo p'an which has a list of its 25 rings, the translation of which is listed below, from inner (right) to outer (left).[1]

1. Heaven Pool [with] South Pointing Needle
2. Former Heaven Eight trigrams
3. Earthly Branches - 12 Positions
4. Sitting Position of the House - Nine Stars [in 24 divisions]
5. [Ring used to] Bring Forth Officials - [24] Heaven Stars [from the Ts'ui Kuan table]
6. **Earth Plate** Correct Needle with Pure Yin Pure Yang [Ch'iu Yen Han's Plate]
7. Four Seasons [divided by the] *chieh ch'i* [24 Mini-Seasons]
8. Earth Record Mountain-Piercing Tigers [72 Mountain-Piercing Dragons]
9. [*Chi Men*] *Tun Chia* Nine Palaces [60 Lo Shu numbers + 12 empty divisions]
10. Inner [Earth] Plate *fen chin* [48 of the best *fen chin* in 120 divisions]
11. [60] Evenly Arranged Dragon Divisions
12. *Na Yin* of the Five Elements [of the 60 Dragons]
13. **Man Plate** Lai Kung Central Needle [Lai Pu Yi's Outer Heaven or Man Plate]
14. Mr Ts'ai's [60] Earth-Penetrating Dragons [*Ts'ai Shen Yü's Plate*]
15. Threes and Sevens riding the ch'i
16. Ch'ing Adoption of the [360 Jesuit] New Degrees [to measure *Hsiu* boundaries]
17. 'Bird Star' Boundary Positions [new *Hsiu* boundaries designed for a Ch'ing epoch]
18. **Heaven Plate** Yang Kung Seam Needle [Yang Yun Sung's Plate]
19. *Fen yeh* [stars governing ancient Chinese Provinces] and *fen tz'u* [12 Jupiter Stations]
20. Outer Plate *fen chin* [48 of the most auspicious *fen chin* in 120 divisions]
21. [**Astronomical Plate**] Heaven Record *ying so* [60 Uneven] Dragons
22. Former Heaven Star Degrees of the Five Elements [61 Elements related to *Hsiu*]
23. Degree [numbers of the *Hsiu*, as at the] K'ai Hsi [reign period of Sung basis 960 CE]
24. *Hsüeh* Sitting Position - Auspicious and Inauspicious [positions]
25. The 28 *Hsiu* Divination Degrees [the ancient positions of the *Hsiu* boundaries].

[1] Illustration from Needham (1962), Volume IV, Part 1, Figure 351, page 295. The ring descriptions differ slightly from those of Needham, with reference to the original Chinese. Note this is the only lo p'an ring list in this book which starts its numbering with the central Heaven Pool.

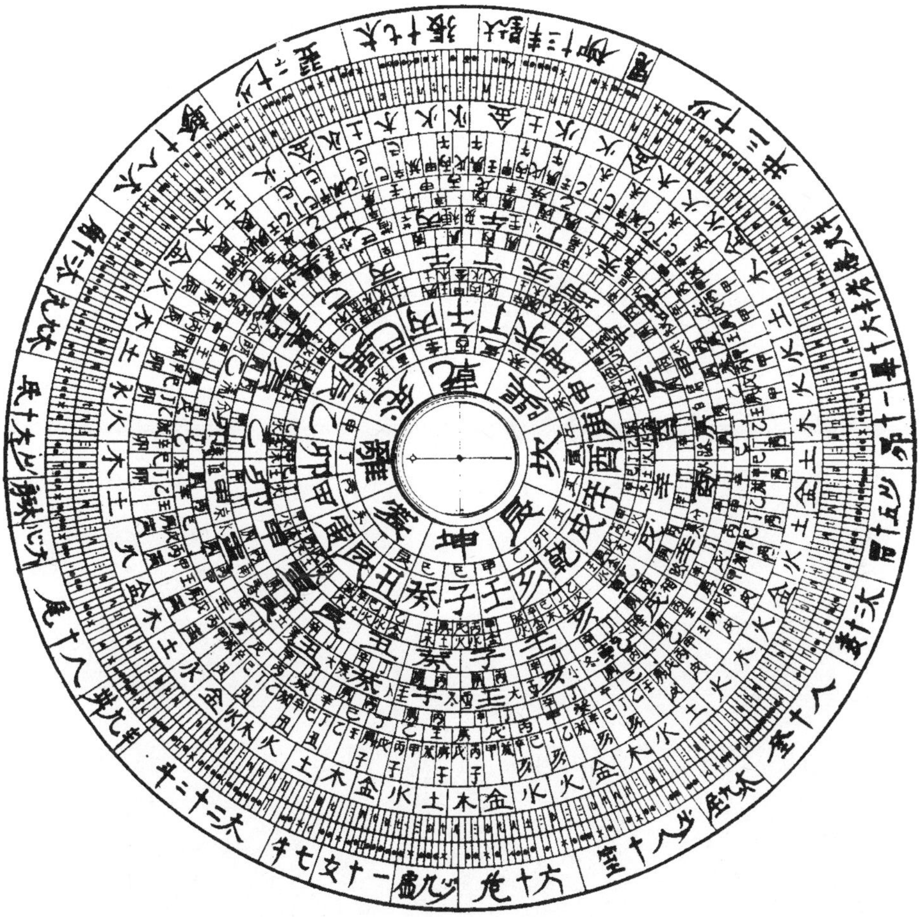

Figure 48: De Groot's San He lo p'an from Amoy (Xiamen) dating from circa 1890.[1]

1. Former Heaven Sequence of trigrams (as characters rather than as images)
2. 24 Robbery *sha* ring
3. **Earth Plate** 24 Mountains
4. 72 Dragons
5. 72 Dragons with Five Elements *na yin* attributions
6. Outer Heaven or **Man Plate** 24 Mountains
7. 120 *fen chin* [showing only the Stems of the 48 most auspicious]
8. **Heaven Plate** 24 Mountains (with 24 Mini Seasons in small characters)
9. The 48 most auspicious of the 120 *fen chin* [showing only the Stems]
10. 60 Dragons [showing only the Stems of each *chia-tzu*]
11. 120 *fen chin* [of the Earth Plate]
12. **Astronomic Plate**: 60 *ying so* [Uneven Dragons] with 61 Elements
13. The 365.25 day-degrees of the *Hsiu* showing odd (yang) numbers only
14. The 365.25 day-degrees showing auspicious and inauspicious markings
15. The 28 *Hsiu* with a number showing their extent in day-degrees.

[1] Amoy is Xiamen in Fujian Province. From De Groot (1892-1910), Plate XXVI, Vol. 3, Book 1, page 958.

So you can see that Shen was a very practical man as well as being a scholar, and this was also his approach to feng shui. He was also not afraid to change methods if he thought that one was superior to the other. Shen first studied San He feng shui. Later he researched the *I Ching* (and the associated theories of Shao Yung) and got to understand Hsüan K'ung Hsin Fa,[1] before permanently switching to Hsüan K'ung style feng shui.

Figure 49: Gordon of Khartoum, Shen Chu Reng's mentor, dressed in the robes of a Chinese General. Amazingly Gordon was awarded his rank of *Titu* 提督, one of the highest ranks in the Chinese army, by the Chinese Emperor.

[1] 玄空心法 Xuan Kong Xin Fa.

In 1873, when Shen was just 25, he went to visit Chang Chung Shan's descendants. Chang by then was already deceased. After paying heavily for the privilege, he was finally allowed by the family to read Chang's manuscripts for just 24 hours. He and a friend stayed up all night frantically copying out as much of the text as they could. It is on the basis of that text copy that Shen based much of his Flying Star theories and doctrine, so in that sense he is part of Chiang Ta Hung's lineage, but via the written word rather than by direct master to pupil transmission.

Shen devoted years to studying Hsüan K'ung, and his classic text on this is 'Master Shen's Hsüan K'ung Theory.'[1] In many ways this is one of the clearest texts on Hsüan K'ung, and the basis of much 20th century Flying Star theory, although the order of its chapters and arrangement of contents leaves a lot to be desired. Shen maintained that he learned his feng shui from the four traditional Masters: Kuan, Kuo, Yang and Tsêng.[2] By this he means that he learned it from reading the classics of feng shui rather than direct lineage pupil-ship. As well as studying the works of Chiang Ta Hung, Shen also includes a commentary on the judgements of Chiang's pupil Chang Chung Shan in his book.

Shen Chu Reng had many great talents but didn't always put them to use in the service of feng shui. He hid himself in Shanghai, writing poetry to amuse himself, delighting in calligraphy, drinking wine and reflecting on military tactics. Even his poetry and paintings achieved fame in their own right. His ideal lo p'an is shown in Figure 45. This is very significant as it shows how much of the early San He rings had been stripped away by Hsüan K'ung.

Shen Tsu Mian[3] (c.1875–c.1935), Shen's eldest son, edited his father's manuscripts and finally published them in 1925 and again in an expanded version in 1933. One of the difficulties in reading these early editions is that it is never really clear if you are reading Master Shen's own words or his son's commentary, and furthermore they are not punctuated, so it is often unclear where one sentence ends and another begins. A more recent edition (2002) cures these defects.

---

[1] *Shen Shih Hsüan K'ung Hsüeh* 沈氏玄空學 *Shen Shi Xuan Kong Xue.*

[2] Or Guan, Guo, Yang and Zeng in pinyin. These traditional Masters are Kuan Lo (209-256 CE), Kuo P'o (276-324 CE), Yang Yun Sung (834-906 CE) and Tsêng Wên Ch'an (854-916 CE). These are four of the most influential feng shui Masters of all time.

[3] 沈祖绵 Shen Zu Mian.

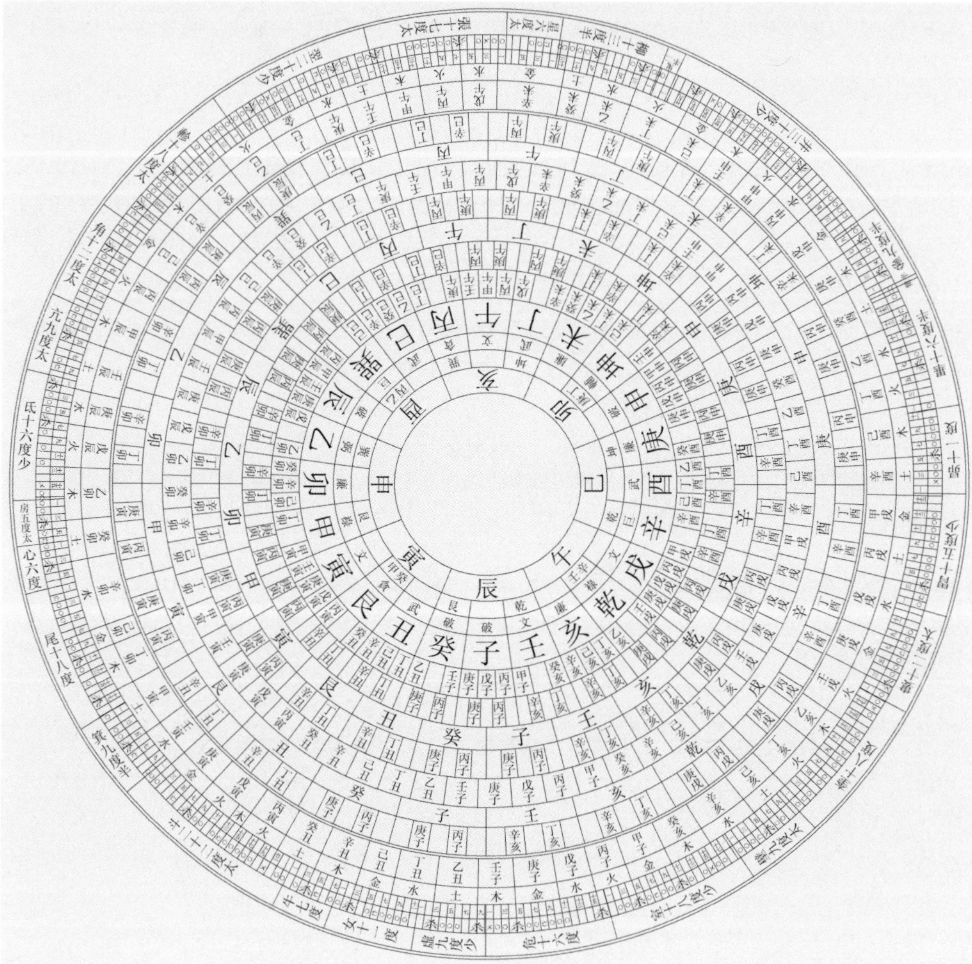

Figure 50: Key to a Classical late Ch'ing dynasty San He lo p'an from the famous Fang Hsiu Shui workshop (shown in Plate 4). This San He design is a lot more complex than the Chiang p'an in Figure 45.

1. *Yao sha*
2. Yellow Springs 8 divisions
3. The Nine Stars
4. **Earth Plate** 24 Mountains (with San He yin/yang colouring)
5. 72 Dragons
6. 120 *fen chin* (Earth Plate)
7. Outer Heaven or **Man Plate** 24 Mountains
8. 120 *fen chin* (Man Plate)
9. 60 Dragons
10. **Heaven Plate** 24 Mountains
11. 120 *fen chin* (Heaven Plate)
12. **Astronomical Plate**: 60 Uneven *ying so* Dragons
13. 61 Elements relating to the 60 Uneven *ying so* Dragons
14. 365.25 day-degrees
15. Auspiciousness indicators of the 365.25 day-degrees
16. 28 *Hsiu* with the number of degrees of extent.

The End of the Imperial Era

The Famous T'ai Pao Illustration

To gain some idea of how Ch'ing dynasty feng shui masters went about their business at the end of the Imperial Era look closely at Figure 51. This is the well known picture of T'ai Pao[1] assessing the feng shui.

The illustration *purports* to illustrate an incident in the ancient Chou dynasty, but the picture looks much more like a scene from the Ch'ing dynasty. T'ai Pao stands to the right (with his name inscribed above his head) supported by two assistants. The lo p'an is placed on a level portable table, which is more precise than holding it in the hands.

The senior pupil is examining the lo p'an, with his hands and clothing held back and kept well out of the way. The other senior pupil gazes intently at the river, making notes on the quality and direction of flow. A pair of assistants use a measuring stave to measure exact distances. In the background a croissant shaped hill is probably one of the reasons why the master is considering this particular site.

This illustration is also sometimes said to capture what Chou Kung[2] did to choose a suitable site for his new capital Luoyang.[3] However this illustration is clearly captioned in Chinese as 'T'ai Pao Assessing a Residence.' Joseph Needham first described it in his essay on the *Shu Ching T'u Shu*[4] as follows: "the use of the lo p'an has been included in this Chou (Zhou) dynasty diagram, is clearly a mistake made by academics of that [Ch'ing] period."[5]

After this picture was first mentioned by Joseph Needham,[6] it was then utilized incorrectly and anachronistically by both Chinese and Western scholars as 'proof' of the importance of feng shui in determining suitable sites for residences in the Chou (Zhou) dynasty.

However, despite the historical inaccuracies, the illustration is valuable for us, as it shows the procedure of consulting the lo p'an as it was practiced at the end of the Ch'ing dynasty.

---

[1] 太保 Tai Bao. T'ai Pao may be a title of the highest rank rather than a proper name, translated as the Great Protector.

[2] 周公 Zhou Gong.

[3] Or Lo I or Luo Yi.

[4] From *Shu Ching T'u Shuo* 書經圖說 *Shu Jing Tu Shuo*.

[5] As confirmed, the *T'ien Ting Shu Ching Tu Shu* was originally handed by Sun Chia Chai (Sun Jia Zhai) to the Empress Dowager in the 2nd month of the 26th year of the reign of Emperor Kuang Hsü 光緒 (Guang Xu) who reigned 1875-1908. It was only in the 31st year of the reign of Kuang Hsü [1906] that the edited version complete with diagrams was printed on paper and stone for various schools. This cannot therefore be considered as *proof* that feng shui was used to assess residences during the Chou (Zhou) Period, but it does record a vision of feng shui consultation around 1901.

[6] In Chinese texts this is credited to Li Yue Se, which is just Joseph Needham's Chinese name 李約瑟.

Figure 51: Late Ch'ing dynasty illustration (printed circa 1906) supposedly of a Chou (Zhou) dynasty feng shui master T'ai Pao and his assistants surveying a site. Note the lo p'an resting on a folding stand like a portable canvas camp-chair. [1]

[1] From *SCTS* Chapter 32, Shao Kao, reproduced by Needham (1962), Volume II, page 362.

Manufacturing the Lo p'an late in the Ch'ing Dynasty

Traditionally, in China the best known centre of lo p'an manufacture was in Hsiuning County[1] in Anhui Province. Even today lo p'an manufacturing continues there, particularly in Wan An town. Here manufacturing of lo p'ans started in the late Yuan dynasty, right through the Ming dynasty, and was still going strong in the Ch'ing dynasty, with a few breaks, up till today.

Perhaps the most famous Wan An lo p'an workshop was the Fang Hsiu Shui *lo ching* shop.[2] An example of the workmanship of this shop (see Plate 4) is from the present author's collection. Another famous lo p'an workshop was founded by Wu Lu Heng[3] (1702-1760) who was a trainee in the Fang Hsiu Shui *lo ching* workshop. He took the formulae and set up his own lo p'an business, which subsequently also became famous. In 1915 a Wu Lu Heng lo p'an won a design Gold medal at the Panama World Fair. Despite a decrease in interest, Wan An continued to make lo p'ans under the Republic, but ceased in 1960 because of changes in the government's attitude to feng shui. It resumed again in 1982, and continues to this day.[4] Their hand crafted lo p'ans are made from *ch'ung yang* wood, but have not yet equalled the quality of their 1915 achievements.[5]

Min School[6] lo p'ans were made in Changchou in Fukien and especially in Amoy[7] where lo p'ans were produced by Hu Ren Shan from the Chen Nan T'ang workshop; Ch'en Jui Yun at the Hsin Yi Chai workshop; and Liang Kuei Yuan.[8] The lo p'an illustrated by De Groot (Figure 48) also came from Amoy. Other notable centres of production include Kanchou in Kiangsi (the town in which Yang Yun Sung settled); Wenchou and Hangchou in Chekiang and maybe Hsingning in Kwangtung.[9] Early Chiang Pans were manufactured by Wang Yang Hsi in Hsin An town in Hsiu Yi in Anhui (see Plate 9).[10]

In the late 20th century there was an explosion of different lo p'an designs, particularly in Taiwan. Almost all the current rings were extant during the Ch'ing dynasty, except those mentioned in the next chapter.

---

[1] 休寧 Xiuning.

[2] 方秀水 Fang Xiu Shui.

[3] 吳魯衡 Wu Lu Heng.

[4] Professor Cheng (1998) mentions Chan Yun Hsiang and Hu Cheng Hao who now run a current day lo p'an shop in Ch'iao, Hsiuning, in Anhui Province, as carrying on the Lao Wu Lu Heng lo p'an tradition.

[5] *Ch'ung Yang Mu* 重陽木 *Chong Yang Mu,* or in Latin *Bischofia polycarpa*, colloquially referred to as 'tiger bone wood' is now a protected species in China. This is valued for its ability to hold ink without smudging,

[6] 閩派 Min School simply means 'Fukien School'.

[7] Changchow is 漳州 Zhangzhou in Fukien. Amoy is the city of 夏門 Xiamen, also in Fukien.

[8] 胡仁山 Hu Ren Shan from 南堂 Zhen Nan Tang; 陳瑞雲 Chen Rui Yun from 新意齋 Xin Yi Zhai.

[9] 贛州 Ganzhou in 江西 Jiangxi; 溫州 Wenzhou and 杭州 Hangzhou in 浙江 Zhejiang; 興寧 Xingning in 廣東 Guangdong.

[10] 新安 Xin An in 休邑 Xiu Yi in 安徽 Anhui. This town was mistakenly located in Kwangtung by Needham.

Figure 52: Drawing steel wire to make lo p'an needles during the late Ming dynasty, but the techniques were still the same in the late Ch'ing dynasty. The needles were sometimes magnetised by the process of thermo-remanence: which consisted of heating till red hot, aligning North-South, then quenching in water .[1]

[1] In *T'ien Kung K'ai Wu* 天工開物 *Tian Gong Kai Wu* or 'Explanation of the Works of Nature' published in 1637. Reprinted in Needham (1962), Volume 4, Part I, page 283.

The New San Yuan Rings

The late Ch'ing dynasty rings have, in the last few decades of the 20th century, been 'updated with a whole lot of additional material, mainly relating to Hsüan K'ung. Most of this material would have been more suitably calculated by the practitioner on paper, or by using one of the palm calculation methods, without recourse to the lo p'an in the late Ch'ing. Three such rings have been introduced, which are really circular versions of tabular formula, rather than truly directional sector rings.

The first of these new rings is the recent attempt to load the whole Flying Star system on to the lo p'an. The result is not very elegant. Full Flying Star charts, and male and female *kua* number rings, are modern innovations as rings, and not classical rings at all. Certain lo p'ans made in the last decade or so now show complete Flying Star charts for different Periods on their surface. Periods 7 and 8 are always included, and the most ingenious lo p'an designs even show Period 5 to Period 9 (see Plate 17). No lo p'an, as far as I am aware, shows all Periods. Such a ring is therefore always incomplete. Although this makes the process of drawing up a Flying Star chart very rapid, from a purist point of view this is a misuse of a lo p'an ring.

From a practitioner's point of view, these lo p'ans save a lot of time drawing up the chart and flying the stars. However as there are nine possible charts (nine Periods) for each of the 24 Mountains, and each chart has nine cells, each with only three Star numbers in each cell, there are a possible 5832 numbers in all. You can imagine how cramped these rings might be if every one was shown. In fact they are not. One space saving is achieved by amalgamating the second and third Mountain charts for each direction, as they are effectively the same chart. For example there will be one set of charts for N1 and a second set for N2 and N3 combined. This reduces the number of charts to 144, but still requiring the inscription of no less than 3888 Star numbers in all (144 x 9 x 3). The most extreme example of chart compression is shown in Plate 17 where Master Huang's lo p'an shows all of Periods 5 to 9.

The second recent development is the attempt to put the Eight Mansions formula on the front of the lo p'an. Previously, masters were content with inscribing this essentially tabular formula on the reverse of the lo p'an (See Figure 42). To do the formula justice on the surface of the lo p'an, and to keep each Travelling Star (auspice) pointing in the correct direction, you need to generate 8 rings (one for each sitting direction), and this is not really viable.

The third 'improvement' is the recent arrival of the Dragon Gate formula on the lo p'an. The formula for this also varies according to the sitting/facing of the house, and it is therefore again not easy or appropriate to encapsulate in one ring. Also there are many variant versions of this formula.

Relating the Lo P'an to the Almanac

The rings of the lo p'an are still very much a part of popular Chinese culture. Figure 53 and Figure 54 show the opening pages of a 1911 and a 2004 Almanac respectively. The Ch'ing dynasty Almanac or *Tung Shu* (1911) looks just like the 5th century *Chai Ching* Earth Board, and the 2004 Almanac shows that not much has changed even in the last century. The 24 Mountains of the lo p'an and the four Gates can be clearly seen on both. Thus the Almanac carries the most important rings of the lo p'an, which are reproduced every year, together with the position of the changing stars.

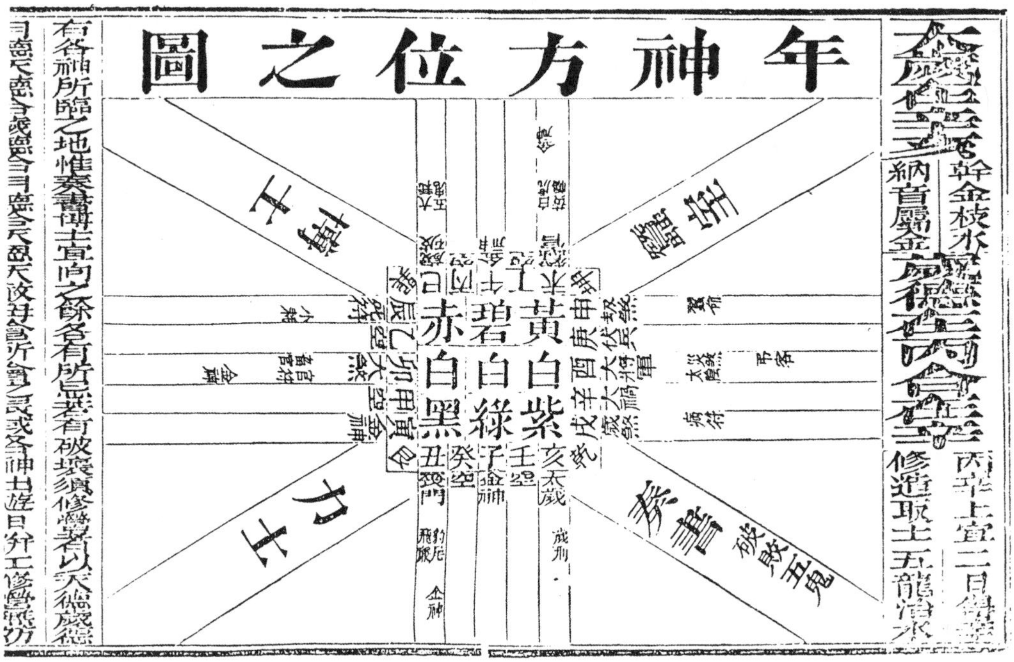

Figure 53: A Ch'ing dynasty Almanac for 1911 (the last year of Ch'ing dynastic rule) showing the feng shui configuration for that year. It presents the lo p'an in a square format, showing all 24 Mountains as the main square 'ring.' The corner Gates have four special path attributes attached to them which rotate from year to year.[1]

In the 1911 Ch'ing dynasty Almanac, the Flying Stars of the year shows three 8-white Stars across the centre three Palaces. Here the older convention of just showing the colour is adhered to, so across the centre you can see three 白 or 'white' characters. These represent 6-white, 8-white, and 1-white respectively, but you could only be expected to know that if you know how to 'fly' the Stars.[2] The line above shows the 7-red, 3-jade, and 5-yellow Stars. The line below shows the 2-black, 4-green and 9-purple Stars. Moving outwards, the

[1] *Shi Hsian Shu* 時憲書 *Shi Xian Shu*, 1911, as reproduced in Smith (1991), page 78.
[2] See Skinner (2003), Chapter 9.

next square 'ring' is the familiar 24 Mountains, beyond which are a selection of other fate stars. Additional Star auspice details are shown on the side columns.

The four Path attributes at each corner for the year 1911 Almanac are:

NW	Ch'ien trigram	Merit Record Keeper	moral qualities
SE	Hsun trigram	Scholar	intellectual abilities
NE	Ken trigram	Strongman	strength and physical wellbeing
SW	K'un trigram	Silkworm Room	qualities of a more yin nature! [1]

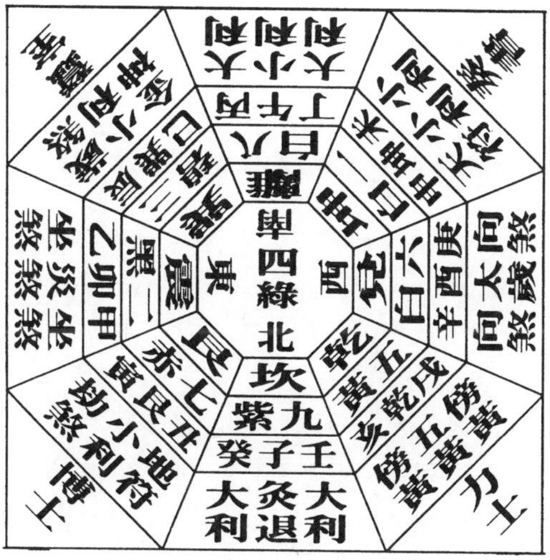

Figure 54: The opening page of a modern 2004 Chinese Almanac or *Tung Shu* showing from the middle: 4 directions (South at top); 8 trigrams; Nine Flying Stars; 24 Mountains; and Fate Stars for 2004, with the four Paths at the corners.[2]

The inner octagon of the 2004 Almanac shows the 4 directions, with South at the top. Also in the centre is the Flying Star for that year, 4-Green. The first octagonal 'ring' working outwards contains the familiar 8 trigrams. The next 'ring' shows the Annual Flying Stars for that year, with for example 8-White at the top (S), and 5-Yellow in the bottom right corner (NW). The following 'ring' holds the 24 Mountains, with Ping-Wu-Ting at the top (S). The outer double 'ring' contains the good and bad Stars for the year (over and above the 9 Flying Stars). At the corners are the usual four Paths, and in this year the Strongman star is located in the bottom right corner (NW).

All of these, the *Shih*, the *Chai Ching* Earth Boards and the long running annual Star configurations on the first page of every Almanac (be it Ch'ing or modern) are very much concerned with the same feng shui influences as the lo p'an.

---

[1] The 'silkworm room' was a polite euphemism for a place of recovery after suffering castration, among other meanings.

[2] *Tung Shu* 通書, Hong Kong, 2004.

Post Imperial China to the 21st Century

The rise of rationalism and Western education in China since the end of the Imperial era have seen the destruction of a lot of traditional knowledge in the fields of religion, medicine and feng shui. It culminated in the official banning of feng shui in 1927 as a "superstitious practice" likely to hamper the increasingly Westernised modernisation of China.

When the Communists succeeded in 1949 in ousting the Kuo Min Tang,[1] who fled to Taiwan, the latter took with them much of the Imperial art, antiques and library, with its many feng shui classics. With the formation of the People's Republic of China, opposition to what was seen as an antiquated and superstitious practice was increased and feng shui was effectively driven underground in China itself. Similar pressure was applied to traditional Chinese medicine (TCM), which has only recently begun to reassert itself in China. Many masters of feng shui went to Taiwan or Hong Kong where the political climate was not so determinedly materialistic. Some set up flourishing practices in Taiwan and Hong Kong in the 1950s and 1960s.

Since then the history of feng shui has been mostly set outside of the People's Republic of China. As the contemporary scholar He Xiaoxin once said: "now the West sets a fashion of studying and imitating it [feng shui] while in China it is almost neglected."[2] To this day, as far as I know, the ban has not been lifted, and conferences wishing to involve feng shui do so under the banner of one of the other more respectable facets of ancient Chinese metaphysics like the *I Ching*.

The so called Cultural Revolution of the 1960s and 1970s did even more to persuade practitioners of feng shui to leave mainland China and migrate to either Taiwan, Hong Kong, Singapore, Canada or Australia. This migration had the secondary effect of helping to spread the knowledge of feng shui throughout the world. Persecution was most severe during this time, when feng shui was identified as one of the so-called 'Four Olds' (Old Customs, Old Culture, Old Habits, and Old Ideas) scheduled for destruction in 1966, along with many other Chinese cultural artefacts, books, paintings, temples and even family genealogies. Feng shui practitioners were beaten and abused by Red Guards, or marched through the streets to be vilified, and their books burned. Fortunately the gates of the Forbidden City were ordered to be closed before the advancing gang of Red Guards arrived there.

---

[1] Kuomintang 國民黨 Guomindang. The flag of this political party consists of a twelve-rayed star symbolic of the 12 Earthly Branches or double-hours of the day.

[2] He Xiaoxin, *Fengshui tan yuan* ('Exploring the Source of Fengshui'), Dongnan, Nanjing, 1990.

After the death of Mao and the end of the Cultural Revolution, the official attitude became more tolerant, but restrictions on feng shui practice are still in place in today's China. For example, it is illegal in the People's Republic of China today to register feng shui consultation as a business, and similarly advertising feng shui practice is banned. There have been frequent crackdowns on feng shui practitioners on the grounds they were "promoting feudalistic superstitions." Some Communist officials who had previously consulted feng shui practitioners apparently lost their jobs and were expelled from the Party.

In China today the pendulum is beginning to swing back the other way, and some value is being seen in traditional knowledge, especially in TCM. There are now departments at various universities which house ongoing academic feng shui research, but with a few notable exceptions this is treated as historical research rather than an enquiry into a living and usable tradition.

Until recently, the most incisive academic works on feng shui were being produced by Chinese students attending British, Australian or American universities.[1] In China itself, architectural and geography departments are increasingly open to this kind of research. Interestingly, apart from Chinese sources, those works most often quoted are the books of just three Westerners: Joseph Needham, Derek Walters and the present author.

Predominantly, the Chinese academics permitted to research feng shui are anthropologists or architects by trade, studying feng shui from the point of view of history, or the theories behind the design of ancient buildings. These academics include Yu Xixian from Beijing University, who was one of the first Chinese academics to study feng shui as part of Chinese culture. Han Zeng Lu is interested in feng shui from an urban planning point of view. Professor Cheng Jian Jun,[2] of the Department of Architecture at South China University of Technology, was interested in feng shui for its own sake and produced a book on the lo p'an in 1998 in conjunction with Adriana Fernandes-Gonçalves entitled *Chinese Feng Shui Compass Step by Step Guide*.[3]

Cao Dafeng, the Vice-President of Fudan University; Liu Shenghuan of Tongji University; Professor Wang Yu De,[4] Director of Historical Research at Wuhan University; and Professor Wang Yang, of the Centre for Disease Control and Prevention in Chongqing,[5] have all done work on feng shui. Wang Yu De has also organised feng shui seminars in China which attracted a contingent of foreigners. Another such seminar was held at Beijing University in 1992.

---

[1] The first such American thesis was by a geographer Dr Hong-key Yoon, *Geomantic Relationships Between Culture and Nature in Korea*. Subsequently published in book form by the Orient Culture Service, Taipei, 1976.

[2] See Cheng (1998).

[3] This guide was useful at the time, but suffered from poor editing, a lack of terminological consistency and overall structure.

[4] 王玉德.

[5] He wrote, with Jon Sandifer, *The Authentic I Ching*, Watkins, London, 2003 about the Plum Blossom oracle.

Nanjing University (in Kiangsu/Jiangsu) announced a feng shui training course in collaboration with the China Architectural Culture Centre, but political pressure resulted in its cancellation despite considerable interest. As Kiangsu Province has historically been involved with feng shui (it was here that Yang Yun Sung finally settled down) such a course would have been very appropriate.

Fudan University flirted with the idea of introducing a feng shui course, mainly I suspect to earn foreign student dollars, but the establishment of full time Chinese university courses in feng shui is still a way off.

From Shanghai to Malaysia

Let us leave the world of academia and return to that of practitioners. Just to recap one lineage, Chiang Ta Hung's successor Chang Chung Shan passed on his knowledge to Yang Chiu Lu,[1] who in turn taught T'an Yang Wu[2] (1891–c.1945). T'an was therefore a disciple of the Wu Ch'ang School. T'an was born in Kwangsi,[3] but set up a School in 1922 at 716 Chentu Road,[4] in Shanghai to teach feng shui. He learned his Hsüan K'ung from the Chiang Ta Hung lineage, but also learned a different variety of Hsüan K'ung Purple-White Star[5] feng shui from Li Chian Hsü.[6]

T'an has the rare distinction of being honest enough to publicly admit his mistakes. He learned that one of the branches of Yin feng shui he had been practicing was in fact wrong, and so he bravely published a public apology in the Shanghai newspapers of the time, offering to compensate wronged clients, and correct his mistakes for free. He wrote three significant books:

> 'Master T'an's Clear Road to San Yuan Ti Li Great Hsüan K'ung'[7]
> 'Great Hsüan K'ung Experiments'[8]
> 'New Commentary on [Chiang's]"Ti Li Distinguishing the Correct"'[9]

It is interesting to note that even at this point in the post Imperial period, the preferred subject name was *ti li* rather than feng shui. T'an was primarily a practitioner, and he is most interesting because he recorded many documented case studies in the second book listed above, rather than just outlining the principles. These case studies have been preserved and are currently the object of detailed research by a current holder of that same lineage, Master Francis Leyau.

In Shanghai, T'an Yang Wu had two pupils: Reverend Hsü Ming[10] (1920-1998) and Yu Hsi Yin[11] (1873-1957), who had the more familiar Buddhist name of Reverend Yen Pen.[12] They both subsequently migrated to Malaysia where

---

[1] 楊九如 Yang Jiu Ru.

[2] 談養吾 Tan Yang Wu.

[3] 廣西 Guangxi.

[4] Chengdu Road.

[5] Tzu Pai Hsing 紫白星 Zi Bai Xing.

[6] 李虔虛 Li Qian Xu.

[7] *T'an Shih San Yuan Ti Li Ta Hsüan K'ung Lu T'ou,* 談氏 三元 地理大玄空路透 *Tan Shi San Yuan Di Li Da Xuan Kong Lu Tou.* Printed in China in 1923, and recently reprinted in Taiwan.

[8] *Ta Hsüan K'ung Shih Yen* 大玄空實驗 *Da Xuan Kong Shi Yan.* Experiments and casebook.

[9] *Ti Li Pien Cheng Hsin Chieh* 地理辨正新解 *Ti Li Bian Zheng Xin Jie.* A commentary on the same title by Chiang Ta Hung. Zeng Yong Xing (aka Terence Chan), one of Joey Yap's students, recently translated this under the title 'Earth Study Discern Truth.'

[10] 虛明法師 also spelled Sui Beng.

[11] 尤惜陰 also spelled Eu See Ying.

[12] 演本法師.

they gave rise to different branches of the Wu Ch'ang P'ai lineage in that country. Yu Hsi Yin had three disciples: Chen Chuan Hui, Hung Ch'uan (Hong Choon)[1] and Rong Po Yun. Reverend Hsü Ming, who first arrived in Penang in 1958, founded Buddhist temples in both the Cameron Highlands and in Johor Bahru. He passed on his knowledge to Master Francis Leyau Yoke Sai,[2] who currently teaches and practices feng shui in Melaka and Singapore.

Master Yap Cheng Hai[3] (c.1928-) also learned his San Yuan feng shui from Chen Chuan Hui, who was part of the lineage of T'an Yang Wu, but drew his earlier Eight Mansions practice from books like the classic 'Eight Mansions Bright Mirror.' He learned San He and Water Dragon feng shui from Tan Chuan Hui from Taiwan. Master Yap Cheng Hai founded the influential YCH Academy in Malaysia in the late 1990s, which has been very effective in teaching and promoting the spread of authentic traditional feng shui worldwide.

He also offered his assistance and collaboration to feng shui author and motivational speaker Lillian Too (1946-), who sought his advice when writing her early books. Lillian Too helped popularise feng shui in Malaysia, and originally claimed Master Yap Cheng Hai as her master. She went on to popularise feng shui and to open a number of franchise shops selling her feng shui books and associated Chinese cultural items.

Master Joey Yap[4] (1977-), who originally worked with and helped to promote Master Yap Cheng Hai, has subsequently branched out on his own and become a very popular and successful lecturer both in Malaysia and around the world. He has researched feng shui in considerable detail, and is helping to spread traditional feng shui worldwide. Joey has done a lot of painstaking research on many different methods and formulae, as well as studying with many feng shui masters in Hong Kong, dating back to his university days in Perth, Australia. Most of his masters come from the Wu Ch'ang School, as well as some from the Kong Miao, Li and T'ien Tong Schools. Joey has written a large number of excellent books on feng shui and designed a precise and accurate range of lo p'ans, examples of which are shown in Plate 8 and Plate 13. His *Chinese Metaphysics Compendium,* a huge volume detailing and tabulating almost all feng shui and Chinese astrology formulas, is the most detailed and clearly laid out book of its kind in any language.[5]

His teaching emphasis has changed in the last few years. It is now focused upon showing his students how to get real and impressive practical results, not upon just learning detailed classical knowledge. After all, what use is the learning of

[1] See next chapter for more details.
[2] 劉育才.
[3] 葉清海.
[4] 葉威明.
[5] Yap (2008).

tables of arcane feng shui secrets, or belonging to a lineage, if it does not result in real increases in wealth, happiness and fertility for the student?

Joey has also been working at bringing Chinese feng shui classics into English. Zeng Yong Xing (aka Terence Chan), one of his students, recently translated two major feng shui classics. One being the Chiang Ta Hong (Jiang Da Hong) commentary *Ti li pien cheng (Di li bian zheng)* under the title 'Earth Study Discern Truth.' The other being the *Pa chai ming ching (Ba zhai ming jing)* 'Eight Mansions Bright Mirror' by Jo Kuan Tao Ren (Ruo Guan Dao Ren). The latter classic is the source of the Eight Mansions method of feng shui, used by many modern masters including Yap Cheng Hai. Both are substantial contributions to the availability of Chinese feng shui classics in English.

A rather more wide-ranging approach to feng shui has been taken by the very prolific Malaysian writer Ong Hean Tatt. One of his first books was a study of *The Chinese Pa Kua,* published in 1991, which had a heady mix of classical Chinese material, with the *kameas* of Cornelius Agrippa, the Kabbalah of William Postel and the gods of the Taoist pantheon. Books from the same pen have been appearing at the rate of about two per year, examining the true meaning of various feng shui classics, and the influence of Confucius on that tradition. As a welcome benefit of his research a number of feng shui classics such as *Hsue Hsin Fu* ('Snow Heart'); the *Han Lung Ching* ('Classic of the Moving Dragon') and the *Shui Lung Ching* ('Water Dragon Classic') have been translated into English as part of his series of books.

My own contributions to the translation of Chinese feng shui classics were also written whilst I lived in Malaysia. These were four classics all written by Master Chang Ping Lin (Zhang Binglin) in 1739 under the Emperor Ch'ien Lung (Qianlong). The titles are *The Water Dragon; The Original Eight Mansions Formula; The Key San He Feng Shui Formulas* and *The Mountain Dragon.* The original Chinese title which means 'Yi Li Fully Complete Series Books' indicates that Chang Ping Lin felt that he had covered *all* the main formulae of San He feng shui as were available to him in 1739.

A number of modern masters still use water dragon formulae (first volume), Eight Mansion feng shui (second volume), and other San He formula (to locate the *hsueh*, avoid *yao sha* and robbery sha, place the kitchen stove correctly, and calculate the *na yin* of the 12 Palaces - all in the third volume), and a few still do yin feng shui (fourth volume). However few of these masters use the original formulae available in these four volumes, preferring to rely on more modified later versions instead.

Singapore is blessed with one of the best feng shui bookshops, Wan Li in Golden Mile Tower on Beach Road. It stocks a range of Chinese feng shui titles, which would otherwise only be obtainable in Taiwan or Hong Kong, plus a selected range of the more serious feng shui titles in English.

Serious Business in Singapore

Singapore was always fertile soil for feng shui. Not only does it have a large Chinese population, but a Chinese population that for the most part did not undergo the materialistic suppression of Chinese metaphysics which was experienced in the People's Republic of China. Although in many ways Singapore is very westernised, there is still a strong bedrock of traditional Chinese thinking coupled with a very practical can-do outlook. Looking around the streets of Singapore it is not hard to find examples of the serious application of feng shui to everything from small shop-houses to major public buildings.

In the early days when Singapore was a British colony a lot of thought was put into the feng shui positioning of graves, particularly those of wealthy Chinese families. As a result of this, a number of private burial grounds (often belonging to just one family or clan) were opened on the higher ground, for feng shui reasons, near to the developing city of Singapore. In 1887/1896 a Burial Bill was drawn up to attempt to regularise and control the opening of such burial grounds. It was felt that graveyards were taking up a disproportionate amount of the good land near the city, leaving the often swampy (and unhealthy) lowlands for occupation by the living. The Bill received considerable opposition especially from the wealthier Chinese families who relied upon the good feng shui of their immediate ancestors to preserve their wealth and status, not only in Singapore but also in other Straits Settlements in Malaya.

Eventually those burial areas close to Singapore city were removed, and in 1922 a relatively large cemetery (213 acres) was opened at Bukit Brown in the north of the island. A number of very impressive graves were built there over the intervening years, including those belonging to the families of important politicians and businessmen, many them designed according to the rules of San Yuan or San He feng shui. However even Bukit Brown is now threatened by the continual expansion of Singapore.

The second of T'an Yang Wu's pupils, Yu Hsi Yin (1873-1957), taught the Reverend Hung Ch'uan (Hong Choon)[1] (1907-1990) a well-known monk and feng shui master of considerable talent. Reverend Hong Choon came to Singapore in 1938, and afterwards went to Penang in 1943 to be the abbot of Mio Hiong Lim Temple where he met Wu Ch'ang Master Yu Hsi Yin from whom he learned Hsüan K'ung feng shui. He returned to Singapore in 1965 to take charge of the building and expansion of the Kong Meng San Phor Kark See Monastery[2] in Bishan. Some of the early temple buildings built in the

[1] 宏船法師 Hong Ch'uan (also spelled Hong Choon).
[2] 光明山普觉禅寺.

grounds of that Monastery in the 1950s appear to have utilised Period 5 Flying Star principles in their door orientations. His memory is fittingly commemorated at that monastery by an impressive free-standing memorial, and in a huge and futuristic building which includes on its top floor the magnificent and austere meditation Hall of No Form.

Figure 55: Reverend Hong Choon's memorial portrait at the Kong Meng San Phor Kark See Monastery in Bishan, Singapore.

Hong Choon was also credited with doing a successful feng shui assessment of the Singapore Hyatt in Scotts Road, which resulted in them tilting the angle of the main doors.[1] In August 2007, that work was updated (because of the changing feng shui that accompanies changing of Period in 2004) as part of the overall renovation started in 2006. An explanatory notice was apparently attached to the wooden partition (put up to enclose the construction work) which stated that the renovation was done so as to reap the feng shui benefits for Periods 8 and 9. The notice also stated that the original feng shui design was done by the Venerable Sek Hong Choon for Period 7 (1984-2004), and that the main door now requires to be tilted to face 313 degrees.[2] This does not quite match up with a recent analysis of the Hyatt's feng shui:

---

[1] There were rumours that although Hong Choon was called in to bless the hotel, the actual feng shui was done by a lay Chinese master who subsequently lived for a while on the penthouse floor of the hotel. I have met that master but cannot confirm the story.

[2] With acknowledgements to Alvin Chua.

> The original architectural facing of the hotel building, according to Google Earth, is 298 degrees (NW1). The hotel was built in 1971, in period 6.
>
> In Period 6 (1964-1984), the natural facing to Scotts Road gives unsatisfactory facing stars of 4 - 8. Therefore during this period it would have been very beneficial to tilt the doors clockwise by 15 degrees to a facing of 313 degrees (NW2), giving double Period stars 6 - 6 at the facing.[1]
>
> In Period 7 (1984-2004), the natural facing to Scotts Road gives a reasonably satisfactory Wang Shan Wang Shui configuration, but with a 5 Mountain star at the front. During this period it was not necessary to change from the NW2 facing, as the building remained a Period 6 building (based on construction date), even though current time had moved on to Period 7.
>
> In Period 8 (2004-2024), the natural facing to Scotts Road gives acceptable facing stars of 8 - 1. But it would have been beneficial to tilt the doors clockwise by 15 degrees to a facing of 313 degrees (NW2), giving again a Wang Shan Wang Shui configuration. The building may have updated itself to a Period 8 building because of the major refurbishment carried out in 2006.[2] Part of the feng shui improvements consisted of placing huge slabs of rock with water running over them inside the front windows of the hotel.[3]

Dr Evelyn Lip Mong Har (1938-), architecture lecturer, researcher and author at the School of Architecture Studies, National University of Singapore, wrote one of the earliest books on feng shui in 1979. It included colour photos of lo p'ans and temples, and was followed by other books on the subject with an architectural slant, also published in Singapore. Her teaching of architecture, which included segments on feng shui, would have been of considerable use to her students who would have to deal later in their professional lives, with clients who raised feng shui objections to their plans. Once characterised in an interview in the *Straits Times* (September 1981) as "Superwoman Evelyn," she paints, draws, writes, and teaches architecture as well as being well-informed about feng shui. In 1986, she became the first person to obtain a Ph.D. from the University's architecture faculty, for her thesis *Chinese Temple Architecture in Singapore*. She was the first person to survey over 120 Chinese temples in Singapore, and her thesis traced the architectural, religious and feng shui influences on temple building. She was also probably the first person to write about Flying Star feng shui in English, although she did not initially refer to it by that name. Although her books were heavily illustrated with photos of temples and lo p'ans, the quality of the reproduction made it very difficult to derive any detailed knowledge of their rings from these illustrations.

[1] Under some circumstances, to have both Period Water star and Period Mountain star at the facing is better than a Wang Shan Wang Shui formation.

[2] Alvin Chua suggested that the 2007 work was done by Victor Li, possibly using Hsüan Kung Ta Kua (Xuan Kong Da Gua) instead of Flying Star.

[3] Feng shui analysis by Gregory Wei.

In the early 1980s, Reverend Hong Choon, Reverend Lim Koon Hian, Peter Gwee Kim Voon and You Long Zi[1] were perhaps the best know Singaporean feng shui practitioners. The Reverend Hong Choon passed away in 1990 and Reverend Lim retired about the same time.

Among the best known Singaporean masters of the next generation is Master Tan Khoon Yong[2] (1954-) who pioneered the use of precision methods, theodolite accuracy, computer-generated architectural plans and modern advertising to promote feng shui. His offices have always looked more like those of a successful architect than those of a feng shui master, and he has more than once experimented with large advertisements on the back of Singapore's commuter buses. He inherited his forefather's expertise in feng shui at 30, and founded the Way Chinese Geomancy Centre in the Fu Lu Shou Centre in 1984.[3] To date, Master Tan has delivered more than 1000 talks and seminars worldwide on various aspects of feng shui. In 1997, Way Geomancy became the first feng shui consultancy to be awarded the coveted ISO 9001:2000 Certification, a very modern affirmation of the quality of his services. In 2000, Master Tan set up www.WayOnNet.com, providing perhaps the first bilingual feng shui portal in the world. He reorganized and re-named his company Way OnNet in the following year.

Master Tan has also published a number of books and booklets on topics like the Four Pillars of Destiny, as well as his regular annual publication of the *Way Bilingual Almanac*. Master Tan's broad feng shui and Chinese cultural knowledge have earned him accolades from several prestigious institutions. He is the Advisor to the Department of Philosophy at Beijing University and Vice Chairman of the Organisation for Promoting Global Civilisation. He is also serving as an honorary committee member at the Singapore Association of Writers. Master Tan was also made a 20th generation disciple of the *Quan Zhen Hua Shan* Taoist Sect in China by Reverend *Min Zhi Ting* and he is currently serving as the President of the Singapore *Quan Zhen Hua Shan*.

Master Tan was also part of the Committee that set up the IFSA on 8th May 2004. The official list of founders included: Master Yap Cheng Hai (Malaysia); Master Vincent Koh (Singapore); Master Raymond Lo (Hong Kong); Master Adelina Pang (Singapore); Master Shang Zong Wei (Singapore); Master Stephen Skinner (United Kingdom, now Singapore); Master Gahle Atherton (Australia); Dr Cui Yong Qiang (China), with Secretary Mr Eng Buck Keng (Singapore) and President Mr Darren Ng Hung Meng (Singapore). The IFSA ran its first International Feng Shui Conference (IFSC) later that year. The 9th such Conference just ran in Singapore in November 2012.

---

[1] 游龍子.

[2] 陳軍榮.

[3] 'Way' of course refers to the Tao.

Figure 56: The founding Committee of the International Feng Shui Association 2004.

One of the founders, Master Vincent Koh, opened his Singapore Feng Shui Centre (SFSC) in 1997. His first major contribution to feng shui in the English speaking world was his *Hsia Calendar 1924 to 2024* which he brought out through Asiapac in 1998. There were other English almanacs before this one, but Vincent's was eminently clear and easy to use, with useful introductory chapters on feng shui terminology and Flying Star charts. His *Basic Science of Feng Shui* came out in 2003. He also taught the first formal academically recognised feng shui courses in Singapore, at the Singapore Polytechnic, with a well-designed syllabus. He has thus been responsible for teaching traditional feng shui to a large number of students. He has also produced a partly-English San Yuan lo p'an.

Other notable feng shui masters in Singapore include Master Chong, who combines a design and interior construction practice with feng shui, and Master Yun Long Zi from the Lotus on Water chain of feng shui shops who evidently believes that the larger and more expensive an item is the more likely it will be able to confer affluence. New faces on the Singapore scene include Brandon Chua, and Master Tan's four instructors: Goh Guan Leong, Jet Lee Yi Xue, Chew Keat Leng and Lam Swee Cheong.

Feng Shui and Scandal in Hong Kong

It is not much of an exaggeration to say that almost everyone in Hong Kong is crazy about feng shui. Many feng shui masters moved there from the less accepting culture of the People's Republic of China, and have been richly rewarded for doing so. Practitioners range from the almost itinerant fortune tellers of Temple Street, in Mongkok, Kowloon, up to the practitioners whose fees and penthouses rival that of any of the other professions. I am indebted to Master Raymond Lo for much of the information in this chapter.

Hong Kong has often been referred to as a 'feng shui city' as its landform matches a number of classic feng shui formations. It has generally been agreed among feng shui masters that the position of Hong Kong at the Pearl River estuary is the mouth of the Southern Dragon of China. It is the location where the head of the massive Southern Dragon formed by the land between Yangtze river and the Pearl river ends at the South China Sea. Victoria Peak on Hong Kong Island is often characterised as the head of the dragon, turning back to face the motherland. This very auspicious feng shui configuration is called "Dragon turning its head to greet the ancestors" (廻龍顧祖) which is often the term used to describe the unique feng shui landscape of Hong Kong. Victoria Peak creates a natural shelter to protect the energy of the dragon in the Harbor, with the most powerful dragon energy concentrated in both the Central district and Tsim Sha Tsui area on the Kowloon side, making both sides of the harbor very prosperous.

Many famous feng shui masters have left their mark on the landscape by creating famous feng shui sites and auspicious tombs and graves in various parts of Hong Kong. As of today, we can still find some famous graves of great feng shui interest. The grave of Dr. Sun Yat Sen's mother at Kowloon Peak, and the auspicious grave of the Tang family in the New Territories (with the Tortoise on the Lotus leaf formation) are two such examples.

Famous feng shui masters in Hong Kong in the earlier years of the nineteen fifties and sixties include Master Ng Sze Ching (吳師青) and Master Choy Pak Lai (蔡伯勵). Master Ng is very famous for feng shui as well as Chinese Astrology and he has written a great book on the relationship between feng shui and the celestial bodies. His books include *A Treasure Guide for Houses* and *The Mountains and Landscape of Hong Kong*. Master Choy is especially famous because he produces the annual Chinese *Tung Shu* Almanac, used by many other masters, and he is generally regarded as the most respected living feng shui grand master.

In the nineteen seventies and eighties, feng shui become more popular among public people, as famous masters such as Master Paul Lam (林國雄) and Master Lam Cheung (林真) made feng shui and other Chinese metaphysical subjects such as palmistry and face reading available to the general public. They made feng shui a popular topic in media such as newspapers and radio programs. Both masters conduct regular feng shui classes which have provided training for many people who are interested in exploring these subjects. Master Paul Lam was said to be the first feng shui master in Hong Kong offering classes to educate people in Flying Star feng shui.

In the nineteen eighties and nineties, feng shui began to appear on TV programs. One of the most famous feng shui personalities is Master Rocky Sung Siu Kwong (宋韶光) who is also a scholar and professor of the Chinese University. His promotion of feng shui on TV has brought the subject to a higher academic status. At the same time, Master Raymond Lo started writing a feng shui column in the English newspaper *Hong Kong Standard*, and started promoting feng shui, four pillars of Destiny and *I Ching* to the Western world.

Master Raymond Lo is perhaps the most widely known Hong Kong feng shui master in English speaking circles, and he has been responsible for teaching feng shui and *pa tzu* (*bazi*) (Four Pillar astrology) to many thousands of students around the world. Raymond's lo p'an was one of the earliest part-English lo p'ans and it contains both San He and San Yuan rings.

Master Wong Ting Chee (王亭芝) was responsible for making Purple Star Astrology or *Zi Wei Dou Shu* very popular in Hong Kong and South East Asia generally in the nineties. He conducts classes with many students and he also promoted his branch of feng shui, which is well-known as the Central Continent School (中洲派), and which remains one of the most respected Hsüan K'ung (Xuan Kong) feng shui schools today.

A bit of light relief was provided in 1998 by Sherman Tai whose illustrated guide *Principles of Feng Shui,* done in a cartoon style, explained all the basics of feng shui such as Heavenly Stems and Earthly Branches, very clearly. Tai is a graduate of the Hong Kong Technological University, and has pursued further studies in California, but his book was published in Singapore. He has subsequently become a professional feng shui master in Canada.

Many people in Hong Kong, especially businessman, more or less believe in applied feng shui, but they may be a little shy of openly admitting this in public. In a recent year, there was an incident in which the Government Audit department criticized the Science University of Hong Kong for spending money on feng shui.

The year 2010 brought to light the famous court case surrounding the feng shui master Tony Chan who laid claim to the 13 billion US dollar estate of the very wealthy business woman Nina Wang. This incident points up how very common it is for rich business people in Hong Kong to engage the services of a feng shui master. However, there was more to this case than just feng shui, as Tony Chan became Nina Wang's lover, and on her death, at 69, produced a Will that indicated that she left her entire estate to him.

After a long drawn-out trial in Hong Kong, and in the High Court in London, a judge in January 2010 finally rejected the feng shui master's claim to the huge riches of the late billionaire. Although the real issue should have been the validity (or otherwise) of the Will that Tony Chan produced in his favour, instead the trial turned out to be more of a trial of feng shui itself, with the opposition trying to blacken Tony Chan's reputation by painting him as a con man, and by implication, someone who might easily forge a Will. The charity's lawyers said Chan was a charlatan who duped Wang, arguing that she did not have the mental capacity to execute the 2006 Will because of health problems.

It is certainly true that his feng shui methods were unorthodox to say the least, and that he often charged Nina huge fees for his advice, but that did not necessarily mean that the Will was bogus. His methods included burning large amounts of real money, and burying talismans in the basements of some of Nina's buildings.

High Court judge Johnson Lam wrote in his ruling that the signature on the 2006 Will was a 'highly skilled simulation,' and handed the entire estate to a charitable foundation run by Nina Wang's siblings. Wang, the owner of the Chinachem empire, who at one stage was Asia's richest woman (a fact that should have reflected well on Tony Chan's skills as a feng shui master) died of cancer in April 2007 at the age of 69, triggering a bitter feud between Chan and the charity.

Drawn in to give evidence was a well known feng shui master from Canada, who made comments about Tony Chan's lack of real feng shui knowledge, and an academic who wrote the first detailed thesis on feng shui in 1974. The judge rejected the evidence of the former, as he admitted having learned 90% of his feng shui from experience and books, albeit Chinese classics. On the other hand the judge accepted the evidence of one Szeto Fat-Ching, an expert feng shui witness called by the Chinachem charity. He was said to be registered with the government of China, to have 30 years of experience in feng shui, and had allegedly done 400+ related ritual ceremonies.

In Chinese-speaking circles in Hong Kong, Pa He Ming (Pak Hok Ming) who also produces a range of lo p'ans, and Peter So Man Fung (蘇民峰), are well-known for their books. Other current famous masters include Master Mak Ling Ling (麥玲玲) and Master Li Shing Chak (李丞責).

Dr Jin Peh, who grew up in Singapore, and took his medical degree in Australia decided that life as a doctor was not for him. He therefore apprenticed himself to Chen Chein Lee, a well known feng shui master in Taipei, plus several other masters specialising in classical feng shui styles like San He, San Yuan, Nine

Star, Hsüan K'ung Ta Kua. In March 2005 he took up the position of resident feng shui columnist with the *South China Morning Post,* the best known English language newspaper in Hong Kong. A collection of his columns has recently been republished in book form as *Feng Shui: a Hong Kong Perspective.*

So great is the impact of feng shui on daily life in Hong Kong that it has become customary for international corporations to hire feng shui masters at the inception of any new building project. The prestigious Mandarin Oriental Hotel used to have its own resident feng shui master, Joseph Chau, and a statue of a *chi lin* (*qiren*) on its reception desk facing out to its main doors. At a more popular level, the basic rules of household feng shui seem to be known to most people in Hong Kong, especially the older generation.

An Almanac is of course essential for the time calculations of feng shui. The first time parts of this intriguing annual publication appeared in English was in 1986 when Martin Palmer, Mak Hin Chung and Kwok Man Ho selectively translated parts of it.[1] Understandably missing from this translation was the all important tables for each day, as they change every year. Raymond Lo and Ricky Than rectified this with their regular annual publication in English of the Almanac in 2003, through Ricky's company, Thomson House, which had been publishing the same information in Chinese since they were established in 1980. They were the first full scale lo p'an manufacturing company in Hong Kong, who are able to produce lo p'ans from computer graphics right through to the finished product. Thomson House made the world's first non-Chinese lo p'an (in German) in 1994. Later they produced a English/Chinese lo p'an which they called an "I Ching Compass." With Master Raymond Lo they produced another lo p'an with a full instruction manual in English.

Raymond Lo wrote a popular feng shui column in the *Hong Kong Standard* between 1988 and 1991. In this column he made several notable forecasts about world events, including the outbreak and the result of the Gulf War, the fall of Mr. Gorbachev and Mrs. Thatcher's resignation, many of which have later proved to be accurate. He made appearances on TV programs such as BBC, ASC, CNN and CNBC. He is often invited to give talks and lectures at world-renowned conferences such as the World Economic Forum and the CEO University. He is a feng shui lecturer at S.P.A.C.E. under the University of Hong Kong, and is a consultant to the Hong Kong Tourist Association for their Health and Fortune Expo and Feng Shui Tour. Raymond has written several books in Chinese, and a number of books in English on Chinese astrology, the *I Ching* and feng shui including: *Essential Four Pillars of Destiny; Four Pillars of Destiny for Healthy Life; Feng Shui Essentials; I Ching: Divination for Feng Shui and Destiny; The Thousand Year Calendar for Feng Shui & Destiny; Feng Shui and Destiny.*

---

[1] Palmer, Mak Hin Chung and Kwok Man Ho, *T'ung Shu: then Ancient Chinese Almanac,* Rider, London, 1986.

Traditional Feng Shui in Taiwan

Taiwanese feng shui was derived directly from late Ch'ing dynasty mainland Chinese feng shui, and uses the same classics. However, in Taiwan there was no examination in feng shui, but rather an apprenticeship system. Under Japanese occupation (1895-1945), feng shui was very much controlled and suppressed in both Korea and Taiwan, as the occupying country did not want the local Chinese population benefiting from such knowledge. From 1945 to the present day, a professional association, the Association of Astrology, Divination and Feng Shui, regulates feng shui knowledge and records lineages. The quality of lo p'an manufacture in Taiwan is the best in the world, and certainly better than many modern lo p'ans emanating from the People's Republic of China. Until recently these were still either rather roughly hand made, or just meant as tourist curios, quite often sold without even the base plate.

In Taiwan the attitude to feng shui is one of acceptance, and a large number of practitioners flourish. Precisely because of this the standard of work and training is high. However, Taiwanese state propaganda encourages cremation and the interment of the body in bone pagodas or *ling ku t'a*,[1] which helps reduce both the use of expensive land plots for traditional burials, and the use of *yin chai* feng shui. Yin feng shui is not effective in the case of cremation, as the bones and marrow, upon which yin feng shui depends, are destroyed. Burial sites in Taiwan, which are not part of a formal cemetery, are becoming increasingly expensive, especially where their feng shui is perceived to be particularly good.

Yin feng shui even plays a part in local politics. During the elections of 2004, a number of feng shui masters appeared on Taiwanese TV to comment on the chances of one or other candidate, based on the tombs of their immediate ancestors. One feng shui master was reported as having placed nine iron nails around the family tomb of a competitor politician, resulting in recriminations and mutual accusations. Neither of the parties involved won the election. In the event Chen Shui-bian won the election, and ended 50 years of Nationalist Party rule. He later stepped down over corruption charges in May 2008. Tactics such as damaging the tomb of an opponent's immediate ancestors are common, and armed guards are often posted at sensitive times on sensitive graves.

A recent study entitled *An Estimation of the Impact of Feng-Shui on Housing Prices in Taiwan: A Quantile Regression Application* carried out by three academics,[2] showed that feng shui is a very important factor in house pricing as well as politics:

---

[1] 靈骨塔 *ling gu ta.*

[2] : Professor Chu-Chia Lin, Professor Chien-Liang Chen and Ya-Chien Twu, M.A.

> Feng-shui has a significant influence on many aspects in daily life for most Chinese [in Taiwan], including choosing locations for dwelling units, offices, burial sites, and so on. However, there have been few studies on the impact of feng-shui on housing prices. By applying a housing hedonic equation and a data set of 77,624 observations in Taiwan, we have attempted to estimate the impact of feng-shui on housing prices. We find that all six types of bad feng-shui have a significantly negative impact on housing prices. Moreover, by applying a quantile regression, we find that most of the bad feng-shui has a stronger negative impact on expensive dwelling units. Our findings confirm that people who buy expensive housing units care about feng-shui more than those who buy less expensive housing units.

The types of bad feng shui most feared by potential house buyers are *lu-chun* (end of road or T-junction), cutting blade elevated road, anywhere on a dead-end road, location on the fourth floor, near a temple, and proximity to funeral parlours or hospitals. These can easily cut an *average* of 10% off the asking price of a house in Taiwan, or even more if the affliction is pronounced.

Although one Taiwanese newspaper calculated that there are up to 30,000 practitioners of feng shui in Taiwan, this is undoubtedly an inflated figure, as only about 3,000 are actually licensed by the feng shui Association which keeps track of lineages and levels of skill.

Pungsu in Korea

Korea has a long history of using feng shui, imported from its near neighbour China. In the last couple of decades some very detailed research work has been done on feng shui in Korea, including one book that includes the Chinese texts of Yang Yun Sung's four books.

The national flag of Korea carries 4 trigrams in a *pa kua* format, with a *tai chi* yin-yang symbol in the middle. It is obvious from this that feng shui is definitely part of the national consciousness. The four trigrams are those representing the cardinal points and four seasons: *Ch'ien, K'un, Kan* and *Li.*

Figure 57: Two versions of the South Korean flag showing just the 4 cardinal trigrams: the modern version (left) and the Doseon inspired version, used 1882-1911 (right).

Korean feng shui is called *pungsu-jiri-seol* ('Wind-Water Earth-Principles').[1] It is supposed to have been developed by the Korean master Doseon-guksa in the late 900s. But it is also likely that some Koreans studied Chinese Taoism during the Three Kingdoms period, and brought it back to Korea with them. Due to the absence of Taoism in Korea, feng shui became associated with Seon (Zen) Buddhism instead. Doseon adapted the various Chinese Taoist schools of feng shui to the Korean landscape and cultural traditions. He placed greater emphasis on the spiritual and material energies of mountains, and their resultant effect on the destinies of families, communities and the nation as a whole, rather than on personal fortunes or interior furniture placement.

Taejo Wang Geon, who founded the Goryeo dynasty in 918, used Doseon's feng shui recommendations, and (possibly as a result) the family remained politically and socially powerful till 1396. Around 70 monasteries, both large and small, are claimed to have been founded either under Doseon's supervision and direction, or by the orders of Taejo Wang Geon, and most of them still thrive. Four Goryeo-dynasty Confucian scholars of the 12th Century, led by Kim In-jon and Bak Seung-jung, wrote the book entitled *Haedong-Pirok*

[1] I would like to acknowledge Professor David A. Mason's excellent book *Spirit of the Mountains*, Hollym, 1999, as the source of much of my information in this section.

('Secret History of Korea') that repeated and extended Doseon's theories, and that book remains the oldest complete *pungsu* text.

One of the key concepts of Doseon's *pungsu* is the existence of the Baekdu-daegan, the mountain range dragon or spine of the Korean Peninsula. This is believed to feed essential ch'i throughout the nation, from its mountains into its lowlands, affecting its spring-waters, crops and air, and thus its people. Unimpeded flow of this ch'i is considered necessary by traditional Koreans for the birth of virtuous citizens, and thus for the health, strength and prosperity of Korea.

Doseon taught that building temples and stone pagodas on particular sites (or strategically located *hyeol*) could amplify their positive energies or at least reduce/neutralize their negative energies, thereby benefiting the kingdom. Accordingly these structures were erected according to his directions and are still called *Bibo-sacheol* and *Bibo-satap*. None of Doseon's original writings survive, but a number of later documents quoted from them survive, and so his ideas have been preserved. The currently most famous temple said to have been founded by Doseon himself is Seoul's Samgak-san Doseon-sa, one of Korea's 'top-20 temples.'

Hyeol is defined "a spot where the influences on one's fortune converge," and so is the equivalent of the Chinese word *hsueh*. It's like an acupuncture point on the mountain. The word is even used to name mountains, so that Hyeolgu-san mountain is so named because it has nine prominent *hyeol* present on it. The *hyeol* is surrounded by the same four landform animals as is the Chinese *hsueh:* the Black Tortoise (with snake or dragon genitals) peak to the rear (north); a rocky White Tiger ridge on the right (west); a winding Blue-green Dragon ridge on the left (east); and a good open view in front, with beyond it a protective hill, the Red Phoenix (in the south).

The ch'i of a *hyeol* is said to swirl in a clockwise direction, which gives positive effects, while an anti-clockwise motion gives negative energy, while straight-moving is just considered neutral, which calms the wind in that area, and attracts water to it. Details like this about the direction of the ch'i flow and its relationship to wind are often missing from modern Chinese feng shui texts.

Hyeol is also defined in non-specialist Korean dictionaries as a 'hole,' and is also used by Koreans to refer to the 9 openings of the human body through which energies can pass in and out: 2 eyes, 2 ears, 2 nostrils, the mouth, anus and genitals. As with Chinese medicine it also means the points on the body for use in acupuncture. Both mountains and humans were thought to breathe ch'i in and out, and these *hyeol* are the main passageways.

Associated with *hyeol* are the *myeong-dang* (literally 'shine bright' or 'light-space'), which are obviously the *ming tang* of Chinese feng shui. 'Bright' was always considered good, and there is a preference for words like 'bright' and 'gold' in both Chinese and Korean cultures. This has lead to a preponderance of white (*baek*) and gold (*geum*) in Korean place names for towns, counties, mountains, temples, shrines, and people. The popularity of the family name Kim ('gold'), (now owned by 21% of Koreans), which uses the same Chinese character for gold, is another indication of this preference.

As in Chinese feng shui, the *myeong-dang* is a topographically flexible concept. It can be as large as an entire valley holding a city, or as small as the front of a temple. There may be a number of suitable *hyeols* in one large *myeong-dang*. This throws some interesting light on the interpretation of some Chinese feng shui terms. In fact I am of the opinion that at least landscape feng shui, and probably the understanding of specific rings of the lo p'an have been better preserved in South Korea than in many modern Chinese books.

Korean feng shui masters express their judgement of landscape features in anthropomorphic terms, using animal metaphors to express the character of the landform. For example, a shape might poetically be said to be "a crane sitting on its eggs;" "a white tiger crouching, ready to spring;" "a black ox content to lie and sleep;" "a rabbit about to run away;" "a stately king on his throne" or "an ancient pine bending in the wind." This is also true of masters in Taiwan, and older classical Chinese feng shui texts.

Figure 58: A traditional figure of a Korean *pungsu* master drawn in Taoist style. He is holding a mountain recluse's staff in one hand and a feng shui compass in the other. His hat is that of a Joseon dynasty fortune-teller, which is derived from Chinese Taoism. His robes with their chest-belt are like those of a government official, but are gray like a Buddhist monk. Over them is a red sash with royal circular gold embroideries.

Large *hyeol* or *myeong-dang* found on the southern slopes of mountains frequently become the sites of Buddhist, Taoist or Confucian temples, with smaller ones being used for traditional tombs. Somewhat less frequently, those found on eastern or western slopes are used in this way, but rarely those on northern slopes, for the same reason as Chinese feng shui masters do not favour the cold northern side of a mountain.

The greatest sacred mountains have three *hyeol* (upper, central and lower) on a ch'i-line running down their southern slopes. Typically major monasteries will be found on the lower *hyeol*, and hermitages on the central and upper. These temples will have unusually high levels of spiritual energies, allowing those who live, meditate and worship there closer access to the mountain ch'i and to Heaven ch'i.[1]

The classic ideal Chinese feng shui landform configuration surrounding a *hyeol* is referred to as a *baesan-imsu* site, which is a low altitude site backed by a mountain to the north, and facing a river running laterally in the south (preferably flowing from west to east). Because of the north-south orientation of Korea, such sites are rare, and will mostly be on the eastern side of the country. One good example of such a configuration is the southern slopes of mount Jiri-san, which end at the eastern-flowing Seomjin River. Hannam-dong (Hwagye-dong), where many business tycoons live, is currently thought to be one of the hottest feng shui places to live, and is touted by the Hadong County government as being an ideal *baesan-imsu*. Other excellent examples are the sites of the main royal palaces in Seoul and Sogni-san's Beobju-sa Temple.

However, the auspicious ch'i of sites can fade away with the changing of time Periods, or deliberate human abuse. This can cause a family to lose its fortune, a king to lose his crown, or a nation to be ruined by war or famine. During the Japanese occupation of Korea, feng shui came to the forefront and allegedly feng shui was used as a weapon by the Japanese.

> In order to ensure that the occupation would be successful, Japanese geomancers dug deep shafts into the earth, inserted, then buried upright, long iron poles to act as collectors and re-distributors of the land's *qi*. This was intended as a sort of destructive geomantic acupuncture. To this day, Koreans are trying to find and remove these poles, in order to restore their country's original *qi* flow.

The issue of time periods is also important, as for example the recent change from Period 7 to Period 8 in 2004, as measured by Chinese feng shui, made considerable changes to the quality of the feng shui. The Korean system of

[1] One example is the southern slope of mount Nogo-dan, with the sites of Sangseon-am hermitage on the upper *hyeol*, Sudo-am hermitage on the central *hyeol* and the great Hwaeom-sa Monastery on the lower *hyeol*.

measuring such periods is not quite the same, but the understanding that time causes changes in the quality of the feng shui is the same. The ability of feng shui masters to correct damage done to the national feng shui, or to allow for Period changes has resulted in regular recommendations. The book *Jigi-soewang-seol* ('Theory of Waxing and Waning of Energies') was derived from Doseon's teachings and greatly expanded upon in subsequent centuries. It become a main concern of Korean *pungsu,* together with the many socio-political controversies arising from it.

Pungsu was instrumental in the founding and citing of the capital cities of both of Korea's subsequent dynasties, Goryeo and Joseon, and there was constant debate between kings and their ministers relating to it. Sejong-daewang (reigned 1418-50), one of Korea's best and wisest kings, was deeply concerned with it and personally investigated the feng shui layout of Seoul.

In the middle of the Joseon dynasty, scholar Yi Chung-hwan (1690-1752) surveyed the entire Korean peninsula in both geographic and feng shui terms, and then wrote *Taengni-chi,* a book giving advice on the best places to live – based on *pungsu* ideas. Another book from the mid-18th century is the *Cheon-ch'i-daeyo* ('Great Digest of Heavenly Indications'). Up to today, *pungsu* continues to assist in siting buildings, shrines and tombs, and it has become the object of increasing interest by Korea's modern academic geographers.

Throughout the last 1100 years, the construction of nearly all Korean villages, towns, temples and tombs has been influenced by *pungsu*. Many Koreans are reputed to have paid fortunes, committed crimes, and even risked their lives in endeavours to secure sites with good feng shui. The famous Neo-Confucian scholar Jeong Yak-yong (1762-1836) once commented that around half of the litigations brought to the courts in those days were due to assaults and disputes over supposedly auspicious feng shui sites.

Probably the most detailed survey of Korean feng shui was written by a Japanese scholar, during the occupation of Korea by Japan (1910-1945), Murayama Chijun's *Chosen no Fusui* ('Korean Feng Shui') published in 1931. One presumes that the Japanese thought a knowledge of Korean customs a useful ingredient in effective colonial rule. The former Korean court feng shui master, Chon Kiung, was co-opted as a consultant. *Koryo sidae ui yongu* ('A Study of the Koryo Period') is also a rich source of Korean feng shui lore. Hong-key Yoon's thesis and its republication with additional material in 2006, embody the modern academic tradition of Korean feng shui writing.

Korea is now producing feng shui technical manuals which not only throw a lot of light upon the details of Korean *pungsu* but can also be used to help explain many details of Chinese feng shui. One of the best is *Hsüan K'ung Feng Shui: Theory and Practice* by Ts'ui Ming Yu which has the most amazing clear illustrations which are a considerable advance on corresponding Chinese texts.

八卦	坐	分金	度
兌宮	+庚	甲申	248
			249
			250
		丙申	251
			252
			253
		戊申	254
			255
			256
		庚申	257
			258
			259
		壬申	260
			261
			262
	−酉	乙酉	263
			264
			265
		丁酉	266
			267
			268
		己酉	269
			270
			271
		辛酉	272
			273
			274
		癸酉	275
			276
			277
	−辛	乙酉	278
			279
			280
		丁酉	281
			282
			283
		己酉	284
			285
			286
		辛酉	287
			288
			289
		癸酉	290
			291
			292

卦	爻	吉
渙 환 ⑥	1	●
	2	
	3	
	4	●
	5	
	6	
坎 감 ①	6	●
	5	
	4	
	3	●
	2	
	1	
蒙 몽 ②	1	●
	2	●
	3	
	4	●
	5	●
	6	
師 사 ⑦	6	
	5	
	4	●
	3	
	2	
	1	●
遯 돈 ④	1	
	2	
	3	●
	4	
	5	
	6	●
咸 함 ⑨	6	●
	5	
	4	
	3	●
	2	
	1	
旅 려 ⑧	1	
	2	●
	3	
	4	
	5	●
	6	
小過 소과 ③	6	
	5	●
	4	●
	3	
	2	●
	1	●

八卦	坐	分金	度
乾宮	−戌	甲戌	293
			294
			295
		丙戌	296
			297
			298
		戊戌	299
			300
			301
		庚戌	302
			303
			304
		壬戌	305
			306
			307
	+乾	甲戌	308
			309
			310
		丙戌	311
			312
			313
		戊戌	314
			315
			316
		庚戌	317
			318
			319
		壬戌	320
			321
			322
	+亥	乙亥	323
			324
			325
		丁亥	326
			327
			328
		己亥	329
			330
			331
		辛亥	332
			333
			334
		癸亥	335
			336
			337

卦	爻	吉
漸 점 ⑦	6	
	5	
	4	●
	3	
	2	
	1	●
蹇 건 ②	1	●
	2	●
	3	
	4	●
	5	●
	6	
艮 간 ①	6	●
	5	
	4	
	3	●
	2	
	1	
謙 겸 ⑥	1	●
	2	
	3	
	4	●
	5	
	6	
否 비 ⑨	6	●
	5	
	4	
	3	●
	2	
	1	
萃 취 ④	1	
	2	
	3	●
	4	
	5	
	6	●
晉 진 ③	6	
	5	●
	4	●
	3	
	2	●
	1	●
豫 예 ⑧	1	
	2	●
	3	
	4	
	5	●
	6	

Figure 59: Korean Hsüan K'ung feng shui illustration of a few rings of the lo p'an stretched out laterally, ranging over 248 to 337 degrees, that is, the West and Northwest sectors of the lo p'an. This shows 8 rings detailed right down to the half degree.[1]

[1] Ts'ui Ming Yu, *Hsüan K'ung Feng Shui: Theory and Practice,* in Korean and Chinese.

Apart from Hong-key Yoon, the best known contemporary Korean scholar of feng shui is Choi Chang-jo (1950-) who graduated with a master's degree in geography from Seoul National University in Korea in 1975. However, the faculty refused to allow him to take feng shui as the topic of his master's thesis. Nevertheless he worked as a geography lecturer, and finally became a professor at the same university. In 1984 he published what is probably the most influential Korean feng shui book called *Hankuk ui pungsu sasang* ('Korean Pungsu Thought'). His colleagues constantly criticised his teaching of feng shui, and he finally resigned in 1991 to become a private scholar, and an unchallenged authority on feng shui in Korea. He has never given an institutional lecture since, but does do radio broadcasts and private lectures. He carried out a feng shui survey of North Korea in 1999. It is ironic that Hong-key Yoon had to go to the US to do his thesis on feng shui, and is teaching in New Zealand, whilst Korea observes academic silence over one of its great traditions, and prevents scholars like Choi from pursuing this study.

In the 1970s, there were few books on feng shui written by practitioners and available in Korea. In the late 1980s this had expanded to several dozen books, but in 2004 Hong-key Yoon counted 231 books on *pungsu*.

In present day Korea there is a much greater awareness of feng shui, with politicians not only shifting their ancestors' graves to better sites in order to get elected, but actively making publicity out of that fact. Such activity was widespread in 2002. A typical example is that of Kim Dae-Jung who shifted his family graves to a more auspicious site in Yong-in near Seoul, after which he was elected president. Of course the opposite also occurs with attempts to damage the ancestral graves of political opponents.

Ironically, the rebellion of the monk Myocheong in around 1130 was mostly based on his advice to move the capital north from Seoul to Pyongyang, in order to achieve a superior feng shui position according to his *pungsu* readings. This was not done, until that city became the de facto capital of North Korea in 1948, but the results so far do not seem to confirm the viability of his feng shui calculations, although that may well be because of subsequent Period (and regime) change.

In North Korea the ancient Koguryo tombs (located within China's Jilin and Liaoning provinces as well as North Korea) are located with respect to the surrounding mountains and rivers. Some of these tombs influenced younger dynasties such as King Kongmin's Tomb found north of the ancient capital of Kaesong, which was completed in 1372, combining both Korean and Mongolian elements. This tomb is dedicated to this Korean nobleman of the Koryo dynasty and his Mongolian wife Queen Noguk. The eastern tomb is dedicated to that Mongolian beauty.

Fusui in Japan

The Japanese name for feng shui is '*fusui*.' In Japan, a certain amount of feng shui was imported from China during the T'ang dynasty. Japanese books recording the feng shui rules for creating gardens around a residence have preserved more detail than extant Chinese classics. A substantial scholarly literature on feng shui exists in Japanese. Between 1989 and 1993 Yoshio Watanabe organized and served as President of the Japan Association for Geomancy Research. Just like Korea, Japan appears to have preserved certain elements of feng shui that are now absent (or at least very hard to find) in Chinese literature. This is particularly true of garden feng shui. In fact, reading Japanese manuals on the *fusui* rules applied to the structuring of gardens is an excellent antidote to the idiocy of some texts in English written in the 1990s by a well known populariser of feng shui, where she attempts to overlay the colour prescriptions of an interior *pa kua* (or *bagua*) on the outdoor garden.

Probably because of the orientation of the islands that make up Japan, Japanese feng shui utilises a NE-SW orientation rather than the North-South orientation of Chinese feng shui.

One Japanese variant of basic feng shui is 'Nine Star Ki,' a system that has also been applied by the Japanese to personality categorisation. The Japanese transliterate ch'i as *ki,* but the original character is the same in both Chinese and Japanese. This system was devised, or at least popularised, by Michio Kushi (b. 1926), who also promoted the macrobiotic food movement. Nine Star Ki was brought to the UK in the 1980s by the late Jon Sandifer, who lectured on it at the East-West Centre in London, and who later turned his attention to the *I Ching* and more classical forms of feng shui.

Feng Shui goes West to the UK

There are very few pre-1976 writers in English or any other European language writing on feng shui. The only ones were missionaries or colonial administrators working in the 19th century. The first description of feng shui in English was by the missionary Simpson Culbertson in Shanghai in 1857, followed by the Reverend M T Yates in 1868. It was Yates who first decided to mis-translate feng shui as 'geomancy' rather than just simply transliterating it. The first English description of the rings of the lo p'an was published by the German missionary Ernest Johann Eitel in 1873, but the rings he referred to were not illustrated.

Nineteenth century interest in feng shui in the West was stimulated by missionary works, especially that of Ernest Eitel and De Groot, both of whose books carried basic descriptions of the lo p'an. Both however took a very condescending view. Eitel saw feng shui as primitive science, just the "rudiments of natural science" rather than an unknown art in its own right.

De Groot was rather more thorough and set feng shui in the context of Chinese religion and burial customs. Jan Jakob Maria De Groot (1854-1921) in his massive *Religious Systems in China*[1] (1897) published the first clear engraving of a lo p'an together with a commentary on its rings (see Figure 48). This in turn provided an image source for Paul Carus (1852-1919) in his *Chinese Astrology*[2] where he expanded on the details of all 16 of the rings. Even so the descriptions were rather sketchy, and no indication of their use is given. In 1932 Charles Williams in a small item in his *Outlines of Chinese Symbolism and Art Motifs* listed a lo p'an with 19 rings, but without an illustration.

Feng shui in the UK was then ignored by an increasingly rationalistic world, until in 1958 a lecture on feng shui was delivered at London University, and attended by Fred Gettings. Fred objected to the lecturer using the term 'geomancy' to translate the word 'feng shui.'[3] Fred was fully aware that 'geomancy' had been applied for over a millennium to a totally different practice unrelated to feng shui.[4]

Sir Joseph Needham (1900-1995) pioneered the Western academic recognition of China's scientific past with his voluminous *Science and Civilisation in China* series. In Volume IV, Part 1 of this series, which he designated 'Physics,'

[1] Volume 3, Book 1, Chapter XII.

[2] First published as *Chinese Thought*, 1907, later abridged in 1974. See pages 58-62 for a description of the 15 rings of J J M de Groot's lo p'an. See Figure 48 of the present book for a ring list for this lo p'an.

[3] 'Geomancy' was a well established term for divination by sand, or from a row of random dots, and had only been mistakenly pressed into use as a translation of 'feng shui' by a late 19th century missionary who could not find a suitable translation in the dictionary.

[4] For details of Western divinatory geomancy, see Skinner, *Geomancy in Theory & Practice,* GHP, Singapore, 2011.

published in 1962, he included a study of the development and understanding of magnetism and the compass in China, a study which inevitably went on to describe the lo p'an and its use in feng shui.[1] Although he constantly looked for parallels between Western and Chinese science, his thoroughness has provided much of the information on the history of the lo p'an available in English up to the present time.

In his section on astronomy, Needham described how the Chinese built advanced observatories. When the help of Jesuit missionaries was sought in order to input Western astronomy during the reign of the Emperor Ch'ien Lung,[2] the missionaries were stunned at the precision and beauty of the Chinese astronomical devices. Western astronomy of the vintage of Tycho Brahe (1546-1601) was added to the existing Chinese equipment. There are many drawings and photographs extant of the resulting amazing structures with their very refined instruments, an example of which is shown in Figure 32. Such instruments enabled the Chinese to make very exact star maps, which are very relevant to the Astronomical rings of the lo p'an.

In his second volume, Needham outlined the history of feng shui, but listed it as a pseudo-science.[3] In this same section he observes that "there is now no doubt that the magnetic compass was first developed for fêng-shui purposes," confirming that one of the most important scientific discoveries of all time sprang originally from the practice of feng shui. Maybe the reason for his dismissing feng shui as a pseudo-science is that he could not quite grasp its purpose and method, even though he understood its technology and history.

Around this time Dr Hugh Baker at SOAS London University began to write a series of articles on feng shui which appeared in English in the *South China Morning Post.*

Maurice Freedman, having spent time in China in the early 1960s, made feng shui the subject of his Presidential Address to the Royal Anthropological Institute in 1968.

In turn, he influenced Stephan Feuchtwang, who in 1974 published his excellent thesis on feng shui. For some obscure reason he chose to publish it in Laos, so that despite being republished in Bangkok in 2002 it is still largely unappreciated and unavailable. It contains the first detailed analysis of the rings of the lo p'an since Needham. I bought a copy in London soon after it was published, but I have heard stories of one keen enthusiast who travelled from the UK to Thailand in a vain attempt to secure a copy. He was greatly disappointed by being refused permission to enter Laos at the land border.

---

[1] Volume 4, Part I, Pages 229-325. Part of this is devoted to the fallacious 'magnetic soup spoon theory' of Wang Chen-To (1948-51) which we will examine in greater detail later.

[2] 乾隆 Qian Long.

[3] Needham (1956) Volume 2, pages 359-363.

Professor Stephan Feuchtwang, in his 1974 doctoral thesis *An Anthropological Analysis of Chinese Geomancy,*[1] provided the best 20th century survey of the contents of the lo p'an in English, with some partial translations of key Chinese texts. He used as his main Chinese source the Ming dynasty classic *Lo Ching Chieh*[2] by Wu Wang Kang.[3] Unfortunately he did not always relate this material ring by ring to a corresponding illustration of a lo p'an, although several other lo p'an reproductions do appear in his thesis. Fortunately Feuchtwang seems to have been more interested in feng shui than in anthropology, and so he deals with his subject sensitively and lucidly. The anthropological content gives the impression of having been added as an after-thought to justify the subject matter of his thesis to his faculty. That observation is in no sense meant as a criticism of this ground-breaking work.

Two years later, my first book on feng shui, the *Living Earth Manual of Feng Shui,* written in 1976, explained some of the intricacies of the lo p'an, and outlined the key 7.5° differences in orientation between the three Plates of the San He lo p'an. My book was reprinted by RKP in 1982 in a very badly produced edition, but it was the first book entirely devoted to feng shui published in English in the 20th century. It concentrated equally on landform and lo p'an feng shui, from a San He perspective, but with very little mention of the internal house decorative feng shui that was later going to become so popular.

In the same year the first ever thesis on feng shui was submitted to an American university by the Korean Dr. Hong-key Yoon. In 1979 the architect and academic Evelyn Lip published her *Chinese Geomancy* in Singapore, which used full colour illustrations of various lo p'ans. Although the rings were not explained, some of the nomenclature of feng shui was.

In the 1980s two books were published which threw some light on aspects of Chinese astrology which forms some of the main building blocks of the lo p'an. The first was *The Way to Chinese Astrology: the Four Pillars of Destiny* by Jean-Michel Huon de Kermadec in 1983, followed four years later by Derek Walters who published *Chinese Astrology*. This still remains perhaps the best treatment of that subject in English. After an excursion into the 5 Elements, Derek explains the construction of the two Chinese calendars. Much of this material is useful to the practitioner of that form of Chinese astrology called 'Four Pillars' or more correctly 'Eight Character' *Pa Tzu*[4] which utilises the Heavenly Stem and Earthly Branch of the year, month, day and hour of the subject's date of birth. These Earthly Branches and Stems will also be found in a

[1] Vithagna, Laos, 1974.

[2] 羅經解 *Luo Jing Jie*.

[3] 吳望崗 Wu Wang Gang.

[4] 八字 *Ba Zi*.

number of the rings of the lo p'an. The book also contains a detailed description of the 28 Lunar Mansions which form one key ring of the lo p'an.

Despite the existence of my book *The Living Earth Manual* on classical feng shui methods published in 1976, and again in 1982, the initial interest in feng shui in the UK, was locked into a very simplified Life Aspirations School. This had its birth in Hong Kong, but was popularised by Lillian Too in her ambitiously titled *Complete Illustrated Guide to Feng Shui* (1990). This book outlined several simplified versions of feng shui, including Eight Mansions, and although it was far from complete, caught the mood of the time.

The Life Aspirations School was easy to understand as it simply divided the house into eight locations, attributing one aspect of life to each sector. The system functioned by putting a symbolic or actual expression of one of the classical 5 Elements in the sector it was desired to 'activate.' This seemed to work, helped along by the focused intention accompanying the action. The 8 trigrams were then overlaid on an 8 sector grid. This was not exactly classical feng shui, but it was derived from a school of feng shui in Hong Kong. In the same book, a basic form of Eight Mansions theory was outlined. The resulting mixture, put together by a very smart UK book designer did very well, and was republished later in the US. This book also stimulated an interest in symbolic feng shui, which provided Lillian Too with fertile ground on which to later plant her chain of shops selling Chinese cultural items and feng shui cures.

An even greater simplification of this system was generated by Thomas Lin Yun in the US, was popularised in the 1990s. He used the above scheme without reference to the actual compass directions of a building, and simply orientated North (or NE, NW) to the main door. The progress of his 'Black Hat Sect' brand of simplified feng shui will be examined in the next chapter.

In, or soon after, 1996 Jon Sandifer (1953-2012)[1] introduced Nine Star Ki to the UK, which he and William Spear taught at the East-West Centre in Clerkenwell, London. Nine Star Ki was a Japanese variation on Chinese feng shui which had been modified by Michio Kushi, the founder of macrobiotics. Instead of dividing the site into 8 equally divided segments (or Palaces), the cardinal points were give a much wider arc, and the inter-cardinal directions (NW, SW, NE, SE) were much narrower. The system concentrated on birthdates and personality types, and is really more like a form of astrology than feng shui. In the early days, a certain amount of 'soft' feng shui[2] was also taught by the same people involved in Nine Star Ki,[3] such as William Spear's 'intuitive feng shui.' This is not feng shui in any classical sense of the word, as feng shui is a very

---

[1] Sadly Jon passed away just as this book was being prepared for press on 15th September 2012.

[2] By 'soft' feng shui I mean that which concentrates upon colours, furnishings, crystals and intuition, rather than the precise rules and directions of classical feng shui.

[3] 'Ki' by the way is exactly the same word, and the same character as ch'i (*qi*).

precise subject involving accurate measurement, not a matter of intuition.

In contrast with this approach, Tony Holdsworth was largely responsible for organising the teaching of real classical feng shui and *pa tzu* (*bazi*) in London in the late 1990s. He first encountered feng shui in 4 or 5 weekend courses on 'soft' feng shui given by William Spear in 1994/95. Tony then read one or two of the Victorian feng shui books written by missionaries who had visited Hong Kong in the middle and latter part of the 19th Century and began to think that there must be far more to feng shui than William Spear was teaching, or even knew.

A number of students from the East West Centre got together to learn more, and Gina Lazenby set up the Feng Shui Network and then the Feng Shui Society. Gina was a professional PR, and so made sure that the Society was properly launched and promoted. She was later to become the author of a number of feng shui interior design books including the *Feng Shui House Book*, which sold very well. Tony took an active part in opening up branches of the Society in Stratford-upon-Avon, Cheltenham and Edinburgh. Subsequently Graham Dunn and Jan Cisek took over the Society from Gina and reformed a committee with a few other people. For a while the Society was run by Simon Brown, then Sylvia Bennett, and in 2012 the current chairman was Raymond Catchpole.

It was during these courses held by the Feng Shui Society in 1995 and early 1996 that Tony began to search for a serious feng shui master. Derek Walters, who knew a lot about Chinese astrology, and who had written a *Feng Shui Handbook* as well as the classic book on *Chinese Astrology*, had spoken at one London meeting of the Society, so Tony contacted Derek in the early summer of 1996. They decided to start a serious course in Stratford-upon-Avon teaching genuine Chinese astrology and feng shui. By this time, Derek had started teaching feng shui and Chinese astrology in Munich, Germany, and so the course was planned with him teaching 6 weekends. Other guest teachers (Roger Coghill, Peter Firebrace, Fred Gettings and Richard Creightmore) taught associated subjects over a further 3 weekends.

Derek Walters came from a family with long standing sinological interests, and had originally learnt his feng shui and Chinese astrology from Master Richard Tsui in Hong Kong. Richard practised as a diviner and feng shui man at the temple of Wong Tai Tsin in Kowloon, Hong Kong (built in 1921 and recently refurbished), where his niece still practises to this day.

At the same time, Tony was still actively searching for a Chinese feng shui master. Tony interviewed Lam Kam Chuen, who taught Ch'i K'ung (*Qigong*) and practised acupuncture and herbal medicine in London. Lam had written a book entitled *The Feng Shui Handbook*, which was, of course, confusingly the same title as Derek's own book published some years earlier. However, whilst

Master Lam was plainly an expert in his field, his knowledge of feng shui maybe seemed rather superficial.

It was in the autumn of 1996 that Tony found Master Chan Kun Wah, a Chinese feng shui master. The story of how Master Chan began practising professionally is rather amusing. Master Chan's master from Hong Kong, Master Chue Yen, had, before he died, told Master Chan that he would become a professional feng shui master from a very specific date in July 1996. By this time, Master Chan owned a Chinese restaurant which was very popular in Edinburgh. However, with the prediction that he should begin to practice feng shui professionally from that date in July, he sold his restaurant and leased the premises to a Spanish restaurateur. Apparently his wife, Yin Yi, was extremely concerned, since she really didn't think they would generate sufficient income to live on. The appointed date in July passed with no telephone calls or contacts requesting consultations, but at 9am on the following day, the *Scotsman* newspaper called and asked for an interview in order to immediately publish a one page article on him.

It was from this article that he met Tony who helped to launch his professional career. After meeting up in Edinburgh it was decided that Tony would organise feng shui consultations for him in England: up to that time, he had not consulted for any Westerners. Master Chan accordingly went south to England in October 1996 and Tony proceeded to organise all his consultations. At one time they had a waiting list of 18 months.

While Tony was organising Master Chan's consultations, he was also running the classes in classical feng shui and *pa tzu* (*bazi*) being taught by Derek Walters. Derek also had sufficient command of Chinese to read relevant feng shui texts, and be able to interpret the *Tung Shu* or Almanac for his students. These classes ran fortnightly, for up to a year, and gave students a good grounding.

At the same time Master Chan continued to do consultations. I published the details of one such consultation in the first issue of the magazine *Feng Shui for Modern Living*. On this occasion I went with him, as an observer, whilst he did the feng shui of a 6 million pound house in London's Holland Park. I was impressed by his careful recording of the house's features in fine Chinese calligraphy, although a bit surprised that he did not have a detailed plan of the house to work from. We discussed the ch'i flow of the adjacent street, the lack of support behind the house, and the usefulness or otherwise of mirrors from a feng shui perspective (there were a number of mirrors in the house).

Tony soon realised that Master Chan knew far more than had been published, or made available in the West up to that time, and persuaded Chan to teach Yuen Hom style feng shui,[1] to students who had done the first year course

[1] Cantonese for Hsüan Kung (Xuan Kong) feng shui.

with Derek. These courses (which soon developed into a three-year syllabus) were run by Tony's School of Feng Shui in Stratford-upon-Avon, beginning at Chinese New Year, on February 7th 1997. In 1998, they opened in London as well, with more advanced courses running from 2000. Tony handed over the running of the School and the main teaching to Kajal Sheth in 2001/2002, but from those early days in Stratford-upon-Avon, some 23 schools teaching classical feng shui in 19 countries have since evolved.[1]

In 1996 Michael and Helen Oon invited Lillian Too to come to the UK. In those days she was not very well known even in her home town of KL. I remember one of the first things she said to me when we met, was that my *Living Earth Manual of Feng Shui* was the first feng shui book that she had read. Several years later, I ran a number of promotional articles and special offers in *Feng Shui for Modern Living,* which helped establish her on the international scene. I also arranged to connect her with Cico, one of her main UK publishers. Meanwhile Michael and Helen Oon also arranged for Master Raymond Lo to visit the UK in the late 1990s after he had been teaching in Hong Kong.

The most detailed book on the lo p'an published since Feuchtwang and Needham was the translation of Professor Cheng Jian Jun's book on the lo p'an into English in a limited edition organised by Adriana Fernandes-Gonçalves in Perth in 1998. This was however sadly afflicted by many errors.[2]

Man Ho Kwok, an excellent Chinese scholar who certainly knew better, and for whom I have great respect, collaborated with Joan O'Brien in 1999 to produce a little book called *Feng Shui: an Introductory Guide*. Surprisingly they only copied their lo p'an ring descriptions from a previous and inadequate English source, and in doing so, abbreviated the ring descriptions so much that she completely destroyed the meaning of many of them. Errors abound, such as the confusion of 'Pool' and 'Plate' or 'hexagrams' and 'trigrams.' It is a great pity that Man Ho Kwok allowed his co-author to butcher existing but sketchy English sources, rather than writing ring descriptions translated directly from his own knowledge, or from reliable Chinese sources.

Interest in feng shui in the UK came to full fruition with the publication in 1998 by me of the magazine *Feng Shui for Modern Living*.

[1] Apart from Master Chan, the main master Tony Holdsworth studied with was Master Chen Ho Chou from Taipei, who he originally met, with Derek, at the World Yi Jing Conference in 2001, which was held in Wu Shan, not far from Luoyang, in China.

[2] The English edition suffered from a fairly disorganised layout and a number of translation errors, and was only available in a limited edition. The main information sources for this book were Pa He Ming (1997) in Chinese; and in English, books by Joseph Needham, Derek Walters, and the present author.

Figure 60: Two issues of the magazine *Feng Shui for Modern Living*, the original English edition (1998-2001).

Figure 61: Two issues of the syndicated Chinese edition (1999-2003) of the magazine *Feng Shui for Modern Living*.

This magazine was predominantly sold in the UK and US, but at its peak it was distributed in 42 counties worldwide with sales of more than 120,000 audited copies monthly. In addition to these sales, I licensed a Chinese edition, which was printed in Taipei, and a German edition, both of which sold well in their respective markets. The Chinese edition in fact ran for longer than the original English edition.

To promote the magazine we ran a poster campaign in the London underground with full-size posters running in every central tube station, and most outlying stations. We backed that up with a PR campaign that saw massive coverage in national newspapers, and full pages in the Express, plus TV appearances on every TV channel but one. The launch party in the Gardens on top of the old Biba building in Kensington High Street, London, was filmed by Sky TV and even China TV. Martin Wood helped with the promotion of both the Conference and the magazine, having been responsible for finding the amazing PR company who got us so much TV and newspaper exposure. By the time the first issue hit the streets, a lot more people in London knew about feng shui than had ever known just a few months before. We outsold *Elle Deco*, by a considerable margin, and had to rush through a second printing to meet the demand, something almost unheard of in magazine publishing. In 1999, I was nominated by PPA for 'Publisher of the Year,' the print equivalent of getting an Oscar nomination.

Figure 62: The program for the London International Feng Shui Conference from 21-23 May 1999 which had 23 speakers and 46 lectures or workshops running over 3 days.

At the same time as publishing the magazine, I launched the ambitious London International Feng Shui Conference in May 1999. Over 23 lecturers were invited to present more than 46 lectures and workshops. We kept 4 lecture halls running continuously every day for three days, giving the attendees a choice at any one time, of a Beginners, Intermediate or Advanced lecture.

The fourth hall hosted rather more specialised seminars such as 'On Reading Ancient Feng Shui Texts' given by Dr Michael Paton of Sydney University, or a seminar on the San He lo p'an ably given by Howard Choy. The Beginners lectures, as one might have guessed, were more concerned with feng shui symbols, colour, and Eight Mansion feng shui.

There were also talks on 'Flying Star and San Yuan' (Tony Holdsworth); the 'Four Pillars of Destiny' (Master Raymond Lo); the 'Application of the *I Ching* to Modern Living' (Master Koh Pu Lin); 'Eight Mansions Feng Shui' (Master Yap Chen Hai); 'Chinese Astrology' (Derek Walters) and 'Compass Feng Shui' (Roger Green). Martin Wood helped with the promotion of both the Conference and the magazine, having been responsible for finding the amazing PR company who got us so much TV and newspaper exposure.

The publication of the magazine helped to introduce readers to the *Tung shu*, (sections from which were featured and explained in each issue), the lo p'an, and more advanced form of feng shui such as Flying Star. At around the same time Mark Shakelford contacted me at the magazine, as he had started to program some of the first feng shui programs, based on my earlier books. Whilst my magazine was being published from 1998 to 2001, feng shui practitioners began to attract quite serious clients, like British Airways, Hiscox Insurance, Jerry Hall (ex-wife of Mick Jagger)[1] and the famous China White nightclub.

It was Renuka who did the feng shui of a rather unpromising basement under the Café Royal in Regent Street, London, which became China White. Its main entrance was a non-descript door opening into Air Street, a side alley. Renuka realised that the initial feng shui of the premises was not brilliant and set about remedying that in Autumn 1998. Because it was a very yin site, feng shui adjustments had to be made more definite, so for example, instead of one wind chime, a small forest of wind chimes was employed in the appropriate position. China White opened as a club just before Christmas, for one or two test parties, and then opened for real in January of the New Year. Within a week it was jam-packed. A combination of much improved feng shui and good marketing meant that by February it was the talk of the town. Renuka did warn the owners Rory Keegan and John Snow that after Period change in 2004 it would need a revamp, but that was not acted on, so when it moved to

[1] Done by Robert Gray.

a new site off Oxford Street, it never retrieved its earlier success. On the strength of her earlier successes, Renuka was also hired to do the same for Movida nightclub and the Cinnamon club in London.

An Indian restaurant in the fashionable Kings Road called Vama became hugely successful after Renuka did the feng shui for the opening. The owners were dubious about also having the feng shui of their office changed, but within a month of doing that the restaurant became very fashionable. The owners happily confirmed a 30% increase in takings. Masala Zone received the same treatment and became another success, now with multiple branches in London. Nightclubs and restaurants were definitely Renuka's speciality. She did a 'resuscitation' on Riccardo's restaurant, and its VIP room specially designed for Al Pacino, which is still going strong.

Renuka's feng shui also helped a lot of couples to conceive the babies they wanted. Other clients included a Swiss bank, and the accounts man on the Formula 1 racing team.

Jimmy Choo, the well known shoemaker to the stars, kindly wrote a preface to my 2001 book, *The KISS Guide to Feng Shui.* In the preface Jimmy, who had long been very concerned with the feng shui of his office and shops, attributed much of his good fortune to this practice.

In 2003, when my book *Flying Star Feng Shui* was published, Mark Shakelford completed a series of sophisticated programs which generated Flying Star charts from simple inputs like build year and facing compass reading, based on that book.[1]

[1] These programs are still available on www.fengshui-magazine.com.

European Feng Shui

At the same time as feng shui was flourishing in the UK, it was also making huge strides in Europe. For some unaccountable reason the French never seemed very interested in the subject, except for François Martel, who in 1972, described and analysed some of the rings of a lo p'an from the Collection Musée de l'Homme.[1]

However, Germany and particularly Austria could not get enough of it. A long history of sinological interest in Germany must have helped, but the initial breakthrough came with the publishing of a German translation of my *Living Earth Manual of Feng Shui* by Trikont Verlag under the title *Chinesische Geomantie: Die gesamte Lehre des Feng-Shui* in 1986.

People were not very clear about what feng shui was in those days, so soon after I got invited to give a lecture on feng shui in Austria on the strength of the German edition of my book. The lectures were very well supported, being held in a magnificent schloss deep in Austria, with attendees from around the globe. When I arrived I realised that most of the other lecturers were there to talk about ley lines and megalithic monuments. Far from feeling left out, many of the audience seemed to be intrigued by my illustrations of sinuous curving rivers and mountain dragons, whilst the other lecturers were concerned only with straight alignments, or megalithic circles. When I explained that straight alignments caused *sha ch'i* a lot of ears pricked up. Although I gave my talk in English there were simultaneous translations into German and other European languages.

Other lecturers included the late John Michell, whose *View of Atlantis* had sparked the original interest in ley lines, following on from the work of Alfred Watkins. John had also published a reprint of Eitel's *Feng Shui,* and so he was well aware of what I was talking about. Later that night, after a sumptuous meal, we were driven to yet another schloss which was reserved for lecturers and the family of the Graf (Count) von Thurn und Taxis who were hosting the event. Conversations late into the night in front of a roaring log fire set in a huge stone fireplace in a 17th century setting are amongst my fondest memories of that particular lecture trip.

From May 1998 there was an International Feng Shui Congress at Starnberg, in Bavaria, near Munich in Germany. The event included a number of lecturers from a mix of classical feng shui (Evelyn Lip; Derek Walters; Jes Lim and Roger Green) plus a BHS and 'soft' feng shui contingent (led by Lin Yun; David Kennedy; Jami Lin; Denise Linn; Angel Thompson and Nancy Santo Pietro).

One of the most memorable European feng shui Conferences, however, was

[1] Martel, François. "Les Boussoles Divinatoires Chinoises" in *Communications*, 19, Paris, 1972.

the World Congress & Exhibition: Feng Shui Experience 2000 held in Innsbruck, Austria. A lot of thought was put into this event by Andreas Hager, and apart from a hall of exhibitors, large sculptures and water features abounded. This time classical feng shui predominated (with Derek Walters; Roger Green; Master Yap Cheng Hai; Master Raymond Lo; Master Victor Dy; Marc Häberlin; Jes Lim and Master Chan Kun Wah) with a smattering of BHS and 'soft' feng shui (represented by Lin Yun; William Spear; Denise Linn; Jami Lin). Added to these was an interesting range of vaguely associated subjects (Thomas Schopf on 'Feng Shui Design'; Dr Balikrishnan on 'Revitalisation of Towns and Cities'; Marc Häberlin on 'The Psychology of the Five Transformations'; Sashikala Anath on the 'Principles of Vastu Design,' and many others). One of the most interesting academic speakers was Dr Manfred Kubny who spoke on date selection. He was a very knowledgeable sinologist who read classical Chinese and had written extensively about ch'i in German.

Both Poland and Russia began their interest with classical feng shui, rather than BHS. In Poland Jacek Kryg, originally an academic, was to a large extent responsible for the spread of feng shui in that country, with some of the first book translations into Polish. My *Water Dragon* translation was translated into Polish by Malgorzata Bladek.

In Russia, in the early days of feng shui Derek Walters taught Chinese astrology. More recently Anatoly Sokolov was responsible for importing a number of well-known S E Asia feng shui masters to talk in Moscow. At a one week seminar he arranged, which I conducted on Flying Star feng shui, I was surprised at the high level of knowledge and questions which I experienced.

Other organisers arranged classes for imported masters in St. Petersburg and Kiev in the Ukraine. A number of feng shui books in English have been translated into Russian, including ones by Master Raymond Lo, and at least four by me.

Feng shui in Italy has been slow to take off, but a weekend seminar I did in Bologna in 2011 showed that whilst BHS surprisingly still has a considerable hold there, the number of classically trained feng shui practitioners is steadily increasing.

It is easy to tell immediately from where an audience has come for a feng shui lecture. An American or Russian audience will be almost 90% female, a UK audience will be mixed but with a preponderance of females, but a German or Austrian audience will for the most part be male. I can only think that this is a reflection on the sort of feng shui taught originally in each of those countries.

Feng Shui goes Pop in the US

I have to declare that I could not have written this chapter in such detail if it was not for the help of my old friend Dennis Fairchild. Denny was the US columnist for the magazine *Feng Shui for Modern Living* which I published from 1998-2001, and he also used to write a long running feng shui column for another magazine. Therefore he had his finger very much on the pulse of what was going on in feng shui in the US. He is the author of more than ten books, including *Healing Homes* and *Feng Shui Here & Now,* and has appeared on National Radio, CNN, and the Tonight Show with Johnny Carson.

At the beginning of 1849 there were, according to the statistics, only 54 Chinese in California. By 1876, news of the gold rush had spread across the world and the Chinese in the United States numbered 151,000, of whom 116,000 were in the state of California. This increase was partly due to the presence of gold, and partly to the fact that prior to 1869 it was faster, and safer, to travel from China to California than it was to travel overland from the east coast of the US. An additional incentive for Chinese to migrate was the huge disruption and subsequent poverty caused by the Taiping Rebellion from 1850-1864. Suffice it to say that many Chinese customs, including feng shui, travelled with those migrants. However, with very few exceptions, the knowledge of feng shui, especially burial feng shui, was kept a closely-guarded secret within the Chinese community.

Even the missionary books written about feng shui in the late 19th century did not make much impact in the US, and there does not appear to have been any academic interest in feng shui except for that of the geographer Andrew March.[1]

In the 1960s, the *I Ching,* acupuncture, Buddhism and kung fu, especially the latter, opened the eyes of America to the fact that western scientific knowledge was not the sum human knowledge. People began to realise that a civilisation such as China, many thousands of years older than the US, had a lot to offer.

1976

Globe-trotting astrologer Angel Thompson begins teaching feng shui classes in Los Angeles, and edits a New Age glossy newsletter with a feng shui focus, called *Gentle Breeze.*

The first thesis on classical feng shui is submitted to an American university, by Korean Dr. Hong-key Yoon.

1982

Some copies of the Routledge edition of my *Living Earth Manual of Feng Shui* begin to cross the Atlantic and spark interest in feng shui in the US.

[1] See March (1968).

1983

Feng shui first becomes a household word in the US thanks to Sarah Rossbach's book, *Feng Shui: the Art of Placement.*[1] It was this book that introduced Lin Yun and 'Black Hat Sect' feng shui to the American audience.

1985 - 2004

Launch of the first syndicated feng shui newspaper column, *Making Waves with Feng Shui* by Dennis Fairchild.[2]

1986

'Professor' Thomas Lin Yun founds the Yun Lin Temple in Berkeley, California, which is referred to as a reformist 'Black Hat Sect Tantric Buddhist temple.' Lin Yun set about simplifying classical feng shui, by removing the lo p'an or feng shui compass, and thereby destroying its basic rationale. The resultant 'Black Hat Sect Tantric Buddhist' (BHS) feng shui struck a chord with the American public and the movement begins to grow. Lin Yun becomes a millionaire. Soon, to the confusion of many readers, there are books on both BHS feng shui and classical feng shui on the bookshelves.

1987

Sarah Rossbach's *Interior Design with Feng Shui* came out. With this book the floodgates really opened with the hundreds of BHS feng shui books to follow.

1989

A number of feng shui schools are set up, mostly derived from Lin Yun's BHS feng shui, with an increasing and irrelevant input of environmental and New Age concerns. Typical of these is the still active Pyramid School of Feng Shui, founded by Nancilee Wydra with a mix of traditional feng shui tenets and socially aware environmental sciences.

Of the more than 1000 books on feng shui published in English since 1989, few have been written on traditional feng shui. Most of these (especially those produced in the US) have been written from the point of view of either simplified 'Life Aspirations' feng shui, or 'Black Hat Sect.' This movement will be examined in the next chapter in more detail.

Angi Ma Wong, author of 25 books, who has appeared on Oprah, CNN, CBS, establishes a feng shui consultancy.

1990

Lillian Too and Evelyn Lip books arrive in American bookstores; both were

[1] Sarah Rossbach currently writes for the *New York Times, Washington Post, House & Garden* and *Harper's Bazaar.*
[2] *phenomeNews*, a national New Age monthly.

highly promoted authors in Borders. Too's *Complete Illustrated Guide to Feng Shui* achieves record sales, and spreads a more traditional '*Pa Kua Lo Shu*' and simplified Eight Mansion view of feng shui.

1991

The American Feng Shui Institute is founded by Master Larry Sang in Monterey Park, California to teach Compass School feng shui as a scientific discipline.[1] It brings an awareness of yin feng shui (ancestor and grave feng shui) to the US. He publishes his first book, *The Principles of Feng Shui* in 1994. Currently, Master Sang is the Yin House feng shui consultant for SCI, one of the largest memorial park companies in the world. In 2005 Master Sang was appointed to an advisory position on the board of the China Architectural Culture Centre in Beijing. He also received a Ph.D. for his work on the *I Ching*. He has spoken at seminars which were jointly sponsored by the University of Southern California and the Northrop University.

Nancilee Wydra launches the Feng Shui Institute of America (FSIA), one of the first professional feng shui certification schools in America. Throughout the 1990s, Wydra's writings appeared in *Cosmopolitan, Better Homes and Gardens* and *Natural Health*. She has been consulted by Fortune 500 companies including Coty and Bed, Bath and Beyond.

1993

James Moser debuts America's first feng shui product company, the Feng Shui Warehouse, retailing feng shui cures like wind chimes, flutes and crystals from the East.[2]

1995

James Moser publishes the first US feng shui magazine, the *Feng Shui Journal*.

1996

Eva Wong, an American originally from Hong Kong, brings out *Feng-Shui: the Ancient Wisdom of Harmonious Living for Modern Times*. By explaining the lo p'an and the setting up of a Flying Stars chart, and integrating it with Form feng shui, Eva brings a breath of fresh air to the subject by setting feng shui in the context of its Taoist roots.

Kwan Lau's *Feng Shui for Today* is published. Lau is reputed to have applied feng shui to the renovation of the Empire State Building.

---

[1] Notable instructors taught by Master Sang include Lorraine Wilcox and Kartar Diamond (author of some dozen books on traditional feng shui).

[2] James had moved from the Big Island of Hawai'i, where land he owned on the rather remote Kalapana side had got buried under a lava flow, rendering it totally uninhabitable. Fortunately for James, the lava flow was slow in reaching his homestead and he had plenty of time to stuff his 4-wheel drive as full of his possessions as he could possibly fit, before fleeing to safety.

Karen Kingston makes 'clutter clearing' fashionable, and moves to Bali for 20 years, where she gives classes on the subject. Her two international bestselling books, *Creating Sacred Space with Feng Shui* and *Clear Your Clutter with Feng Shui* (1998) have each sold over one million copies worldwide since.

Lin Yun establishes the Lin Yun Monastery in Long Island, New York.

James Moser organises America's First International Feng Shui Conference in San Diego, California.

The Western Guide to Feng Shui, a 'soft' feng shui title by Terah Kathryn Collins sells 100,000 copies in 10 weeks.

1997

James Moser organises America's Second International Feng Shui Conference in Palm Springs, California.

1998

Feng Shui For Modern Living magazine comes to American bookshelves and raises the bar on standards, ethics, and public interest. The magazine almost sells out at a price far higher than many other US magazines.

Yap Cheng Hai, Larry Sang, and Raymond Lo are frequent teachers to a variety of national venues, and become the strongest advocates of classical feng shui in the US throughout the late 1990s.

Sarah Rossbach's *Feng Shui Design: From History and Landscape to Modern Gardens and Interiors* becomes another hit.

Donald Trump, interviewed on national TV, on NBC's Nightline, says feng shui "was recommended by our Asian buyers, and people started asking about feng shui. I don't have to believe in feng shui, but I use it because it makes me money." Trump subsequently hired Manhattan feng shui Master Pun-Yin to work on the Trump Tower. As a result the main entrance was placed facing Central Park which then acts as its *ming tang* to receive positive ch'i.

National Feng Shui Awareness Day instituted in North America.[1]

1999

In May, James Moser organises his 3rd Annual International Feng Shui Conference in Monterey California, gaining considerable national media recognition and attention in the US.

The *Miriam-Webster Collegiate Dictionary* includes 'feng shui' as a main entry.

Oprah announces that she won't let her boyfriend have a TV in her Lake

---

[1] National Speaker's Board.

Michigan condo bedroom, "because it's bad feng shui."

Master Yap Cheng Hai's Feng Shui Center of Excellence begins teaching in the US.

US books on traditional classical feng shui start appearing in the US, beginning with the *Idiot's Guide to Feng Shui* by Elizabeth Moran and Val Biktashev (and in later editions Joseph Yu). These books concentrate upon Eight Mansions, Four Pillar analysis, Flying Star, and associated techniques. Few mention the lo p'an in any detail, and if they do, still restrict their remarks to the first two or three rings only, just taking in the basic 8 trigram ring and its relationship to the Lo Shu.

2000

David Twicken publishes his book on the *Flying Stars.* Lily Chung publishes *Calendars for Feng Shui,* and teaches a updated form of *pa tzu (bazi).*

Chuck Lorrie of ABC TV reveals to reporters that he hired James Moser and Angel Thompson to feng shui and 'space clear' for the sitcom, *Dharma & Greg.*

2001

James Moser's 4th International Feng Shui Conference, Orlando, Florida.

In California the Getty Center opens to the public, with feng shui design by architect Richard Meier. *Feng Shui for Modern Living* does a major article on it.

Juan Alvarez publishes a feng shui Almanac: *Feng Shui: the Ten Thousand Years Manual.*

2003

Nancilee Wydra dubbed "most published American author of feng shui" by Amazon.com.

2004

California Assemblyman Leland Yee proposes a resolution that would require California's building standards to promote feng shui principles. It fails to pass, but draws a lot of attention to feng shui.

2005

In August, Roger Green hosts an International Feng Shui Conference in San Diego, with a range of teachers, 400 attendees, but poor reviews.

2007

Fun Shui, US's premiere weekly feng shui TV decorating show, begins its first season on HGTV; hosted by Stephanie McWilliams, with a BHS orientation.

2008

Multi-billion dollar company Canon Europe enlists US based consultant, Dr.

Simona F. Mainini, for a re-design to remedy employee office stress and rage.

2009

Master Chi-Jen Liu completes a feng shui remodel for Hacienda Heights, California McDonald's franchise.

2010

New York's Metropolitan Institute of Design becomes the only US feng shui certificate program to be licensed by the New York State Department of Education.

2011

The following businesses publicly acknowledge their use of feng shui in 2011: ABC; AT & T; Borders Bookstore; Chase Manhattan; Citibank; CNN; Coca Cola; D. R. Horton Homes; Eli Lilly; Federal Express; Fuji; Hill Holliday; Honeywell; Hyatt Hotels; Hyatt Regency; IBM; Intel Corp; Lucent Technologies; MGM Grand Hotel and Resorts; Mercedes Benz; Merrill Lynch; Business Guides Microsoft; Motorola; Nike Corp; Shell Oil; Trump Towers; Universal Studios; W Hotels; Walt Disney.[1]

2012

It was announced that the Bellagio and the Wynn Hotel, both built by Steve Wynn, were constructed under the watchful eyes of feng shui masters.

Figure 63: The late James Allyn Moser was largely responsible for the spread of feng shui in the US. He organised the first four influential International Feng Shui Conferences in the US.

[1] According to Polaris media records.

Black Hat Sect Tantric Buddhist Feng Shui

Black Hat Sect 'feng shui' needs to have a section by itself, because although it is not part of the history of classical feng shui, the fact that it, for a while, took centre stage in the US as a sort of over-simplified feng shui, makes it a part of that history. I contemplated leaving it out entirely, but it affected so many people in the US (and some outside), that I felt I had an obligation to record its progress. Elliot Tanzer very kindly responded to my queries about Black Hat Sect feng shui (BHS for short), and so I have him to thank for some of the following chapter. It helped spread feng shui in the US, for which we can be thankful, but delayed an appreciation of what feng shui was really about.

BHS basically did away with the lo p'an, the feng shui compass, and by doing so disqualified itself from being considered as part of real classical feng shui. It involved a lot of practices borrowed from Buddhism such as prayer, blessings, red packets, beads, crystals and so on. However the mere fact of a home owner deliberately re-arranging the contents of his home with the firm intention to improve his marriage, wealth, luck and so on, backed up by blessings and prayer would have had an effect anyway. This effect, however, is due to the religious and magical elements of the procedure, rather than the redirection or accumulation of ch'i according to the rules of feng shui.

By claiming Buddhist and Tibetan roots, the true Taoist origin of feng shui, and its precise methods which require exact compass directions, are obscured. The title of his movement neatly sums up what was then the current aspirations and interests of the American New Age public. Buddhism, which had been made famous by Jack Kerouac's novels in the 1960s, had become popular in the US, with a number of genuine monasteries setting up in California. 'Tantric' obviously had attractive sexual overtones. The 'Black Hat' referred to the Kamapa lineage of Tibetan Buddhism, and 'Sect' reflected the rather inward turning guru worshipping aspects of BHS.

However Chinese feng shui has much deeper roots in Taoism, than in either Buddhism or Tantra. It is certainly true that many Buddhist monks know and use feng shui, but the cosmological basis of feng shui is totally Taoist. The only historical connection between feng shui and Tibetan Buddhism is a method of 5 Element Divination contributed to Tibetan culture in the 9th century CE,[1] a method which anyway does not appear on Lin Yun's syllabus. Despite the fact that Lin Yun later began to refer to himself as 'His Holiness Rinpoche,'[2] he had no direct lineage links with Karmapa Black Hat Sect

[1] For details of this see Stephen Skinner, *Tibetan Oracle Pack,* Carroll & Brown, 2005.

[2] Although Lin Yun is definitely not part of the Tibetan Karmapa Black Hat Sect lineage, as confirmed by an email exchange I had with Tai Situ, he does have a Bon entitlement to adopt the title Rinpoche. In 1998 His Holiness Lungtok Tenpai Nyima Rinpoche, the supreme leader of the Bon religion, led four high lamas to the United States from India to conduct enthronement ceremonies, one in the Yun Lin Temple in Berkeley, California, and the other in the Lin Yun Monastery in Long Island, New York.

Tibetan Buddhism. In due course he attempted to drop the 'Hat' from the title of his movement.

His version of the art (which has little if anything to do with Tibetan Black Hat Karmapa Sect teachings, and not much to do with classical feng shui), was devised as recently as 1986 by Thomas Lin Yun (1932-2010). This version specifically removes the difficulties of teaching the lo p'an to Westerners. The basic premise of "Black Hat Sect Tibetan Buddhist feng shui" is that you don't need to know the compass directions, but simply interpret the front door as 'North' (or NW or NE), and proceed from there. Practitioners accordingly sometimes refer to the system as '3-Door Bagua.' Although this helped greatly to promote feng shui in the US, it delayed any real understanding of traditional feng shui, or knowledge of the lo p'an, for some considerable time. Even now, the majority of Americans who have heard of feng shui still think of Black Hat Sect as the real thing.

Lin Yun was born in Beijing of Taiwanese parents working for the Taiwan Cultural Association. At the age of six he was enrolled at the Yonghe Gong Lamasery of the Yellow Hat Sect of Lamaist Buddhism in Beijing. At the lamasery he was introduced to feng shui, and at the age of 17 he left to return to Taiwan. Because he attempted to combine elements of Buddhism, Taoism, fortune-telling, medicine and colour theory to construct his own brand of feng shui, he was (according to himself) ostracised by other practitioners.[1] He also took to prophesying the outcome of various political races, rather unsuccessfully, and in one interview referred ruefully to himself as a failed prophet.

He moved to Hong Kong where a rather less regulated atmosphere allowed him to practice his unique brand of feng shui. Although classical feng shui relies simply upon physical elements, location and direction, Lin Yun's version incorporated blessings and forms of practice much closer to spiritual practices than classical feng shui. The same newspaper report confirmed that "although his Black Sect beliefs have been widely rejected in Asia, Lin Yun has found a more receptive following in the West."

It was in Hong Kong in 1977 that he met Sarah Rossbach, who encouraged him to come to the US to teach, an invitation that formed the entrée to his later career. By opening his temple in Berkeley, California he was able to take advantage of the free-thinking student population of that town. As Ole Bruun put it, "Lin Yun swopped the Hawaii shirts of his Hong Kong days with [black] Chinese silk Mandarin jackets."

An indication of the degree of confusion introduced by BHS feng shui can be seen in the book of one of its students. Susan Levitt's *Taoist Feng Shui* had very little Taoist material in it. She proceeds to retail various pieces of ill-digested

[1] *Chinese Daily News,* Issue 7110, 8 July 1997, Tainan City, Taiwan.

Buddhism, derived from Lin Yun, and re-label them as 'Taoist,' enough said.

According to Elliot Tanzer, even before Sarah Rossbach discovered him, Lin Yun often came to the US to teach at various university including Harvard and Yale. His subjects included T'ang Dynasty poetry, *I Ching*, Tantric Buddhist meditation, and feng shui. Although I have not been able to verify that, it was on this basis that he referred to himself as Professor.

Figure 64: The late Lin Yun photographed demonstrating a mudra whilst being interviewed by the editors of the Chinese edition of my magazine *Feng Shui for Modern Living* in 2001.

It is revealing however that Black Hat Sect feng shui never attracted any Chinese converts: all of Lin Yun's students were American. His mixture of so many disparate elements, like Buddhism, Tantra, meditation, mudra, mantra and blessings, made BHS an ideal New Age product.

However, things have begun to change. Of the 130 feng shui US practitioners listed recently (2012) on a well known website, 103 claimed to practice Classical compass based feng shui, but only 23 adhered to the Black Hat School of feng shui. Strangely, four practitioners maintained that they practiced both systems, without apparently seeing any conflict in that view.

Feng Shui Down Under in Australia

Although I was born and grew up in Australia, I have been away from that country for many years. Accordingly, the following brief history of feng shui in Australia is drawn largely from the work of feng shui scholar Tyler J Rowe.

Feng shui had an early beginning in Australia, which is perhaps one of the first countries outside of Asia where it was practiced. Before the American gold-rush, in the mid-1850s, thousands of Chinese immigrants flocked to Victoria, Australia, in search of gold. Many of these came from Fukien and Kiangsi,[1] provinces close to the coastal ports, both of which were also intimately associated with the history of San He feng shui. The country town of Bendigo in Victoria, Australia which was known as 小金山 *Hsiao Chin Shan* (*Xiaojinshan*) 'Little Gold Mountain' (second only to California in the US, the 'Big Gold Mountain'), became the location of the first Chinese settlements in Australia. With this came two important structures whose location was determined by feng shui: the gravesite and the temple.

Two of Australia's oldest Chinese temples dating to the 1860s and known locally as 'Joss Houses,' still stand in their original locations showing evidence of feng shui orientation. Both the Emu Point, Bendigo and the South Melbourne sites demonstrate southward orientations, are situated on elevated land (originally with rear support from local landforms, now lost to later developments) and bodies of water in close proximity facing them. Their architecture is designed to auspicious measurements, arranged to prevent the ingress of *sha ch'i* (*shaqi*) or 'noxious vapours' and the interiors are decorated extensively with Chinese colours and symbols of prosperity or fortune.[2]

A number of Chinese gravesites of the same gold-rush era also display feng shui influences. While the graveyard sections made available for Chinese burial at the White Hills, Bendigo, Maldon and Campbell's Creek sites were limited, they are all situated on gentle slopes with support to the North and headstones facing southward. All have natural water courses situated in the facing directions and nearby hexagonal burning towers for the offering of joss paper. The goldfield Chinese were known to possess and utilise the *Tung shu,* the Chinese Almanac, for the purposes of selecting the best interment dates.

Over the years that followed feng shui's use continued within the Chinese communities of Australia, as is evidenced by numerous examples of door tilting, *pa kua* mirror placement and auspicious statues, especially in the Chinatowns of Sydney, Melbourne and other state capitals.

The practice of feng shui was still largely unknown and unseen by the

[1] Fujian and Jiangxi.
[2] Groves (1991).

Western population, though one possible exception may be in the planning of the nation's capital, Canberra. It is known that the Chicago based architect credited with the initial design in 1911, Walter Burley Griffin, used the principles of geometry, perhaps sacred geometry, in designing the layout of the city. It has been suggested that his team may also have employed feng shui techniques in the project. It is clear that the husband and wife duo had long been exposed to eastern architectural principles and landscape artwork in their education and professional work. This lead them to create concept drawings on this theme, applying ideas of a north-south central axis, a hierarchical system of building placement, consideration of the location of five sacred mountains and the creation of a central lake.[1]

As Chinese business interests began to arrive in Australia so too did a plethora of Cantonese feng shui masters bought in to consult on a number of big projects including offices, hotels, casinos and an authentic Chinese Garden, one of the few outside of the mainland.

The 谊园 Yi Yuan Chinese Garden of Friendship, Darling Harbour Sydney, was originally designed in the early 1980s, utilising the combined efforts of local Chinese community groups, the state government and 'experts' from Guandong in Southern of China. Investigations undertaken in a recent redevelopment of the gardens revealed that these Chinese consultants, while purporting no expert knowledge of feng shui (which was likely to have been a political necessity at the time), appear to have utilised at least two compass formulas, including the Flying Star and *Lung Men Pa Chü* (*Longmen ba ju*) Dragon Gate Eight Formation Water methods in its planning.[2]

In the early 1990s, Caucasian practitioners, initially trained overseas, began to emerge and it wasn't long before feng shui was taught openly in Australia for the first time. With this came a number of dedicated associations as well as training programs from visiting Asian masters. The creation of a large number of associations seems to have been a hallmark of the growth of feng shui in Australia.

The first key group to emerge was the Feng Shui Society of Australia (FSSA) established in the early 1990s. The society was formed after a visit to Australia by William Spear, whose brand of 'soft' feng shui was already being taught in London.

Howard Choy is one of the best known Chinese practitioners. Howard was born in China, and studied architecture in Sydney, whilst travelling back to Hong Kong and mainland China to apprentice himself in feng shui, *Taichi* and *Qigong*. He later founded the company Feng Shui Architects, and began the

---

[1] Proudfoot (1994).

[2] Choy (2011).

Feng Shui College of Sydney, which along with the Feng Shui College of Melbourne taught some of the first classical feng shui in Australia. Howard now lives and consults in Berlin where he has been instrumental in producing the Kan Yu and Architecture International Conference since 2010, taking over from where Dr Michael Mak's conferences left off. Howard still regularly visits Australia to run specialty workshops as well as venues throughout Europe and study tours to China.

Roger Green, perhaps best known for his inverted 'feng shui for the Southern Hemisphere' model,[1] began as a natural therapist before studying abroad and later teaching his own unique brand of feng shui at his Sydney School of Feng Shui. Roger also includes principles of Sacred Geometry in his teaching, resides in the US and teaches throughout America and Europe. With Marc Häberlin he designed an English version of the lo p'an which attempted to include BHS feng shui, Eight Mansions and a number of other things on a highly coloured, multi-ringed compass. Although this was extremely inventive, it did not catch on, as its design was so far from the traditional lo p'an that it was really only useful as a teaching aid.

Julie Rocka studied extensively with masters in South East Asia before opening the Feng Shui College of Melbourne in the early 1990s, along with the Feng Shui College of Sydney, one of the first complete schools teaching classical feng shui in Australia. With her partner and British dowser Richard Creightmore, Julie has taught in Australia and the UK which she now calls home, being based in both Sussex in the UK, and in Australia.

Gahle Atherton, a former student of Raymond Lo, was one of the first to teach the Flying Star methods in Australia in the mid 1990s. She went on to establish herself in the tough SE Asian male dominated feng shui world and now consults internationally on big developments and corporate relocations. She was one of the group that founded the IFSA in Singapore.

In late 1998 another significant group came on the scene, this time headed by Jodi Brunner. Jodi is a well known local consultant and student of Joseph Yu. The Feng Shui Network (FSN) became a global community linking feng shui practitioners and enthusiasts worldwide, at its peak boasting nearly 500 members. The FSN produced 25 regular newsletters, ran 10 Australian State Conferences and instituted the first accreditation and CPD development scheme.

---

[1] The system, which mostly reverses and inverts the existing paradigm based on seasonal, tidal and weather differences between the two hemispheres, has been widely criticized and never gained much credence outside of his own students. I did several experiments using this system, including checking the feng shui of Chinese temples in Sydney, and following Roger's ideas to their logical conclusion, by reversing my own *pa tzu* (*bazi*). I feel that climatic associations are simply helpful analogies, and not the root of the system. The sun still rises in the East and sets in the West, no matter which hemisphere you are in. As an ex-geography lecturer I was not convinced by Roger's logic.

In 1999, a new school, the Australian College of Environmental Studies (ACES) opened. It was significant as being the first college in the country to offer a government accredited certification in feng shui. The founder, former naturopath, acupuncturist and tertiary lecturer, Nicole Bijlsma, also offers recognized qualifications in Building Biology, a subject not directly related to feng shui, but dealing with the built environment from a partly scientific point of view, which had its genesis in Germany.

As a direct result of the College a fresh Association was founded in 2005: the Association of Feng Shui Consultants (AFSC) would from humble beginnings go on to become the biggest feng shui association yet in Australia. It held regular conferences and hosted seminars from national and international presenters, put out a regular newsletter and eventually went on to absorb the FSN, as well as to officially supersede the long in hibernation FSSA. In 2011 the AFSC would join forces with the Feng Shui Society (UK) and the International Feng Shui Guild (USA) to become a founding member of an innovative international initiative, the Global Feng Shui Alliance.

With the influx of international visitors teaching feng shui in Australia over recent years, particularly from Hong Kong, Singapore and Malaysia, interest grew and a place was found in 2010 for an entirely different entity to establish itself in Australia. An Australian Chapter of the International Feng Shui Association (IFSA) was set up by Janene Laird and her very competent committee. The local Chapter has since held two national Conventions highlighting local and overseas talent bringing the two regions together in lectures, social events and seminars. The popular online magazine *Feng Shui Today*,[1] is also a product of the Australian Chapter of the IFSA, and Janene's brainchild. The recent Feng Shui Convention put on by them in May 2012 had an interesting line up of speakers including Khor Tong Nee, Jerry King, Dr. Jin Peh, Juliana Abram, Melynda Munro, Tyler Rowe and Nicole Biljsma. I contributed a post convention workshop on utilising the Heaven and Man Plates of the San He lo p'an.

In recent years Australia has not been without its share of feng shui academics. Whilst many locals have produced dozens of popular manuals, the more serious academic works that are of note include:

Dr Michael Paton of the University of Sydney – his background in geology guarantees some interesting insights into feng shui classics. He has translated no less than five major feng shui classic texts of the Form School including Kuo P'o's (Guopu) *Tsang Shu* (*Zangshu*) 'The Book of Burial' and Chiang Ta Hung's (Jiang Da Hong) compilation the *Shui Lung Ching* (*Shuilongjing*) 'The Water Dragon Classic.'

[1] http://www.fengshuitoday.org/.

Zeng Yong Xing (aka Terence Chan), an Australian student of Joey Yap's, has done some important translations, already mentioned in the Malaysian chapter.

Dr Michael Mak of the University of Newcastle, is an architect, researcher and author responsible for developing Research into Scientific Feng Shui and the Built Environment analysing feng shui from a scientific perspective. He has produced two books on the subject and, in association with the City University of Hong Kong, produced a series of International Conferences bringing together some of the world's brightest academic feng shui minds.

Derham Grove's (Melbourne University department of Architecture) text *Feng-Shui and Western Building Ceremonies* has a little on some of the early practices of the Chinese in the gold rush era.

Feng Shui Around the World

In India there is a totally different tradition to feng shui, but with similar objectives, called Vastu. Its way of dividing the home into 9 or 81 squares is quite different to that of feng shui. Its 'cures' are more likely to be the placement of a god's statue or the saying of *pujas* (prayers) rather than anything related to the Chinese five Elements. Anyone who says the two systems are compatible, obviously has not studied them in depth. Nevertheless, because of the sudden fame of feng shui, a strange compromise has grown up in India. This compromise consists of using traditional Vastu to diagnose a problem, then using a feng shui 'cure' to solve it. A lot of feng shui classes now take place in India, and books like Vijayalakshmi Minocha's *Feng Shui Answers* have provided basic background.

Master Mas Kehardtham, President of the Feng Shui Institute of Thailand is reputed to run the largest feng shui teaching organisation in that country, and has a number of high profile clients. He teaches around the region in Singapore and in Australia. One of his recent talks at the 2011 IFSC in Singapore had the audience scratching its head, as he propounded a much more logical set of associations between the *pa kua* trigrams, directions and Elements. Obviously, if he was serious then the whole basis of feng shui has been called into question. But I think his real purpose was to show that sometimes you have to just accept the basic traditional assumptions, rather than trying to re-engineer them in the light of modern science or 21st century logic.

There is obviously much more that could be said about the growth of feng shui in many other regions and countries, but if I have at least shown that this ancient science is now flourishing and taken seriously outside of its traditional homeland (where it is still treated as a superstition), then I will have achieved my purpose in writing this book.

APPENDICES

Appendix I - Feng Shui Chronology and Chinese Dynasties

Traditional Emperors & Dynasties	Date	Significant feng shui event
Fu Hsi (Fu Xi)	2852-2737 BCE	Invented the 8 trigrams, the Ho T'u and Former Heaven Sequence.
Huang Ti (Huangdi) (the Yellow Emperor)	2697-2597	Hsüan Nü gives Huang Ti a compass. Traditional invention of the calendar, based on the 60-year *chia-tzu* cycle, with epoch of 2637 BCE (the zero point of the *Hsiu* Tou).
Yao	2356-2255	Set up astronomical observatories to help regulate the calendar.
Shun	2255-2205	Attempted to, but failed, to regulate the rivers.
Yü	2205-2197	Discovered the Lo Shu, Later Heaven Sequence of the trigrams, and regulated the floods
Hsia (Xia) dynasty	2150-1557	Hsia solar Calendar devised.
Shang	1557-1027	The 60 day *chia-tzu* cycle devised from 10 Heavenly Stems and 12 Earthly Branches.
Chou (Zhou)	1027-221	King Wen (1122 BCE) arranged 64 hexagrams. His son Duke Chou wrote commentary which became the *I Ching*.
		Chan pu used to found the site of Luoyang (1027 BCE).
Spring and Autumn Period	770-476	Confucius edited the *I Ching* and wrote the *Ten Wings* (c. 550 BCE). Lao Tzu wrote the *Tao Teh Ching*.
Warring States Period	476-221	Chou Yen (350-270 BCE) mentions the 5 Elements.
Ch'in (Qin)	221-206 BCE	Kuei Ku Tzu 'Ghost Valley Master' (c. 220 BCE).
		China unified. Burning of the books by Emperor Ch'in Shih Huang Ti who creates a tomb with a star map on its ceiling and a map of the rivers of his domain in flowing mercury on its floor, and creates the terracotta warriors.
Han	206 BCE - 220 CE	*Shih* Board in use, utilising the 28 *Hsiu*, all the 10 Heavenly Stems, 12 Earthly Branches but no trigrams.
		24 Mountains established with Earth Stems (not trigrams) at the corner positions. Five Element doctrine.
		K'an yü becomes a profession. It uses the *Shih*, Stems, Branches, and *Hsiu* to judge best times and directions.
		Ching Wu, Master Blue Raven wrote the *Canon of Burials* (some fragments survive).
		Writing of *Huai Nan Tzu* (139-122 BCE) and Y*üeh Ling* (with monthly correspondences and prescripts for action).
		Many books written on *K'an yü* like the *Golden K'an yü Thesaurus* (14 chapters, but now lost).
		Wang Ching (Wang Jing) wrote the *Fifty Original Groundstones* summarising burial and building practice.
		Ching Fang (79-37 BCE) established the *na yin* system, and attributes a Combination to every line of the 60 Root *kua*.
Three Kingdoms (Wei, Shu, Wu)	220-265 CE	Chu Ko Liang (181-234 CE) the military strategist, invents/uses *Ch'i Men Tun Chia* style military magic.
		Kuan Lo (209-256 CE) writes classic feng shui text, *Kuan Shih Ti Li Chih Meng*.
Chin (Jin)	265-420 CE	Kuo P'o (Guo Pu) (276-324 CE) writes the *Burial Classic*, first mention of 'feng shui', gnomon, & compass with 8 trigrams. Gets *Book of the Blue/Green Satchel/Bag*.

Traditional Emperors & Dynasties	Date	Significant feng shui event
Southern & Northern	420-589	Wang Wei (415-443 CE) supposedly writes *Huang Ti Chai Ching*, with a square Earth Plate and 24 Mountains.
		Other examples of the *Shih* found. For the first time, the 4 corner trigrams appear on the *Shih*.
Sui	589-618	A dozen feng shui titles extant. The *Water Dragon Classic* sometimes said to have originated c. 600 CE.
T'ang	618-906	Emperor T'ai Tsung (reigned 626-649 CE) establishes a commission under Lü Ts'ai to appraise and regulate feng shui. The results were published in a book of 100 chapters.
		Ch'iu Yen Han (fl. 713-741 CE) refers to the circular Earth Plate with 24 Mountains.
		Trigrams probably added to the lo p'an as an inner ring, as direction indicators only (by the 9th century).
		Yang Yun Sung (834-906 CE) establishes the Heaven Plate and the 72 Dragons ring for 'riding the ch'i.' Writes *T'ien Yu Ching, Ch'ing Nang Ao Chih, Yu Chê Ching*.
		Yang's main disciple Tsêng Wên Ch'an (854-916 CE) writes *Yin Yang Wen Ta, Hsun Lung Chi*.
5 Dynasties & 10 Kingdoms	906-960	The 240 *fen chin,* and then 120 *fen chin* rings developed by a Yang Yun Sung disciple.
Northern Sung	960-1127	Flying Star charts found amongst Tun Huang (Dunhuang) monastery manuscripts (982 CE).
		Wang Chi (990-c.1060) founds the Fukien San He School of feng shui. Establishes a lo p'an with 17 rings. His pupil Yeh Shu Liang publishes his *Heart Classic*.
		Shao Yung (1011-1077 CE) develops circular arrangement of the hexagrams later used on San Yuan lo p'ans.
		Emperor Ren Tsung (r. 1023-1063) restores *Tai Yi, Ch'i Men Tun Chia* and *Liu Ren (Liuren)*, 3 Cosmic Board divinations.
		Shen Kuo (1031-1095 CE) works on declination, the relationship between Magnetic and Astronomic North, magnetism, spherical trigonometry & calendar reform.
		Wu Ching Luan (fl. 1041 -1064 CE) writes *Hsüan K'ung Secret Decree* and *San Yuan One Revision* (but not quite the same theory as presently goes under those titles).
Northern Kin & Southern Sung	1127-1279	Ts'ai Shen Yü (fl. 1135) invents 60 Dragons ring.
		Lai Pu Yi (1131-1162 CE) establishes the Outer Heaven [Man] Plate and defines the 24 Heaven Stars ring.
		Establishment of the K'ai Hsi benchmark for the *Hsiu* ring in 1206 CE as 126.16° but based on 960 CE.
Yuan (Mongol)	1271-1368	Chao P'ang (1319-1369) uses the term *lo ching*, and states that its practitioners radiated out from Fukien Province.
Ming	1368-1644	First Ming Emperor Chu Yüen Chang (r. 1368-1398) kills Taoist feng shui masters & issues false feng shui books.
		12 Sovereign hexagrams ring included in lo p'an.
		60 Root hexagrams ring matched with the 60 *chia-tzu* ring.
		Yellow Springs, *yao sha*, and Robbery *sha* rings devised.
		Dry mounted needle becomes the norm for the lo p'an.

<table>
<tr><th>Traditional Emperors & Dynasties</th><th>Date</th><th>Significant feng shui event</th></tr>
<tr><td></td><td></td><td>Wu Wang Kang (c.1563-c.1620) edits Lo Ching Chieh, the Ming standard text on the lo p'an, with 38 rings.</td></tr>
<tr><td rowspan="13">Ch'ing (Qing) (Manchu)</td><td rowspan="13">1644-1911</td><td>Chiang Ta Hung (Jiang Da Hong) (1620-1714) begins to use the 9 yün cycle and calls his method 'San Yuan.'</td></tr>
<tr><td>Establishment of the Shih Hsien benchmark (1645) for the positioning of the Hsiu on the lo p'an.</td></tr>
<tr><td>Lo Ching T'ou Chieh standard work on lo p'an rings.</td></tr>
<tr><td>Chang Ping Lin (fl. 1739) writes 4 San He classics.</td></tr>
<tr><td>Emperor Ch'ien Lung (Qianlong) rectifies the calendar and feng shui practice with Hsieh Chi Pien Fang Shu (1741).</td></tr>
<tr><td>Chao Chiu Feng's Ti Li Five Formulas (1786).</td></tr>
<tr><td>Jo Kuan Tao Ren's Eight Mansions classic Pa Chai Ming Ching (1790).</td></tr>
<tr><td>Chang Chung Shan (fl. 1820) founds Wu Ch'ang School.</td></tr>
<tr><td>Chang Hsin Yen's San Yuan 9 Yün 64 Kua Method changes lo p'an ring from 60 kua to 64 kua ring (1824-1827).</td></tr>
<tr><td>Whipple lo p'an made (1860) showing two Hsiu epochs.</td></tr>
<tr><td>Shen Chu Reng (1849-1906) writes classic book on Hsüan K'ung Flying Star feng shui.</td></tr>
<tr><td>Western administrators like De Groot, and missionaries like Eitel (1868-1910) bring feng shui to the West. Eitel writes first 19th century English book on feng shui (1873).</td></tr>
<tr><td>Imperial Board of Rites disbanded, removing standardisation of astrology and feng shui.</td></tr>
<tr><td rowspan="3">Republic of China</td><td rowspan="3">1912-1949</td><td>T'an Yang Wu (1891-1945) opens a school in Shanghai, the source of Wu Ch'ang P'ai in Malaysia (1922).</td></tr>
<tr><td>Feng shui suppressed in mainland China (1927).</td></tr>
<tr><td>T'an Yang Wu takes an advert in a Shanghai newspaper proclaiming that his previous feng shui was wrong (1930).</td></tr>
<tr><td rowspan="2">People's Republic of China</td><td rowspan="2">1949 -</td><td>Many feng shui masters begin to move to Taiwan, Hong Kong, Singapore and Malaysia (1949).</td></tr>
<tr><td>The Cultural Revolution closes down most feng shui practice in People's Republic of China (1966-76).</td></tr>
<tr><td rowspan="7">The development of feng shui in the rest of the World</td><td rowspan="7">1962 - 2012</td><td>Joseph Needham publishes Vol. IV, 1 of Science and Civilisation in China, the first Western scholarly study to include detailed feng shui history and theory (1962).</td></tr>
<tr><td>Maurice Freedman writes anthropological studies of feng shui and kinship in Singapore and Malaysia (1966-69).</td></tr>
<tr><td>Stephan Feuchtwang publishes his excellent and very detailed thesis on Chinese Geomancy in Vientiane, Laos (1974).</td></tr>
<tr><td>First 20th century English book on feng shui, Living Earth Manual of Feng Shui, written by the present author (1976).</td></tr>
<tr><td>First thesis on feng shui submitted to an American university, by Korean Dr. Hong-key Yoon (1976).</td></tr>
<tr><td>Sarah Rossbach publishes Feng Shui: the Art of Placement, and introduces Lin Yun from Hong Kong (1983).</td></tr>
<tr><td>Lin Yun sets up his 'Black Hat Sect Tibetan Buddhist' temple in Berkeley, to promote faux feng shui (1986).</td></tr>
</table>

Traditional Emperors & Dynasties	Date	Significant feng shui event
		Derek Walters publishes *Chinese Astrology,* the most complete book on the subject in English to that date (1987).
		Lillian Too's *Complete Illustrated Guide to Feng Shui* published in the UK and later in US. Claimed to be highest selling feng shui book (1990).
		Larry Sang sets up American Feng Shui Institute and starts to teach traditional feng shui in the US (1991).
		James Moser opens the Feng Shui Warehouse (1993) to retail imported feng shui goods.
		First lo p'ans partially in a Western language (German) made by Thomson House in Hong Kong (1994).
		James Moser publishes the *Feng Shui Journal* in the US (1995).
		James Moser organises the First Annual International Feng Shui Conference in San Diego (1996).
		Second Annual International Feng Shui Conference at Palm Springs organised by James Moser (Oct 1997).
		Pun-Yin does the feng shui of Trump Tower for Donald Trump who praises feng shui on NBC (1998).
		First worldwide full colour feng shui magazine *Feng Shui for Modern Living* published by Stephen Skinner, selling 121,000 audited copies per month worldwide (1998-2001).
		International Feng Shui Congress organised by Andreas Hager in Starnberg, Munich, Germany (May 1998).
		Vincent Koh publishes the *Hsia Calendar* in English (1998).
		Roger Green organises a feng shui study tour to HK, Taiwan, China, Tibet, Nepal and India (Apr 1999).
		Third Annual International Feng Shui Conference at Monterey organised by James Moser (May 1999).
		London International Feng Shui Conference, the largest ever European feng shui convention organised by Stephen Skinner (May 1999). 23 speakers and 46 sessions.
		World Congress & Exhibition Feng Shui Experience organised at Innsbruck, Austria (Jun 2000).
		Fourth Annual International Feng Shui Conference at Orlando organised by James Moser (2001).
		First Annual World Classical Feng Shui Conference at Köln, Germany (2002).
		Rick Than and Master Raymond Lo publish their first English Almanac (2003).
		International Feng Shui Association (IFSA) organised in Singapore. First IFSC Convention in Singapore (Aug 2004).
		The present author publishes *Guide to the Feng Shui Compass,* the most complete analysis of the *lo p'an* (2008).
		Joey Yap publishes *The Chinese Metaphysics Compendium,* in Malaysia, the most complete compendium of feng shui formulas in English (2008).
		International Kanyu and Architecture Symposium organised by Howard Choy in Berlin (2010).
		9th IFSC International Feng Shui Convention held at Nanyang University, Singapore (Nov 2012).

Appendix II - The Historical Schools of Feng Shui

It is central to any discussion of feng shui and the lo p'an to identify which rings are associated with which School. The main Schools of thought in feng shui are San He, San Yuan and Hsüan K'ung. Most books in English on feng shui, including several of my own, mistakenly refer to the two main *methods* of feng shui, Form (*luan t'ou* 巒頭) and Compass (*li ch'i* 理氣) as 'Schools.'

The Form method is concerned with the identification of mountains and rivers, the landform configurations and shapes, and their effects on the site under consideration. The Compass method is concerned with determining the complex set of relationships between time, directions and types of ch'i as indicated by the *lo p'an*.

It has also been said that the history of feng shui conveniently splits along geographical divisions into the 'Gentlemen of Kanchow' and the 'Gentlemen of Fukien.' This is true, but both these groups were practitioners of San He feng shui, the 'Gentlemen of Kanchow' (in Kiangsi) being the followers of Yang Yun Sung (834-906 CE) and the 'Gentlemen of Fukien' being followers of Wang Chi[1] (990-c.1060). The San Yuan School on the other hand developed in the Ch'ing dynasty, long after this split.

San Yuan and Hsüan K'ung originally derived from Kiangsu (Jiangsu)[2] and northern Chekiang (Zhejiang). The geographical distinction is very clear - see Figure 66. The practitioners of San Yuan could flippantly be described as the 'Gentlemen of Chekiang' (Zhejiang) whilst the practitioners of Hsüan K'ung could be referred to as the 'Gentlemen of Kiangsu' (Jiangsu).

These Schools are most easy to distinguish based on the arithmetic of their lo p'an rings. San He rings are always arranged by multiples of 5, and 6, producing rings of 10, 12, 24, 60, 72, 120 and 240 sectors. Hsüan K'ung rings on the other hand are always identifiable by rings which are multiples of 8, 64 and 384. Ancient Astronomical rings on the other hand are identifiable by their division into 28 divisions and 365.25 day-degrees.

Finally, Chinese astrology, which is not strictly part of the practice of feng shui, has increasingly become identified with it in the 20th and 21st centuries. This is because feng shui masters increasingly seek to integrate or personalise the feng shui of a site or building, with the *Pa Tzu* horoscope of the owner.

---

[1] 王伋 also known as Chao K'ing or K'ung Chang. Wang Chi originally learned San He feng shui in Kanchow (Ganzhou), but spent the later half of his life in Fukien, hence 'Gentlemen of Fukien.'

[2] Note that Kiangsi 江西 (Jiangxi) in the South, and Kiangsu 江蘇 (Jiangsu) in the North, are completely different Provinces.

1. *San He School* 三合

Description: Concerned with Form and Configuration, rivers, mountains and riding the *ch'i*. 'San He' refers to the groupings of the 12 Earthly Branches into triads (Three Harmonies) by the four Elements (excluding Earth). Has three Plates: Earth, Man and Heaven. Rings are typically divided into 12, 24, 60, 72, 120 and 240 sectors (also the Astronomical 28 *Hsiu*).

Main Ingredients: Predominantly uses the 5 Elements; 12 Earthly Branches; 12 Palaces and the 10 Heavenly Stems.[1]

Other Names: Yang Kung feng shui. Mountain peaks and vital embodiment school (*luan t'ou* or *hsing shih* 形势). Kanchow[2] (old) method. Kiangsi (new) method. This School is effectively a combination of *ti li* (location and direction) and *k'an yü* (time and auspice).

Patriarchs: The Imperial *ti li* Master Yang Yun Sung (834-906) (often called Yang Chiu Pin), and his chief disciple Tsêng Wên Ch'an[3] (854-916) and later Lai Pu Yi[4] (1131-1162). Also Liao Yü.[5] Kuo P'o,[6] an early exponent of *yin chai* feng shui, is also claimed as a patriarch by this School.

Province of Origin: Kanchow (Ganzhou) which is a prefecture-level city in Kiangsi (Jiangxi) Province which was the final dwelling-place of its patriarch, Yang Yun Sung. Also flourished in Fukien and Anhui province, and now in Taiwan.

Methods and Development: Early forms of San He theory and cosmology are to be found in the Han dynasty *Huai Nan Tzu* (139-122 BCE). The current method stems from Yang Yun Sung and the writings of the three patriarchs listed above. Yang Yun Sung added the Heaven Plate and Lai Pu Yi introduced the Outer Heaven (Man) Plate which relates to Astronomical rings. The main subdivisions are:

1. Yang Kung Old Method 楊公古法 (T'ang dynasty)
2. Yang Kung New Method 楊公新法 (Five Dynasties/Sung dynasty)
3. Correct 5 Element San He 正五行三合 (Ming dynasty version)
4. Facing Matched with Water Method 以向配水
   Double Mountain 5 Element 雙山五行 (Wang Tsao)
5. San He T'an Lang Nine Stars 三合九星 (a mixed method)
6. Four Graves Nine Stars 四墓九星 (a mixed method)

---

[1] Trigrams are used by both Schools, but they are much more integral to the rings of San Yuan.

[2] 贛州 Ganzhou.

[3] 曾文辿 Zeng Wen Chan.

[4] 賴布衣 Lai Bu Yi *aka* Lai Wên Chün 賴文俊 Lai Wen Jun.

[5] 廖禹 Liao Yu.

[6] 郭璞 Guo Pu.

2. *San Yuan* 三元 / *Hsüan K'ung School*

Description: Specifically concerned with Compass directions; time cycles; Fate 'Stars;' invisible *ch'i* and the Calendar, hence 'Three Periods' School. Rings are typically divided into 8, 64 and 384 sectors. Plus often some San He Earth Plate and Astronomical rings will be preserved on a San Yuan lo p'an.

Main Ingredients: This School uses the 8 trigrams (*kua*), and the doubling of these trigrams to form the 64 hexagrams of the *I Ching,* supplemented by the Nine Stars and Lo Shu numbers. This School also partly utilises Sha and Astronomical Plate rings, but not the Man Plate or Heaven Plate.

Other Names: Hsüan K'ung

Patriarch: Founder of the *theory* behind San Yuan: Shao Yung (1011-1077) with philosophical input from Chu Hsi (1130-1200); Ch'ing dynasty innovators Chiang Ta Hung (1620-1714); Chang Chung Shan (fl. 1820); T'an Yang Wu (1891–c.1945) and Shen Chu Reng (1849-1906).

Province of Origin: Kiangsu (Jiangsu) and northern Chekiang (Zhejiang) provinces, but now flourishes in Taiwan, Singapore, Malaysia and Hong Kong.

Methods and Development: San Yuan is split into a number of Schools including:

Hsüan K'ung School 玄空派

1. *Hsüan K'ung Ta Kua* 玄空大卦 A practice that uses up to two rings of the 64 hexagrams, and their 6 x 64 = 384 *yao*[1]
2. *Hsüan K'ung Fei Hsing* 玄空飛星 Flying Stars School
3. *Tzu Pai Hsing* 紫白星 Purple White star method.

Pa Kua School 八卦派

1. *Pa Chai* (and *Ming Kua)* 八宅 Eight Houses School or Wandering Star method (the personal *kua* number matched with house *kua*)
   (A modern New Age variant on this School is the non-traditional so-called Black Hat Sect feng shui which was invented in the US in 1986, and does not use a lo p'an.)
2. *Fan Kua* 翻卦 Flipping Trigram method.

Lung Men Eight Gate Formations method 龍門八法 (Also called Ch'ien K'un National Treasure Method 乾坤國寶).

Chiang Ta Hung's original lo p'ans are often assumed to be part of Hsüan K'ung Ta Kua but in fact Chiang P'ans are quite different. They can be identified by their simple design, limited number of rings (usually less than 7), and the absence of hexagrams, Astronomical rings and the Heaven and Man Plates. There will usually be a wide ring showing just the 12 Earthly Branches. Early Chiang P'ans do not have a 64 hexagram ring.

[1] An older San He version of this ring only has 60 hexagrams.

Chinese Astrology, Divinatory and Fate Calculation

Complex astrological theories, based on the Chinese Solar Calendar also interrelate with the above Schools, predominantly with San Yuan Practice. Of the astrological methods, the best known in the West is *Pa Tzu*.

Methods:

1. *Pa Tzu*[1] 八字 also called Tzu Ping (Ziping) after Hsü Tzu Ping.[2] This form of astrology uses the Branch and Stem from the year, month, day and hour of an individual's date of birth. This yields 8 characters which are then arranged in four 'pillars.' Because of this the method is more commonly known in the West as Four Pillar astrology
2. *Tzu Wei Tou Shu*[3] 紫微斗數 or Purple Star or Purple Emperor astrology which uses 12 Houses and hundreds of 'fate stars' the list of which include some of the 9 Flying Stars and some astronomically identifiable stars, as well as many 'fate stars' which have apparently no physical correlatives
3. *Mei Hua Shu* 梅花數 Plum Blossom (based on *I Ching* numerology)
4. *T'ai Yi* 太乙 Big [Stem] Yi (derived from the *Shih*).
5. *Liu Ren*[4] 六壬 Six [Branch] Ren (also relates to the *Shih* board)
6. *Ch'i Men Tun Chia*[5] 奇門遁甲 Mysterious Gates of the Hidden Stems School. This is now taught as a technique for choosing correct times, but it used to be part of the layout of the San He lo p'an, and was also used in conjunction with Taoist magical techniques
7. *Tsê Jih*[6] 擇日. Date selection (derived from Hsüan K'ung Ta Kua, Ch'i Men Tun Chia, and other systems). It is concerned with the timing of construction; selecting best dates for signing a contract; starting a new job; getting married; having surgery; beginning a new project, etc.

Face Reading and Palm Reading are listed alongside Feng Shui and Astronomy under the same broad category Hsiang[7] in the Imperial Encyclopaedia. Hsiang does not mean 'physiognomy' as is often stated, but in this context it means 'judging by patterns.' Face Reading is hence not really a part of feng shui.

---

[1] Ba Zi.
[2] 徐子平 Xu Zi Ping.
[3] Zi Wei Dou Shu.
[4] Liu Ren.
[5] Qi Men Dun Jia.
[6] Ze Ri.
[7] 相 *xiang*.

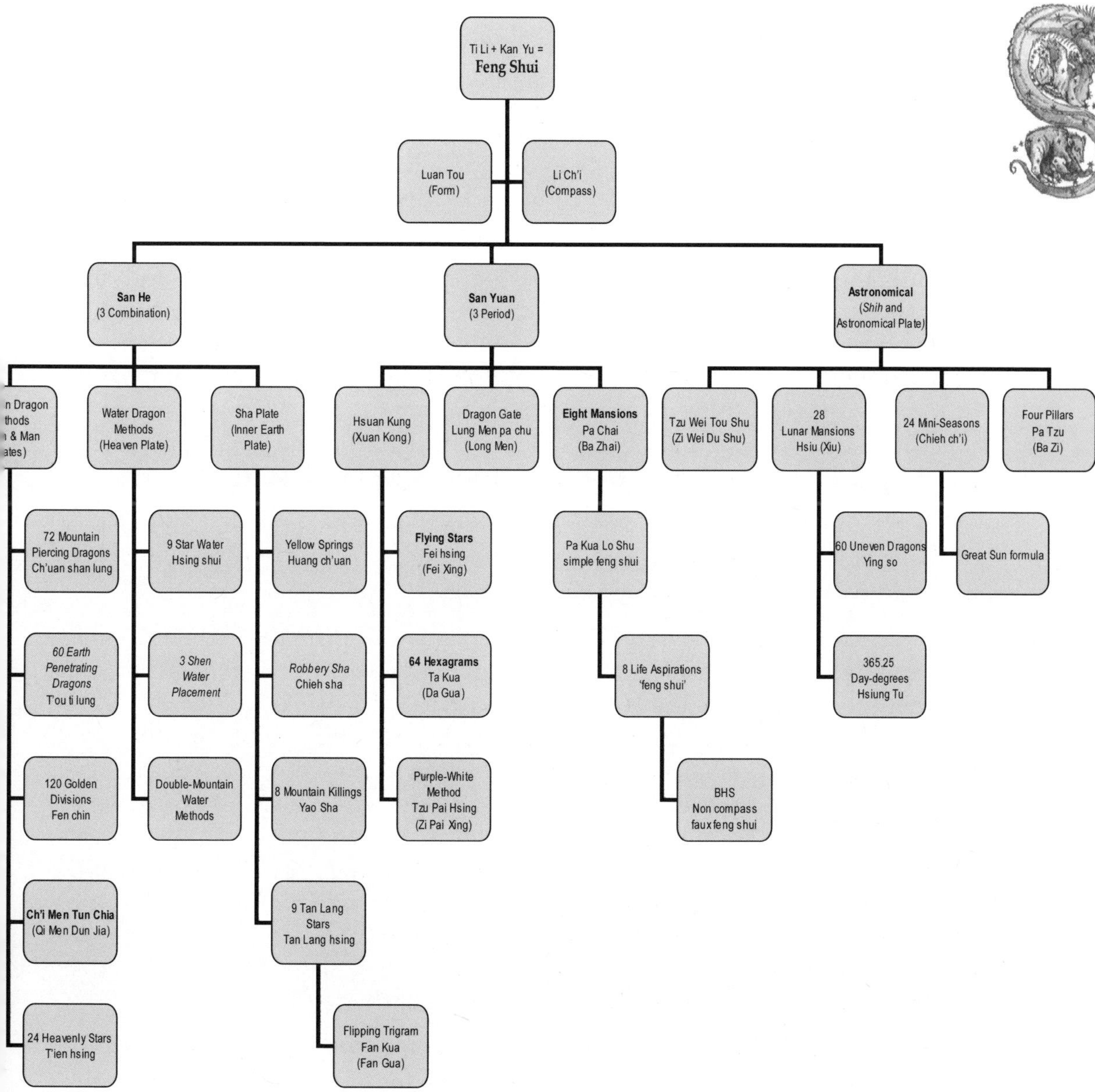

Figure 65: The main Schools and formulae of feng shui.[1] The logo shows the two Bear constellations linked by the constellation Draco and the north pole star. Although of European origin, this diagram encapsulates certain astronomical feng shui formulae.

[1] © Copyright 2012 Stephen Skinner.

Appendix III - Chinese Literature on the Lo p'an

The predecessor of the lo p'an, the *Shih* plate had an extensive literature of its own, although most of those books have long since been lost. The most important extant Han dynasty text for both the *Shih* and the lo p'an is the *Huai Nan Tzu*[1] as it gives the cosmological background of most rings. In the course of examining the cosmology, much of the detailed structure of the rings and Classical feng shui formula become much easier to understand.

There are thousands of Chinese books on feng shui, but only a few specifically examine the rings of the lo p'an. These were published by Chinese authors in the Ming and Ch'ing dynasties. In these classics on the lo p'an there are descriptions, but only a few texts have illustrations. Where there are illustrations, these are fairly rough woodblock illustrations, and they usually only show one ring plus a reference ring (usually the 24 Mountains ring) at a time, and often without any clear segment divisions. They do not usually include the method of using each ring, which will be a matter for oral transmission.

There are five main Chinese classics concerned with the lo p'an. Obviously all of these older texts only describe San He rings, as San Yuan rings were not invented till much later, in the Ch'ing dynasty.[2]

1. The text that Professor Stephan Feuchtwang primarily relied upon for his ground-breaking thesis[3] was the 'Explanation of the Lo p'an.'[4] This was probably written before the Wan Li reign period (1573-1620 CE) by Wu Wang Kang[5] in conjunction with the *k'an yü* master Hsiung Ju Yüeh.[6] 'Wu Wang Kang' is probably an honorific given to Wu T'ien Hung. I will however continue to refer to the author as Wu Wang Kang for the sake of consistency. Wu lived in Hsin An town in Anhui Province, a town which has always been famous for lo p'an production. He later went to Fukien Province to meet the *k'an yü* master Hsiung Ju Yüeh, and he also travelled inland to Kiangsi (Jiangxi). His journey therefore included the three most important feng shui Provinces. His book features 38 rings. Sadly its 1810 edition, as used by Feuchtwang, only has a few illustrations, none of them *lo p'ans*.

2. Hsü Shih K'o (c.1550-c.1630 CE) was the author of one of the earliest Ming dynasty books describing 33 rings of the lo p'an called the 'Top Gate to the Needle.'[7] By the time this was written the lo p'an was a well developed

---

[1] 淮南子 *Huai Nan Zi* (*Huainanzi*). See Chapters 3-5 translated in Major (1993).

[2] Although the theory behind San Yuan rings dates back to Shao Yung in the Sung dynasty, the rings themselves did not appear on the lo p'an till the late Ch'ing dynasty.

[3] See Feuchtwang (1974).

[4] *Lo Ching Chieh* 羅經解 *Luo Jing Jie*.

[5] Wu Wang Kang 吳望崗 Wu Wang Gang.

[6] 熊汝嶽 Xiong Ru Yue.

[7] 徐試可 Xu Shi Ke. See Hsü Shih K'o (1623). This book was probably written in 1580. See Figure 37.

instrument. The title refers to an easy entrance to understanding the needle of the lo p'an, but also has no illustrations.

3. The first text which has detailed ring illustrations appears to be the 'Thorough Explanation of the Lo p'an' by Wang Tao Heng.[1] It describes 36 rings.

4. The next important text is the 'Fixed Explanation of the Lo p'an'[2] by Hu Kuo Chen (1660-1720) which describes 24 rings.

5. 'A South-Pointer to Dispel the Fog about the Lo p'an' by Yeh Chiu Sheng[3] which was published between 1682 and 1693 is also very useful.

The other important sources of detailed lo p'an information, showing the historical progress of feng shui are the several *Imperial Encyclopaedias* produced in the Ming and Ch'ing dynasties which run to many thousands of volumes, and take up so much shelf room that they have to be seen to be believed.[4] Also encyclopaedic in nature is the massive standard work on 'Harmonising Times and Distinguishing Directions' which was produced under the auspices of the Emperor Ch'ien Lung (Qianlong) in an effort to standardise feng shui and Chinese cosmology and astrology.[5] It is an essential reference. The illustrations in the partial English translation are a treasure in themselves.[6]

Amongst modern Chinese texts, the most detailed and most carefully researched one on the rings of the lo p'an is that of Li Ding Xin[7] from Kanchow (Ganzhou) which details and compares 49 rings found in previous classics. A more recent book by him updates this to 52 rings.[8] He limits his survey to San He lo p'ans.

Professor Cheng Jian Jun, from the Department of Architecture at South China University of Technology, is well known for several books in Chinese relating feng shui and architecture, and his work on temples. Professor Cheng also authored a survey of the lo p'an in Chinese and English.[9]

Pa He Ming in Hong Kong includes both San Yuan and San He rings in his

---

[1] *Lo Ching T'ou Chieh* 羅經透解 *Luo Jing Tou Jie* by Wang Tao Heng 王道亨 Wang Dao Heng, early Ch'ing, but I have used the 1823 edition.

[2] *Lo Ching Chieh Ting* 羅經解定 *Luo Jing Jie Ding*, circa 1700. See Hu Kuo Chen 胡國楨 Hu Guo Zhen in the present Bibliography.

[3] *Lo Ching Chih Nan P'o Wu Chi* 羅經指南潑霧集 *Luo Jing Zhi Nan Po Wu Ji* by Yeh Chiu Sheng 葉九升 Ye Jiu Sheng, published between 1682 and 1693.

[4] See Ch'en Meng Lei (1726) and Chi Yün (1773-1782).

[5] Yün Lu 允祿 Yun Lu, Mei Chüeh Ch'eng 梅瑴成 Mei Jue Cheng & He Kuo Tsung 何國宗 He Guo Zong (1741), part translated in Aylward (2007).

[6] Aylward (2007).

[7] 李定信 (1997).

[8] Li Ding Xin 李定信 (2007). His additional three rings are strangely San Yuan rings.

[9] Cheng Jian Jun 程建軍 & Adriana Fernandes-Gonçalves (1998).

work which is written in an easy to follow style.[1]

In Taiwan, two of the clearest writers in Chinese are Wu Ming Hsiu,[2] who writes separately on San He and San Yuan, and T'ien Hsing Chu Shih. The latter is a pseudonym, but his book is exhaustive and gives many detailed lists.[3] Much of his work is based on that of Chen Chein Lee.[4]

---

[1] Pa He Ming 白鶴鳴 Bai He Ming (1994).

[2] Wu Ming Hsiu 吳明修 Wu Ming Xiu (1996).

[3] T'ien Hsing Chü Shih 天星居士 Tian Xing Ju Shi (1995).

[4] 陳建利.

Appendix IV - The Geography of Feng Shui in China

Figure 66: Map of China showing the spread and origins of the different feng shui schools. Key to pinyin Provinces names below. See the next page for a key to the numbered sites.

Anhui	Anhwei	Kiangsi	Jiangxi
Chekiang	Zhejiang	Kiangsu	Jiangsu
Fukien	Fujian	Kwangsi	Guangxi
Honan	Henan	Kwangtung	Guangdong
Hopeh	Hebei	Shangtung	Shandong
Hupeh	Hubei	Shansi	Shanxi
Kansu	Gansu	Shensi	Shaanxi

Map No.	Province	Town	Master	Map No.	Province	Town	Master
1	Shensi	Xi'an	King Wen (1122 BCE)	15	Honan	Luoyang	Shao Yung (1011-1077 CE)
2	Honan	Dengfeng	Kuei Ku Tzu (c. 220 BCE)	16	Chekiang	Hanchow	Shen Kuo (1031-1095)
1	Shensi	Xi'an	Huang Ti buried (d. 206 BCE)	17	Kiangsi	Te Hsing	Wu Ching Luan (fl. 1041 -1064)
			Ching Wu	18	Fukien	Chien yang	Ts'ai Shen Yü (fl. 1135)
3,4	Anhui	Fuyang	Marquis of Yi *Shih* (165 BCE)	19	Kiangsi	Ting Nan	Lai Pu Yi (1131-1162)
9		Huainan	*Huai Nan Tzu* (139 BCE)	20	Anhui	Hsiuning	Lo p'an making & Chao P'ang
10	Honan	Puyang	Ching Fang (79-37 BCE)			Hsin An	Wu Wang Kang (c.1563-c.1620)
5,6	Shansi	Li Shih	*Shih* Boards in N China (8 CE)	21	Chekiang	Chia Shan	Chiang Ta Hung (1620-1714)
7,8	N Korea	Lolang	*Shih* Boards in Korea (25-65 CE)	22	Fukien	Yung Ting	Chang Ping Lin (fl. 1739).
11	Shangtung	Yi Nan	Chu Ko Liang (181-234 CE)	23	Kiangsu	Wushi	Chang Chung Shan (fl. 1820)
12		Ping Yuen	Kuan Lo (209-256 CE)	24		Yen Ch'ang	Chang Hsin Yen (fl. 1827)
13	Shansi	Wen Hsi	Kuo P'o (276-324 CE)	25		Shanghai	Shen Chu Reng (1849-1906)
			Ch'iu Yen Han (fl. 713-741 CE)				T'an Yang Wu (1891-1945)
14	Kiangsi	Kanchow	Yang Yun Sung (834-906 CE)	26	Fukien	Amoy	De Groot & lo p'an makers
		Yü Tu	Tsêng Wên Ch'an (854-916 CE)	27	Taiwan	Taipei	Modern lo p'an manufacture
		Kanchow	Wang Chi (990-c.1060 CE)	28	Hong Kong	Kowloon	

Figure 67: Key to the Map of China showing the origins of different feng shui schools.

The early Han dynasty *Shih* were found in tombs in North China, Korea and in Anhui. Anhui (ancient Huainan) was the origin of the *Huai Nan Tzu*, and the centre of lo p'an making, both ancient and modern. Early *ti li* practice derived from Shangtung. *I Ching* studies and speculation about the *kua* centred on Honan and Shensi Provinces.

Of the two main Schools of feng shui, San He derived from Kiangsi (Jiangxi) and Fukien (Fujian) Provinces. San Yuan and Hsüan K'ung derived from Kiangsu (Jiangsu) and northern Chekiang (Zhejiang) Provinces. Both Schools later spread to Hong Kong, Taiwan, Malaysia, Singapore and thence to other overseas locations.

Bibliography

Aylward, Thomas. *The Imperial Guide to Feng Shui & Chinese Astrology*, Watkins, London, 2007. [a partial translation of the *Hsieh Chi Pien Fang Shu (Qin Ding Xie Ji Bian Fang Shu*), a most important 1741 Imperial classic]

Bennett, Steven. 'Patterns of the Sky and Earth: A Chinese Science of Applied Cosmology' in *Chinese Science*, University of Pennsylvania, Philadelphia, 1978, No. 3.

Cheng Jian Jun, with Adriana Fernandes-Gonçalves. *Chinese Feng Shui Compass Step by Step Guide*, Jiangxi Science and Technology, Jiangxi, [1998].

Choy, Howard. *The Practical Application of Chinese Garden Feng Shui in the West*, World Feng Shui Day Presentation, 2011.

Cullen, Christopher. *Astronomy and Mathematics in Ancient China: the Zhou bi suan jing*, CUP, Cambridge, 1996.

De Groot, J. J. M. *The Religious System of China*, Leyden, 1892-1910. Volume 3, especially Book 1, Part III. Chapter XII. [Best missionary description]

De Kermadec, Jean-Michel Huon. *The Way to Chinese Astrology: the Four Pillars of Destiny*, Unwin, London, 1983.

Eitel, Ernest J. *Feng-shui; or the Rudiments of Natural Science in China*, Trubner, Hong Kong, 1873. Reprinted Cokaygne, Cambridge, 1973.

Feuchtwang, Dr Stephan. *An Anthropological Analysis of Chinese Geomancy*, Vithagna, Vientiane, 1974. [One of the oldest and still one of the best studies of the technical aspects of classical feng shui]

Groves, Derham. *Feng-Shui and Western Building Ceremonies*, Heian, 1991.

He Xiaoxin. *Fengshui tan yuan* ('Exploring the Source of Fengshui'), Dongnan, Nanjing, 1990.

Ho Peng Yoke. *Chinese Mathematical Astrology*, Routledge, London, 2003.

Huang, Alfred. *The Numerology of the I Ching*, Inner Traditions, Rochester, 2000.

Kalinowski, Marc. *Cosmologie et Divination dans la Chine Ancienne: Le Compendium des Cinq Agents*, Paris, 1991.

Koh, Vincent. *Basic Science of Feng Shui*, Asiapac, Singapore, 2003.

Leyau, Francis, *The Luo Pan: Feng Shui's Most Fundamental Tool*, CAFS, Kuala Lumpur, 2007.

Lo, Raymond. *3 Period and 3 Harmony Combined Lo Pan Interpretation*, Thomson House, Hong Kong, 2001.

Lo, Raymond. *Feng Shui Essentials*, Feng Shui Lo, Hong Kong, 2005.

Major, John. *Heaven and Earth in Early Han Thought: Chapters Three, Four, and Five of the Huainanzi*, State University of New York Press, NY, 1993.

March, Andrew. 'An Appreciation of Chinese Geomancy' in *Journal of Asian Studies*, 1968, Volume 27.2, pp. 252-267.

Mason, David A. *Spirit of the Mountains*, Hollym, 1999.

Needham, Joseph. *Science and Civilisation in China,* Volume 4, Part I: Physics, Cambridge University Press, Cambridge, 1962. [A classical work, seen from the perspective of the history of science rather than feng shui.]

Proudfoot, P. *The Secret Plan of Canberra*, University of New South Wales, 1994.

Schafer, Edward. *Pacing the Void: T'ang Approaches to the Stars*, Berkeley, 1977.

Skinner, Stephen. *The Living Earth Manual of Feng Shui,* RKP, London, 1976, 1982.

Skinner, Stephen. *Feng Shui for Modern Living* [the magazine], Centennial, London, 1999-2001. [also the Chinese edition, Taipei, Taiwan 2000-2003]

Skinner, Stephen. *Feng Shui for Modern Living*, Cico, London, 2001.

Skinner, Stephen. *Feng Shui: Before and After,* Tuttle, Boston & Tokyo, 2001.

Skinner, Stephen. *Flying Star Feng Shui*, Tuttle, Boston & Tokyo, 2003.

Skinner, Stephen. *Feng Shui Style*, Tuttle, Boston & Tokyo, 2004.

Stephen Skinner, *Tibetan Oracle Pack,* Carroll & Brown, London, 2005.

Skinner, Stephen. *Feng Shui: the Living Earth Manual,* Tuttle, Singapore, 2006.

Skinner, Stephen. *Water Dragon*, Golden Hoard, Singapore, 2006.

Skinner, Stephen. *Key San He Feng Shui Formulas,* Golden Hoard, Singapore, 2007.

Skinner, Stephen. *Original Eight Mansions Formula*, Golden Hoard, Singapore, 2007.

Skinner, Stephen. *Mountain Dragon*, Golden Hoard, Singapore, 2008.

Skinner, Stephen. *Feng Shui History: the story of Classical Feng Shui in China and the West from 221 BC to 2012 AD,* Golden Hoard, Singapore, 2012.

Skinner, Stephen. *Geomancy in Theory & Practice*, Golden Hoard, Singapore, 2011.

Skinner, Stephen. *Terrestrial Astrology: Divinatory Geomancy*, Routledge, London, 1980. [The last two books are on divinatory geomancy, not feng shui.]

Smith, Richard. *Fortune-Tellers and Philosophers: Divination in Traditional Chinese Society*, SMC, Taipei, 1991, and Boulder, San Francisco, 1991.

Swetz, Frank. *Legacy of the Luoshu*, Open Court, Chicago, 2002.

Ts'ui Ming Yu. *Hsüan K'ung Feng Shui: Theory and Practice,* Korea, 2004.

Walters, Derek. *Chinese Astrology*, Aquarian Press, London, 1987, reissued Watkins, 2002. [The most complete English book on Chinese astrology].

Yap, Joey. *The Ten Thousand Year Calendar*, JY Books, Kuala Lumpur, 2004.

Yap, Joey. *The Chinese Metaphysics Compendium*, JY Books, Kuala Lumpur, 2008. [1078 pages of Classical feng shui and Chinese metaphysical formulae].

Yoon, Hong-key. *The Culture of Fengshui in Korea: an Exploration of East Asian Geomancy*, Lexington, New York, 2006.